T'ai Chi Ch'üan

Harmonizing Taoist belief and practice

The Sussex Library of Religious Beliefs and Practices

This series is intended for students of religion, social sciences and history, and for the interested layperson. It is concerned with the beliefs and practices of religions in their social, cultural and historical setting. These books will be of particular interest to Religious Studies teachers and students at universities, colleges, and high schools. Inspection copies available upon request.

Published

The Ancient Egyptians Rosalie David
Buddhism Merv Fowler
Christian Theology: The Spiritual Tradition John Glyndwr Harris
Gnosticism John Glyndwr Harris
Hinduism Jeaneane Fowler
Humanism Jeaneane Fowler
Islam David Norcliffe
The Jews Alan Unterman
The Protestant Reformation: Tradition and Practice Madeleine Gray
Sikhism W. Owen Cole and Piara Singh Sambhi
T'ai Chi Ch'üan Jeaneane Fowler and Shifu Keith Ewers
Zen Buddhism Merv Fowler
Zoroastrianism Peter Clark

In preparation

You Reap What You Sow: Causality in the Religions of the World Jeaneane Fowler
Jainism Lynn Foulston

Forthcoming

Bhagavad Gita (a student commentary)
Chinese Religions

T'ai Chi Ch'üan

Harmonizing Taoist belief and practice

JEANEANE FOWLER and SHIFU KEITH EWERS

sussex
ACADEMIC
PRESS

Brighton • Portland

2 4 6 8 10 9 7 5 3 1

First published 2005 in Great Britain by
SUSSEX ACADEMIC PRESS
Box 2950
Brighton BN2 5SP

and in the United States of America by
SUSSEX ACADEMIC PRESS
920 NE 58th Ave Suite 300
Portland, Oregon 97213–3786

British Library Cataloguing in Publication Data
A CIP catalogue record for this book is available from the British Library.

Library of Congress Cataloging-in-Publication Data
T'ai chi ch'üan : harmonizing Taoist belief and practice /
Jeaneane Fowler and Shifu Keith Ewers.
p. cm.
Includes bibliographical references and index.
ISBN 1-903900-20-4 (pbk. : alk. paper)
1. Philosophy, Taoist. 2. Tai chi. I. Title:
Harmonizing Taoist belief and practice. II. Ewers, Shifu
Keith. III. Title.
BL1920.F687 2005
299.5′14—dc22

2005005589

Typeset by G&G Editorial, Brighton & Eastbourne
Printed by The Alden Press, Osney Mead, Oxford
This book is printed on acid-free paper.

Contents

Preface and Acknowledgements

Most people today are familiar with the visual expression of T'ai Chi Ch'üan/Taijiquan, or simply T'ai Chi, as it is more familiarly known. Its slow, graceful movements look so easy, so comfortable and so natural that it appears to be a sequence of positions that one can quickly learn in the same way as learning the footsteps and patterns of a dance. But anyone who has ever taken up this art will know that the skills needed to practise Tai Chi are considerable – coordination of movement of different parts of the body, coordination of mind and body, coordination of breathing with movement, for example. It is a practice, in fact, that is multi-layered and multi-faceted, but that ultimately unifies all its elements into a wholeness that mirrors the unified fabric and rhythms of the universe. While we do not see groups of people practising T'ai Chi in the parks and town or city squares of the West – a common sight in China – classes in T'ai Chi are now very popular in leisure centres of the western world. In the busy and somewhat stressful lives that we seem to live in the West, even the sight of people practising T'ai Chi offers an immediate contrast to abnormally tense lives that have come to see stress and hectic living as normal.

This book combines both an academic and a practising approach to T'ai Chi Ch'üan/Taijiquan. On the academic side, students of Taoism will find the beliefs and practices of Taoism itself firmly embedded in the text that follows. At the same time, however, they will be able to travel from a purely academic study of Taoism to explore its practical expressions in T'ai Chi. On the other hand, for practitioners of T'ai Chi – whether teachers or students – the deeper background of Taoism that underpins its practice and that is its foundation can be understood in a way that must surely enrich such practice. Standing in the *Beliefs and*

Practices series, then, the present book truly offers the reader a study of the beliefs of Taoism and the practices of T'ai Chi. It is the view of both authors that T'ai Chi cannot be separated from its Taoist roots, and it is part of the purpose of this book to illustrate just why such a claim is made.

The motif at the head of each chapter represents perfect balance, perfect equilibrium, but at the same time the dynamic vibrancy of potentiality. The familiar *yin* and *yang* symbol is the Taoist and Chinese expression of equilibrium, while the staff and serpent represents the Greek idea of perfection in physical health and well-being. In Greek myth the Messenger of the Gods placed his magic wand between two antagonistic serpents. When the two coiled around the wand the opposing forces of each were transformed to a state of balance and harmony. The Greek healer Asclepius, later to become the God of Healing, supplied the similar traditional symbol of healing. This was a knotty staff around which a single snake was coiled. These two Greek symbols are often combined, and adopted in different forms by the medical professions. In both Chinese and Greek thought, the union and utter complementarity of opposites are epitomized by the respective symbols. Here in this book, the motif is indicative of physical, mental, emotional and spiritual equilibrium and harmony in all dimensions of life.

From the academic standpoint Jeaneane Fowler would like to express her gratitude to her colleagues at the Library and Learning Resources Centre at the University of Wales, Newport, especially to Nigel Twomey, who has been so helpful in procuring texts from Inter-library Loans. Shifu Keith Ewers would like to thank Master Chee Soo for placing him on the path of *Tao* and for passing on to him his knowledge and experience of the Chinese Internal Arts. Keith would also like to thank Professor Ji Jian Cheng of Hangzhou University for furthering his knowledge in Chinese health and holistic arts. Finally, both authors would like to thank the team at Sussex Academic Press for providing the opportunity to write this unique book, and for the professional and friendly dialogue at all stages of its preparation.

Jeaneane Fowler
Shifu Keith Ewers
SPRING 2005

The Tao is something miraculous. Spiritual, it has an essence; empty, it has no form. It is unfathomable whether we follow after it or go forth to meet it. It cannot be found in shadow or echo. No one knows why it is as it is. Supreme sages attained it in antiquity; it has been transmitted to the present by subtle means.

Chang San-feng, translator Thomas Cleary

Go side by side with the sun and moon,
Do the rounds of Space and Time.
Act out their neat conjunctions,
Stay aloof from their convulsions.
Dependents each on each, let us honour one another. . . .
Be aligned along a myriad years, in oneness, wholeness,
simplicity.
All the myriad things are as they are,
And as what they are make up totality.

Chuang-tzu/Zhuangzi, translator Angus C. Graham

If you do not seek the great way to leave the path of delusion, even if you are intelligent and talented you are not great. A hundred years is like a spark, a lifetime is like a bubble. If you only crave material gain and prominence, without considering the deterioration of your body, I ask you, even if you accumulate a mountain of gold can you buy off impermanence?

Chang Po-tuan/Zhang Boduan, *Understanding Reality*,
translator Thomas Cleary

When the mind does not worry or rejoice,
This is the perfection of inner power.
When it is absorbed and does not alter,
This is the perfection of stillness.
When lusts and desires do not fill it up,
This is perfection of emptiness.
When there is nothing liked or disliked,
This is the perfection of equanimity.
When it is not confused by external things,
This is the perfection of purity.

The *Huai-nan-tzu/Huainanzi,* translator Harold D. Roth

In the quiet room I open the mirror of mind;
In the vacant hall I light the lamp of wisdom.
Outside is clear and bright,
Inside is effulgent light.
A tiny grain appears in the glow,
The silver moon is clear in the water.
In the gold crucible, suspended in space,
A grain of great elixir crystallizes.

The Book of Balance and Harmony,
translator Thomas Cleary

The final goal of spiritual cultivation in Taijiquan practice is reaching spiritual enlightenment. Through practicing Taijiquan, you understand the meaning of life until you reach the stage of clarity about your life and the natural universe. When you have reached this stage, your actual practice will no longer be important, since its essence will be infused into your very being.

Yang Jwing-Ming, *Taijiquan, Classical Yang Style: The complete form and Qigong*

To Mum and to my husband, Merv
JEANEANE

To my wife, Geraldine
And to the children, Ryan, Rhys, Arron,
Morgan, Carly and Jordan
KEITH

Introduction

Few people realize when watching or practising T'ai Chi that there is a wealth of Chinese and Taoist culture and traditions that have contributed to its present expression. Paul Crompton makes the apt point that "the world of Tai Chi today is like an enormous warehouse in which the past has accumulated".[1] This is a fact that makes T'ai Chi a fascinating study because of the multiple strands that inform it, strands that reach back into the distant past of ideas and practices that were concomitant with the evolution of Taoism. Two important points emerge from this fact. The first is that the practice of T'ai Chi cannot really be separated from its Taoist context – at least for the serious practitioner. The second is that an academic understanding of T'ai Chi can only come about through a knowledge of Taoism. Either way, for the academic or the practising adept, then, Taoism and T'ai Chi are thoroughly complementary. The purpose of this book is to reflect such complementarity, its authors bringing together their skills in academic analysis on the one hand, and expertise of practice on the other. It is sad that many people do not realize the depth of philosophical thought that underpins the practice of T'ai Chi, and it is the purpose of this book to redress such an imbalance.

For practitioners, the book is designed to enrich their knowledge and practice not only of T'ai Chi, but of martial arts in general. Students and teachers of martial arts will find much in its pages to complement their understanding of their own practice. As to students in schools, colleges and universities, the academic treatment of Taoism, and its practical expression in T'ai Chi, are designed to enrich their exploration of Religious Studies. In writing a book of this kind the task of blending together the work of two quite different authors might seem somewhat daunting, but the result is a smooth amalgamation of the work of two people whose ideas are foundationally alike. The structure of the book would actually enable a student of Taoism *per se* to study only the aspects concerning Taoism. Similarly, the martial arts student could examine those sections related to T'ai Chi, for each chapter is more or less divided into its Taoist background and the application of that background to the practice of T'ai Chi. However, such bifurcated use of the book is not what its authors have in mind.

A few words on the romanization of Chinese characters are essential here. The Chinese language consists of a large number of pictorial symbols. The characters that compose these can be rendered into Western sounds by two methods. One is called the Wade–Giles method, and the other Pinyin. The former is the older of the two systems and has been popular in the West for many years. Hence, we are used to Taoism and T'ai Chi, and for those who have some knowledge of Taoism, Lao-tzu and Chuang-tzu, the great sages of classical Taoism. But Pinyin is becoming very popular, and is much closer to the real sounds of words. It is the method of romanization that is used officially in China, and many writers today use this system. So Taoism becomes Daoism, *Tao* becomes *Dao*; T'ai Chi is Taiji, and the sages Lao-tzu and Chuang-tzu, Laozi and Zhuangzi respectively. Sometimes, the difference is minimal or even non-existent, but on other occasions the difference is so radical that the names bear little similarity. We have decided to use both forms throughout, the Wade–Giles form first, followed by Pinyin, thus Lao-tzu/Laozi. The reader who is used to one form rather than the other is then able to ignore the less familiar form. However, since texts often use one or the other and rarely both, the student will not be bewildered by an unfamiliar form when reading a quotation, or another book.

Despite the decision to use both Wade–Giles and Pinyin romanization throughout, the text would become very cumbersome should *every* Chinese word be written in both methods. We have therefore decided to leave Taoism in Wade–Giles alone as, also, *Tao*. The reader should note, however, that *D*aoism and *D*ao are the correct pronunciations. As far as T'ai Chi is concerned, the correct Wade–Giles form, and the full name of the art, is T'ai Chi Ch'üan. Where *t'* occurs it is indicative of the *t* retaining its sound and not being pronounced as *d*. The Pinyin of T'ai Chi Ch'üan is Taijiquan, a word that looks very different. But since T'ai Chi Ch'üan will be used so frequently in the text, we have decided, as in the case of Taoism and *Tao*, not to add the Pinyin. Further, though strictly speaking T'ai Chi Ch'üan is the correct name of the practice, we shall be abbreviating this further to T'ai Chi purely for the purpose of creating an easier text for the reader. *Ch'üan* is an important word, for it means "boxing", and sets T'ai Chi originally in a martial art context. For this reason we shall occasionally use the full form as a reminder to the reader.

The Western mind has an ingrained habit of thinking linearly and chronologically. However, this book is designed thematically, in a more "eastern" approach. But it begins at *Beginnings* by tracing the origins of Taoism and the origins of T'ai Chi, with the aim of discovering the nature of both in their historical and cultural settings. Chapter 2 takes up the theme of *Harmony* with an exploration of the theories of *yin* and *yang* that are central to Taoist belief and T'ai Chi practice. There are two major strands of Taoism, its ancient philosophy that has surfaced again and again, and its religious expression that developed out of, and alongside, that philosophy. It is the former that has been a great influence on T'ai Chi rather than the latter, though not exclusively so. Chapter 3, *The Way*, examines such a philosophical background and centres on *Tao*, which is what ultimately informs beliefs and practices of both Taoism and T'ai Chi. Chapter 5 takes up the theme of *Phases* and discusses the concept of the Five Elements or Agents, their origins in Taoism and their importance in T'ai Chi. *Energy* is the theme of chapter 6. Energy is called *ch'i/qi*, and is sufficiently important to be mentioned in nearly all the chapters, but is singled out for deeper examination in this chapter. In the Taoist context, *ch'i/qi* is the focus of alchemical practice, and in T'ai Chi it is the essence of the practice. Chapter 7, *Movement in Stillness*, brings the earlier chapters to fruition in concentrating on the practice of T'ai Chi itself and, finally, *Unity*, chapter 8, as its title suggests, brings all the concepts together to illustrate the ultimate goal of Taoism and T'ai Chi. A *Glossary* of important terms is to be found at the end of the book, and a detailed *Bibliography*.

Taoism is informed by multifarious traditions; it has an enormous, encompassing breadth. Similarly, T'ai Chi is a varied phenomenon with a great variety of different schools. While the *Yang Short Style* is the main tradition used in this book to promote T'ai Chi, there is by no means a partisan emphasis, and other schools are not excluded. Like Taoism, T'ai Chi embraces many concepts and practices – alchemy, meditation, spiritual development and martial arts. Like Taoism, too, it is concerned with the holistic evolution of body and mind, the evolution of the physical and the spiritual.

1 Beginnings

What is Taoism?

Taoism originated in China – a land so vast that it is almost the same size as Europe. China has had a long period of prehistory and history and multiple expressions of what it is to be Chinese. Taoism has grown out of that prehistory and history. It is difficult to trace the beginnings of the Taoist religion partly because its roots are varied and complex but also because of the unique interaction of the different religious strands of Chinese culture. China has embraced four religious genres from antiquity – Confucianism, which has been the dominant culture; Taoism; Buddhism, which infiltrated China at the beginning of the first millennium; and popular religion, the religion of the ordinary folk. While each of these has had its own particular characteristics, the cross-fertilization of beliefs and practices between all four has been prolific, resulting, almost, in a fifth genre – Chinese religion. Thus, it is often difficult to extract Taoism from Confucian, Buddhist and popular beliefs and practices. And since, too, Taoism has encompassed so many beliefs and practices it is difficult to define it. Julia Ching aptly remarks that it "may designate anything and everything".[1]

From what has been said so far, then, while we might want to see the term Taoism as indicative of a religion that has a formulated set of beliefs, it is not so. Just as religions like Christianity, Judaism, Hinduism and Buddhism – to name but a few – are characterized by great diversity, so, too, is Taoism. While its origins stretch back into antiquity, Taoism is a relatively late term for a whole spectrum of beliefs and practices. So when Taoism is referred to as a religion of China, the term may be likened to water that encompasses seas, oceans, streams, rivers, rain and clouds. It is the water that is Taoism while its facets are many and varied. So in Taoism, then, there are many pathways, sometimes to the same goal and sometimes to different ultimate goals. In fact, such a perspective reflects well the heart of Taoism for, just as water never flows the same way twice, so Taoism would find one route or path a totally one-sided perspective.

We should view Taoism, then, as one facet of Chinese religion, and Chinese religion as unique in being a special blend of Confucianism, Taoism, Buddhism, and popular practices. To the western mind this may be difficult to understand. In the West we are rather exclusive about religion; Christians are Christians, Jews are Jews, Muslims are Muslims. The idea that the three could blend together at any level of religion is a difficult one, not only theologically, but also psychologically in that most individuals would find it impossible to be all three at the same time. This is not so in Chinese religion, and in examining Taoism as a specific aspect of Chinese religion the particular influences and characteristics that inform it from such a unique blend always have to be borne in mind. Confucianism influenced Taoism from the earliest times, and when Buddhism later arrived on the scene, it too bequeathed a good deal of its beliefs and practices to Taoism. And in the area of popular religious beliefs and practices the dividing line between them and Taoism is often extremely difficult to define. Taoism has been very much people orientated. Barrett describes it as "a natural outgrowth of native ways of thought and action":[2] essentially, it was very much a *Chinese* phenomenon, close to the psyche of the Chinese people.[3]

If we look at the word *Taoism* itself, the first part of the word, *Tao*, lies at the heart of what we call Taoism, and we shall spend some time examining it in a later chapter. The Chinese used the word *tao* in all sorts of contexts, and are thoroughly familiar with it. It was a term that pervaded all Chinese thought, and the word *tao* predates the beginnings of Taoism. Tao-*ism*, however, really refers to two kinds of religious belief, *Tao-chia/Daojia*, which is early philosophical Taoism, and *Tao-chiao/Daojiao*, which is the later religious and ritualistic Taoism. Using the word *Taoism* unites the two, but somewhat anachronistically and ambiguously. While both of these aspects of Taoism inform the development and practice of T'ai Chi Ch'üan/Taijiquan, it will be philosophical Taoism that will be seen to be the dominant influence. In approaching Taoism and especially T'ai Chi, therefore, we need to concentrate on the word *Tao* and not search too hard for the *-ism*. The Chinese character that represents the word *Tao* is made up of two parts, one representing a human, and the other representing forward movement. Thus, *Tao* suggests a "Way" in a very fundamental sense. In Taoist philosophy and metaphysics, *Tao* represents Reality at its ultimate, and all existence both as the "Way" that emanates from that Reality, and as the return to it.

Tao-chia/Daojia, associated with Lao-tzu/Laozi and Chuang-tzu/Zhuangzi – both of whom we shall meet in chapter 3 – belongs to the classical period of Taoism, which began as early as the sixth century BCE. It is clear from the seminal writings attributed to Lao-tzu/Laozi and Chuang-tzu/Zhuangzi that Taoism was very much concerned with naturalism and humanism. Lao-tzu/Laozi has advice for the ruler and for warfare, and Chuang-tzu/Zhuangzi's writings are full of the humour associated with life itself. But also evident is a recognition of the capabilities of the human self for transcending ordinary existence in order to experience the self as a natural part of the universe – a self rooted in *Tao*. Before and after the times of Lao-tzu/Laozi and Chuang-tzu/Zhuangzi there were many influences that contributed to philosophical Taoism, and to religious Taoism, *Tao-chiao/ Daojiao*. Thus, even including its early phase, Isabelle Robinet pointed out that we cannot think of Taoism as a whole, nor can we trace a neat linear growth of it. She wrote:

> It took shape only gradually, during a slow gestation that was actually a progressive integration of various ancient lines of thought. No precise date can be set for its birth, and the integration of outside elements into the religion has never ceased. If we add to this the enrichment of Taoism throughout its history with new revelations or new inspirations, we can see how open a religion it is, constantly progressing and evolving, and how difficult it is not only to date its first appearance but also to define its boundaries.[4]

Despite such obscure development and varied beginnings, there are some characteristics in the archetypal Chinese psyche that are to be found in Taoist thought and practice throughout its history right through to present times – albeit characteristics overlaid by accumulated ideas and practices. These characteristics seem to emerge in spite of the historical silences that pepper Chinese history and the great regional variations in belief and language in the vast lands of China. Underpinning the varied threads that make up the multifaceted religion of Taoism are some strands that reach back to antiquity. China had a great reverence for its ancient past. It is such reverence that enables certain characteristics embedded in the Chinese psyche to emerge again and again.

The Chinese psyche

In searching for the beginnings of Taoism and T'ai Chi we can reach right back to the China of antiquity, to the beginnings of fundamental beliefs that became embedded in the Chinese psyche. Perhaps the most important of these is an inherent affinity with nature and the natural world. Bodde rightly commented: "For the Chinese, this world of nature, with its mountains, its forests, its storms, its mists, has been no mere picturesque backdrop against which to stage human events. On the contrary, the world of man and the world of nature constitute one great indivisible unity."[5] The ancient agrarian background of the Chinese instilled into their psyche a closeness to, and need for harmony with, all nature. It was a harmony that saw animation and spirit in nature as much as in human beings. Mountains, springs, rivers, trees – all had their animated forces that might or might not co-operate with humans.

It was such beliefs that led to worship and propitiation of all kinds of gods and spirits through dance, chant, sacrifice and shamanism. The corners of the home and the niches of the environment had their spirits good and evil – house deities, earth deities, territorial deities, demons, were abundant. But the dominant idea in these ancient practices was a need to harmonize oneself, one's home, family and clan with natural forces, in order for life to run smoothly. Combined with such a perspective of nature was a profound belief in the spirits of ancestors. Ancestor veneration has been a dynamic and continuous aspect of the Chinese psyche, one that held together families, clans, territories and dynasties in the long years of Chinese history, and one that was coupled with Confucian respect for familial ties. What emerged was a reverence for the ancient past and a retention of ancient beliefs in the present psyche.

From ancient times, too, stems the conception of an orderly universe in which all is harmonized and interconnected. Nature is characterized by incessant, regular change that conforms to self-perpetuating rhythms, patterns and cycles: individual, familial and societal life needed to reflect the same kind of harmony. Psychologically, harmonious living is found in the search for harmony of the mind and body, and physiologically in the harmony of the energies that maintain and preserve the body. The *yin* and *yang* theories, associated with Chinese and Taoist religion, reflect these inner searches for balance and harmony. The human being is not estranged from nature or from a reality that is so ultimate that he or she is worthlessly lost. Reality is experienced in the patterns and harmonies of nature and life. Conforming to such patterns and rhythms emerged as meticulous observance of order, right behaviour, ritual practice, honour to ancestors, and so on, which have characterized Chinese life. Fulfilling the best in one's own nature and accepting the unique difference of oneself from another is what it means to be a relevant part of the interconnected and harmonized whole. Yet a belief in fate seems to be characteristic, a belief perhaps informed by the capriciousness and overwhelming force that nature often displays. It was this that engendered the need to remain in harmony with nature, and to use the medium of shamans as well as priests and ritual to maintain the harmonious rhythms of familial, agricultural, political and societal life. The sociologist Granet put this succinctly long ago when he said: "The sense that the natural world and human society are closely bonded has been the basic element of all Chinese beliefs."[6]

The foregoing is not to say that we can stereotype the Chinese psyche. Indeed, contradictions to these generalized characteristics will surely abound. Yet, they are indicators of what we might want to look for in the nature of Taoism in so far as it relates to Chinese culture in general. They are also indicators of the ancient ideas that have contributed to Taoist beliefs and practices that survived to the last century in China. The respect that the Chinese had for their ancient past has meant that the connnective tissue of centuries of tradition has grounded some beliefs firmly in their makeup.

The roots of Taoism in ancient practices

If we look more specifically for the roots of Taoism we shall find them not only in the variety of beliefs that have coloured the Chinese character down through the centuries, but also in a variety of practices from the very earliest strata of Chinese prehistory and history. Three practices stand out as precursors of later trends: divination, shamanism and ancestor reverence – and they are linked by the same kind of human psychological needs. The practice of divination is closely associated with the bond between humans and nature, and the need to know the outcome of a certain action. It is an attempt to understand fate, what will happen in the future, and was widely practised in ancient China. As will be seen later, it was often limited to a negative or a positive response – no or yes. But this was important for the undertaking of serious matters – waging war, for example.

Shamanism was also a major precursor of Taoism; indeed, it was probably the foundation of many religions. Shamanism views the universe as an interconnectedness of spirit and matter. Humans live in the world of matter, along with the phenomena of that world – mountains, trees, the sun, moon, plants, rocks, animals, and so forth. Every entity in existence is affected by one or more spiritual forces on the "other side". Thus, sickness, health, natural disasters, good harvests and the whole welfare of human and agricultural life are dependent on the benevolent or malevolent forces of the spirit world. It is the interconnected nature of, and interaction between, the two worlds of spirit and matter that are at the root of shamanist belief and practice.

So far, this would make life a very arbitrary existence: it would be difficult to know how, when, and which spirits had been offended and brought bad luck, or for what reasons life was going well. It was in situations such as these that the role of shamans became crucial as mediums of contact between the physical and spirit worlds. Through entering into a trance, they were able to come into contact with the spirits, talk to them, and mediate with them for other mortals. Or, a spirit could enter a shaman's body in order to communicate more directly to people. Shamans could ascertain why spirits were offended and, more importantly, what could be done to put things right. Even more so, it was believed that shamans could contact the spirits *before* something was undertaken so that people could proceed with their plans with confidence. Awareness of the fact that life and nature can so easily be hostile, and the need to tread respectfully so as not to offend the spirits of the other world, made shamans a necessary force in society.

Shamanism influenced philosophical Taoism with a legacy of a deep reverence for nature that sees humankind as needing to interact with the whole of the natural world in a very harmonious way. It is an attempt to work *with* nature by assisting the physical and spirit worlds to return to harmony. Palmer puts this point well when he says that shamanism at a philosophical or spiritual level had

> the sense of a relationship between the laws of nature and the ultimate power of the universe. The idea that harmony and balance within nature reflects the harmony and balance of the universe is as central to shamanism as it is to Taoism. Associated with this is the concept that change cannot be forced but only revealed or experienced. The shamanist is not in control of the spirits. They are in charge of him or her. Through the shaman they help humanity to repair any damage it has done and thus to return to the Way. The idea of flowing with the Way, of bending and thus surviving, reflects the shamanistic attitude to life around us.[7]

Reverence for ancestors has been mentioned already above. It has characterized Chinese religions from the earliest times. The continued interaction between the living and the dead meant that the living were protected by their ancestors, who remained interested in the affairs of the family, while the dead continued to be cared for by the living, with sacrificial offerings bestowed with respectful and meticulous ritual. Ancestor veneration gave particular emphasis to the role, unity and stability of the family. It also engendered filial respect and reverence. Bishop's comments concerning this fundamental belief are particularly pertinent: "Religion was predicated on a view of reality as monistic and moral and a belief in the continuity of life and organic natural processes. There was no sharp division between a person and his ancestors. Life flowed on from one generation to another. Similarly, there was no absolute break between past, present and future."[8] Such concepts reinforce the monistic unity in the universe that was to underpin later philosophical Taoism. But for the moment, it is important to note that ancestor reverence was essential to the ordinary person. Bodde called it "the most vital and sincere form of religious feeling" in early Chinese civilization.[9]

The historical roots of Taoism

The earliest period of Chinese tradition is mainly legendary, though evidence of a Stone Age and following Neolithic culture has been brought to light by archeological expertise. It is China that can boast the discovery of "Peking Man", a being likely to date back to the Pleistocene era, 400,000 or 500,000 BCE. Even earlier, approximately a million years ago, some kind of humanoid may have lived in the south-west of China, judging by fossil teeth discovered in 1965.[10]

While there is sound evidence of Stone Age and Neolithic cultures, traditional Chinese prehistory is mostly legendary, full of mythical heroes and legendary emperors and sages. Real facts about China's earliest past date back to about the late fourth and early third millennia BCE. Archeological discoveries have unearthed evidence of divination by the use of animal bones, inscribed pottery, clay phallic objects, and early altars. What is interesting is that many different Neolithic sites have been found in China, suggesting that the streams that fed Chinese civilization were varied and regional. The Neolithic people lived in villages in the river basins where the soil was fertile, or on the higher slopes where water was available but where they were safe from the frequent floods.

However, a common factor would have been dependency on agriculture, a fact that might presuppose an emphasis on fertility and nature. In a world where people were so dependent on the negative and positive powers of nature, it might be expected that earthly and heavenly phenomena were ascribed animated powers. And in the processes of birth, decay and death, it is perhaps here that we see the need for a cult of ancestors who would protect and aid the family and clan.

Of the legendary rulers of ancient China, the most celebrated in the history of Taoism as much as Chinese religion in general is the figure known as the Yellow Emperor, Huang-ti/Huangdi, whom legend dates at around 2500 BCE. He is said to have had secret and divine knowledge. Although the famous Taoist sage Chuang-tzu/Zhuangzi frequently mentions the Yellow Emperor, real evidence to suggest his existence outside myth is impossible to find. But what is important about the Yellow Emperor is that traditionally he is said to have been the founder of Taoism, thus predating Lao-tzu/Laozi, the oldest and most famous sage of Taoism. Although it was Lao-tzu/Laozi who gave Taoism its metaphysical and mystical emphasis, Chinese themselves see the Yellow Emperor as beginning it all. Blofeld wrote: "The majestic figure of the Yellow Emperor looms through the swirling mists of time, for he was one of the Five Emperor-Sages belonging to China's Golden Age (2852–2255 BC) who presided over the birth of the Empire, endowing it with such precious skills as the use of fire, of ploughs, of silk-looms. He personally is credited with having discovered and transmitted the secret of immortality."[11] He was also said to be an expert at *feng-shui*, "earth magic".

The Yellow Emperor was the most important of the legendary emperors, but there were many other legendary figures before and after him, retrospectively cast back into ancient time by later rulers of China. The time of these legendary characters was known traditionally as a Golden Age when people lived in harmony with nature and each other in a life of tranquillity and peace. Since each person's consciousness was harmonized with all other aspects of life, society needed no rules for living: these were introduced only when the Golden Age declined and the consciousness of human beings deteriorated.

The Shang dynasty

The first real Chinese dynasty was the Shang dynasty, sometimes called the Yin dynasty from its later capital. It is dated approximately to 1600–1027 BCE and developed into an advanced Bronze Age culture.

This mature Bronze Age culture produced some beautifully and expertly crafted bronze utensils for religious ritual, for war, and as luxury items. It is from the decorative representations on some of these bronzes that we are able to glean something of the life at the time. Apart from rice and millet, wheat also seems to have been cultivated. Cowrie shells were used as a means of exchange. Divination was an important part of the religious cult, and the practice of it in different ways both preceded the Shang dynasty and stretched down the centuries after it. In Shang times, the undershells of tortoises and turtles or shoulder-blades of animals were heated so that the cracks could be "read" by trained priests, who would then relay the decision of the gods. At first, questions posed elicited only "yes" or "no" or "favourable" or "unfavourable", answers, though later, statements of intent rather than questions became more characteristic. Diviners seem to have been fairly meticulous about keeping records of their transactions, inscribing the divinatory request alongside the cracks and, on occasion, how a king had interpreted it.[12]

Shang religion was pluralistic and polytheistic with a supreme divine being called Ti/Di "Lord" or Shang-ti/Shangdi, "Lord on High", and a host of other deities and spirits. It was, after all, the many nature deities and ancestral spirits that were felt to be closest to the needs of the people, and it was the forces of nature, both benign and malevolent, that were so critical to daily existence. While archeological discoveries cannot project a philosophy of life onto physical artefacts, Donald Bishop has the following to say about the early Chinese direct experience with nature:

> Each day, as the farmer plants his fields and tills the land, he is directly aware of and apprehends the working of nature. But, and very important, intuitive insight is present also. Closely identifying himself with her, the farmer unconsciously knows or is aware of the nuances of nature. He is sensitive to her inner forces. Knowing what the day would bring weatherwise, when the right time to plant the seed is, whether the coming winter will be harsh or mild was a skill so highly developed, among some, that it seemed as if they had an almost miraculous insight into the ways of nature or mother earth.[13]

Bishop's words provide a very simple but an interesting observation. The Chinese, as noted above, were early attuned to nature and, as we shall see, it was these simpler affinities with nature that engendered the later, deeper, metaphysical philosophies. The harmony between the human and spirit world was as essential for effective agriculture, for health, longevity and success, as the harmony between the farmer and the soil. Indeed both were part of the interrelated cosmic pattern. It was in the person of the king that harmony between Heaven and Earth was centred, and his earthly abode was the fulcrum for the important rites that linked the two.

In ancient China there were many gods – gods of the sun and moon, of the rain, the wind, lakes and of clouds. But earthly gods were also very important, not only of rivers, mountains and such natural phenomena, but also of the earth itself, for gods of the soil and of the grain were more immediately effective in daily existence. For the ordinary peasant earth gods and immediate ancestral spirits would have been seen as essential to the ongoing work in the fields. The rain was needed at the right time, and the forces of winter and summer were treated respectfully, "the fecundity of the earth and that of families were interlinked, the same ceremonies which banished the evil influence of winter announced the beginning of both the agricultural season and the marriage season".[14] But we know little of the ordinary peasant in ancient China, for the information we have of the Shang and Chou/Zhou dynasties refers only to the higher class. What we do know is that the family was and always remained extremely important, what Maspero termed "the fundamental cell of ancient Chinese society".[15] What is important for our purpose here, is the fact that harmony between Heaven and Earth, and between human beings and their environment, were considered essential for health, well-being and longevity. These ideas fed into the traditions of the martial arts millennia later.

The Chou/Zhou dynasty

The Chou/Zhou dynasty that followed the Shang is generally dated from 1027–256 BCE. We know a good deal more about these years since it was a dynasty that left us literary sources – including the well-known *I Ching/Yijing* that has had a profound influence on both Taoism and T'ai Chi Ch'üan/Taijiquan, as we shall see in later chapters. The history of the Chou/Zhou dynasty need not concern us too much here, for there was a continuation, though with considerable elaboration, of beliefs and practices from Shang times. But it is important to note that the great philosophers – Confucius, Lao-tzu/Laozi and Chuang-tzu/Zhuangzi – are dated to the later Chou/Zhou times from about the mid-sixth century BCE.

Religious ritual was rhythmic; it complemented the seasons and agricultural cycles on the one hand, and the needs of ancestor worship on the other. It segmented the year[16] into patterns and balances that were predictable, and that were believed to bring about the necessary harmony for existence. By conforming to the rhythms of nature and the patterns for care and veneration of ancestors, life was ensured in a self-creative way. The religious festivals, especially, were intimately linked with agriculture. Divination was still important, but the diviners took to the use of yarrow stalks for divining, rather than the bones of animals and shells of tortoises as in Shang times, though the richer persons might resort to the latter.

The age of the philosophers

The sixth century BCE onwards under the Chou/Zhou witnessed a superb intellectual flowering, producing some of the greatest thinkers and philosophers in the world. There were said to be a hundred schools of philosophers, and their counsel was sought by great nobles at a time of political unrest and social conflict. The age was a crucial period for Taoism proper. Throughout the Chou/Zhou dynasty there had been a growing literati, and by the sixth century BCE such intellectuals had become increasingly concerned with more abstract thought. They were perhaps influenced by the instability of the time, the corrupt Chou/Zhou rulers, and the feeling that their supreme god was impotent in the face of the suffering of so many people. The literati, then, were beginning to be concerned with naturalistic, humanistic and ethical philosophy in contrast to ritualistic religion. Coupled with this was the desire of some to withdraw from the political arena, commune with nature, and follow a more cosmic path.

The late Chou/Zhou period, then, saw the rise of more metaphysical thought. What was behind all the flux and change of life? Was there something behind the constant transformations of *yin* and *yang* in the cosmos? Coupled with this was a belief that life was precious and should be preserved. Death was not the inevitable fate of all. Then, too, the interconnectedness of life gave it a unity, and all things in that unity had their natural "way". It is never really clear whether those that thought this way were religious thinkers or philosophical humanists. For they certainly turned their backs on religious propriety in the sense of conforming to norms of ritual practice. Chuang-tzu/Zhuangzi, for example, was found singing to himself while beating time on a wooden bowl after his wife died, instead of conforming to the usual funeral rites. It is the early Taoist sages like Lao-tzu/Laozi and Chuang-tzu/

Zhuangzi, set in the late Chou/Zhou dynasty, who will absorb chapter 3. With Confucius, Lao-tzu/Laozi and Chuang-tzu/Zhuangzi and others in the three centuries after Confucius, we have the age of classical China, the age of the great philosophers and thinkers in Chou/Zhou times.

But there were other streams of thought and practice that were also feeding into what was eventually to become the expansive sea of Taoism. A passion for longevity was taken up by some and cultivated by control and exercise of the body, along with breathing exercises. It is here that we see the practical beginnings of the martial arts like T'ai Chi. Ideas of immortality had also gained ground, concomitant with harmony of the inner forces of the body. Death, it was believed, occurred because of the disharmony of *yin* and *yang* material forces in the body. But if these forces could be kept in perfect harmony and retained, death would be averted. Morality, virtue, fasting, control of breath – were all thought to promote such harmony.

Taoism in Imperial China

With the end of the Chou/Zhou dynasty China passed into its imperial phase; kings became emperors and, apart from a few periods during its long history, imperial China lasted until the twentieth century. It is from the name of the first Chinese emperor, Ch'in Shih Huang-ti/Qinshi Huangdi, that the word China is derived. But the Ch'in/Qin dynasty was short (221–206 BCE), and it was the following Han dynasty (206 BCE–220 CE) that was to witness the real beginnings of Taoism.

The Han dynasty

The pre-eminence of Confucianism encouraged an emphasis on preciseness in ritual, good manners, and the behaviour of the gentleman. Confucianism became the accepted state doctrine. But the seeds of religious Taoism were certainly blossoming under the Han. There was a considerable move towards a more magico-religious expression at the popular level – a legacy of the ancient shamanic and magical practices. The spirit of the time was one of Confucian supremacy, but a continuing belief in supernatural forces with which Taoism was to be increasingly concerned. The intermingling of the two – Confucianism and Taoism – was to continue for many centuries.

The shared philosophies of the age included a view of the universe as an orderly, interconnected whole that was self-originating and self-generating. Each entity within it was an intimate part of the totality of the cosmos, whether that part was a physical and natural entity or a supernatural one. The interrelation of the many parts necessitated their interdependence. Energy, *ch'i/qi*, pulsated through the universe and gave rhythm and life to it, and the theories of *yin* and *yang* and the Five Elements or Agents, explored in Chou/Zhou times, explained the coming into being and passing away of all matter. No divine being needed to be postulated to explain the universe; it had come into being through its own natural processes. Concomitant with these theories, the acceptance of the Five Elements explained the qualities any existing entities possessed: they were the fundamental categories of reality, accounting for all things. The whole process of *yin* and *yang* and creation and destruction were felt to be reflected in the rise and fall of dynasties, of power, of seasons – in the natural rhythms of all life. These fundamental concepts of *ch'i/qi*, *yin* and *yang* and the Five Elements are essential components of the philosophy that underpins T'ai Chi Ch'üan/Taijiquan, and will be taken up in later chapters.

Fang-shih/fangshi

From the third century BCE until about the fifth century CE China witnessed the presence of a group of diverse men known as *fang-shih/fangshi*. They practised divination, medicine and magic in their early history and, later, astronomy, geomancy and music. Some were specialists in practices promoting longevity and immortality. They branched out, also, into more scientific areas such as calendrics, pharmacology, biology, metallurgy and the like.[17] Some gained status at court as men of learning – as much for their science as for their knowledge of astrology, their familiarity with magic, exorcism, and the world of spirits and immortals. These more supernatural practices declined as the influence of the *fang-shih/fangshi* waxed in higher circles. Their individual specialisms in many skills in Han times meant that their collective knowledge was very broad. Many *fang-shih/fangshi* were famous enough to have acquired the hagiographic state of immortality. Immortality was something that the emperors, especially, hoped to achieve, and this made the *fang-shih/fangshi* useful tools in that pursuit.

Underlying *fang-shih/fangshi* belief was, again, the perception of the universe as an interrelated Heaven and Earth. Harmony and rhythm were the norm of the universe and needed to be maintained in all aspects of life, but especially in that delicate balance between Heaven, the emperor who ruled by the Mandate of Heaven, and the subjects of the empire. The balances and rhythms of *yin* and *yang* and the explanation of all things through the Five Elements were accepted by *fang-shih/fangshi* but often reinterpreted. *Yin* and *yang* and the Five Elements were particularly involved in the biological interpretation of the human body, which was seen as a microcosm that reflected the macrocosm of the universe. The same interactive energies charged both, and it was essential that the energies of the human body were harmonized with the external, but interrelated, cosmos.

Religious Taoism

Amidst the backdrop of the Han dynasty, the roots of a religious Taoism were emerging, embedded in a search for longevity and immortality, and a variety of means was adopted to secure these goals. The search for means to immortality had been a feature of some strands of Chou/Zhou times, but it was clear that, whatever methods adopted to achieve it, immortality still eluded its protagonists. The Han answer came from early Taoists who posited the development in the self of an immortal, invisible "embryo". Essentially, this indestructible spirit soul had to be cultivated and its growth nourished by all sorts of practices – meditation, drugs, breathing exercises, sexual practices, trance, gymnastics, special diets and bodily postures. If such an embryo could be nourished and developed, when death occurred, it would simply rise from the body as the true self, metamorphosed like the butterfly that emerges from the chrysalis. Instead of death, a wonderful life with other immortals would await the soul, or it would have the freedom to wander the universe.

It was in the Han dynasty that the practice of alchemy became important for producing the elixirs that could promote longevity and immortality, and in an inner sense could help nourish the spirit embryo that would ensure immortality. The whole realm of alchemical practices that so attracted Taoism, and their influences on T'ai Chi, are important enough to warrant a separate section (chapter 6) later in this book. Here, it needs to be noted how Han times encouraged alchemical practices both within and beyond Taoism. It was the *fang-shih/fangshi*, especially, which united the many different ideas of alchemy, immortality, the Five Elements, *yin* and *yang*, and the nourishing of a spirit embryo into a primitive religious Taoism.

The development of religious Taoism need not take up too much space here, except to highlight those aspects that were significant in the development of T'ai Chi in much later centuries. The healing cult of Chang Tao-ling/Zhang Daoling in the second century CE linked sickness to wrong doing, and sought to remedy sickness by confession of sins. It was the beginnings of Celestial Masters Taoism. Another, similar, movement was Way of Great Peace Taoism, also a healing cult, which combined meditative practices with confession and repentance of sins.

In the fourth century CE, in the Chin/Jin dynasty, the great naturalist and alchemist Ko Hung/Ge Hong gave his literary name Pao-p'u-tzu/Baopuzi, "the Master that embraces simplicity", to a major work with the same title, completing it in 317. While he wrote many books, and possessed a considerable library, his *Pao-p'u-tzu/Baopuzi* gathered together all previous theories concerning immortals and alchemy, as well as discussing some major philosophical tenets of Taoism. Needham described him as "the greatest alchemist in Chinese history".[18] Most accept him as a Taoist, though some have reservations about this, considering his leanings towards, and erudition in, Confucianism.[19] The "outer chapters" or exoteric chapters of the *Pao-p'u-tzu/Baopuzi*, that is to say those dealing with the outward things of life, show Ko Hung/Ge Hong to have accepted Confucian morality and virtue in social and political living. But he seems to have been a Taoist at heart. The "inner chapters" of the *Pao-p'u-tzu/Baopuzi*, the esoteric chapters dealing with the inner being, are dedicated to the study of immortals, immortality, the nourishing and lengthening of life, and the means by which this can be brought about – alchemical elixirs; medicines; drugs; breathing exercises; dietetics; sexual practices; and talismans.[20] For Ko Hung/Ge Hong, acceptance of *Tao* and living one's life with it within would be pointless were it not for the goal of immortality. Since nature itself shows us that radical change and metamorphosis are natural to life, there seemed no reason why human life, too, could not be metamorphosed to a state of immortality. Death is but the pathology of wrong living; if living could be harmonious, healthy and moral, then life could be extended to the point of immortality.

As to the means to immortality, Ko Hung/Ge Hong believed that self-effort was essential, as well as moderation in all things in life, and assistance from a Master and the gods. A tranquil life, meditation and a good diet were important. Essential to immortality was to "feed" on the *ch'i/qi*, the vital energy of life. On the microcosmic level *ch'i/qi* is the life force of all that lives, and of all inanimate matter. Cosmically, it is that first vital energy, The One, created by *Tao*. As such, it pervades all and is the medium by which *Tao* pervades all. Without *ch'i/qi*, death results, but if *ch'i/qi* can be cultivated, constantly renewed and replenished, then death need not occur or, at worst, longevity can be assured. Human life can only exist in the *ch'i/qi* that is the essence of its being. Nourishing it is essential for energy in life, and this is possible because *ch'i/qi* is not a static but dynamic principle: it changes, fluctuates, diminishes, can be pure or impure. The whole *raison d'être* of T'ai Chi is based on this same understanding of *ch'i/qi*, as we shall see below.

From 316–588 CE China was divided between non-Chinese rulers in the North, and six successive Chinese dynasties in the South – Western Chin/Jin, Eastern Chin/Jin, Liu Sung/Liu Song, Southern Ch'i/Qi, Liang and Ch'en/Chen. Two important Taoist movements occurring in the southern dynasties deserve attention here. These were the Shang-ch'ing/Shangqing school and the Ling-pao/Lingbao school. The Shang-ching/Shangqing school of Taoism was founded by T'ao Hung-ching/Tao Hongjing in the time of the Eastern Chin/Jin. Adherents of the school hoped for life in Heaven, called Shang-ch'ing/Shangqing, from which the school derived its name. The gods could help in the pursuit of salvation, but the means to salvation were more mystical and inward rather than being ritualistic. Inner visualization of the images that would bring salvation were an essential ingredient of Shang-ch'ing/Shangqing practice. The ideal person was the sage who could fly to paradises and mingle with the gods, in his own mind, as much as in person. He could fly to the stars and planets, especially to the Big Dipper, and to the sun and the moon. The sage did not need external stimuli to aid his being, his wisdom came from within, which is exactly where *Tao* is to be found. Livia Kohn graphically writes:

> The aim of their visionary and ecstatic practices is to reorganize their consciousness. From ordinary people, practitioners develop into cosmic beings. No longer limited to their earthly environment, they increasingly make the heavens their true home, wander freely throughout the far ends of the world and soar up into the sky. The mind at one with the rhythmic changes of creation, they go along with all and thereby continue to exist eternally.[21]

The means to salvation were, therefore, prescriptive but thoroughly individual. Each had to work out his or her own salvation. The goal was unity: "The ultimate goal is to arrive at Oneness through the diversity and the multiplicity of forms of the life that animates our body. The human being is conceived as a plurality that must be harmonized, a totality that must be overcome, a oneness that must be constructed while retaining complexity."[22] Visual meditation to secure such goals became the pronounced feature of the movement.

In spite of the emphasis on interiorized development of the self, the Shang-ch'ing/Shangqing school also advocated *tao-yin/daoyin*, "gymnastic exercises", for the benefit of good health. Such exercises were ancient and long known, and were thought to promote the circulation of essential energy, *ch'i/qi*, in the body. T'ao Hung-ching/Tao Hongjing wrote extensively on alchemy and divination, and was interested in martial arts, medicine and herbology. But, from a different view, the meditative emphasis, and the simple and reclusive lifestyle advocated by T'ao Hung-ching/Tao Hongjing, was reminiscent of *wu-wei*, non-action, advocated by the philosophical strands of earlier Taoism, which we shall meet in chapter 3. It was Taoism devoid of excessive ritual, stressing the need to focus calmly without the intrusion of the mind's usual proliferation of thoughts.

Another important school of Taoism was Ling-pao/Lingbao Taoism, a movement also established in the time of the Eastern Chin/Jin. It was this movement that, under its main leader Lu Hsiu-ching/Lu Xiujing (406–77 CE), a great traveller and recluse, incorporated many Buddhist ideas into Taoism – universal salvation; *karma* (the idea that one's good and bad actions reap appropriate merit and demerit for oneself); rebirth; and the idea of perfected beings who could assist the spiritual evolution of the soul. Whereas Shang-ch'ing/Shangqing Taoism emphasized an internalized journey of the individual self, liturgical ritual was the main emphasis of Ling-pao/Lingbao Taoism. Importantly, the liturgical ritual laid down in the scriptures formed the basis of future Taoist liturgy down to the present day, when Lu Hsiu-ching/Lu Xiujing gathered together all Taoist texts and standardized Taoist rituals, drawing heavily on the Ling-pao/Lingbao scriptures for this dimension of his work. It was the first collection and systematized collation of Taoist scriptures, the beginning of the *Tao-tsang/Daozang*, the Taoist canon. Ling-pao/Lingbao Taoism *externalized* the interiorized meditative ritual of the Shang-ch'ing/Shangqing school, initiating highly complex, symbolic, dramatic and vivid ritual characterized by colour, music, dance and chants, and based on ancient praxis. The ritual symbolizes the unity of Heaven, Earth and the interior organs of man.

Much later, after the end of the Sung/Song dynasty (960–1279), three new schools were established – Complete Reality Taoism, which has survived to the present day; Grand Unity Taoism; and Great Way Taoism. Of these, Complete Reality Taoism, sometimes called Complete Realization, Perfect Realization, or Perfect Truth Taoism, advocated equal study of the "Three Teachings" of Confucianism, Taoism and Buddhism in order to gain the complete realization that would result in immortality. Rather influenced by Ch'an/Chan Buddhism, the movement incorporated ascetic practice and frugal living into its regime. The nourishment of stillness of mind, devoid of desires for things in the world, was the primary aim of the movement, second to which was the lesser aim of physical well-being. There was an emphasis, too, on the kind of serenity and naturalness of the self that were expressed by the great philosophers Lao-tzu/Laozi and Chuang-tzu/Zhuangzi. Wang Ch'ung-yang/Wang Chonyang in the twelfth century said:

> In all action there should be no overexertion, for when there is overexertion, the vital energy is damaged. On the other hand, when there is total inaction, the blood and vital energy become sluggish. Thus a mean should be sought between activity and passivity, for only in this way can one cherish what is permanent and be at ease with one's lot. This is the way to the correct cloistered life.[23]

The most well-known branch of the school today is Lung-men/Longmen Taoism.

Supreme, or Grand Unity, Taoism was founded by Hsiao Pao-chen/Xiao Baozhen, and lasted for approximately two hundred years. Important characteristics of the school were its use of talismans for the purpose of healing and exorcism, and its use of registers of good and evil deeds. It also advocated celibacy. Great Way Taoism (Ta-tao chiao/Dadaojiao) was founded by Liu Te-jen/Liu Deren. The movement advocated a modest and simple lifestyle in all respects, obtaining food from tilling the soil. Monastic chastity, inner stillness and emptiness were characteristics of the sect that seem to have been influenced by Buddhist thought and practice.

Taoist movements such as those briefly mentioned above are important in that they reflect the trends of the past. Notable amongst these trends are magico-religious practices that had their roots in shamanism; continued veneration of ancestors; the profound belief in the necessity for harmony between Heaven and Earth; and a multiplicity of gods, albeit more systematically organized than in ancient times. Importantly, however, we need to note those trends that would be taken up by T'ai Chi Ch'üan/Taijiquan. Shang-ching/Shangqing Taoism, for example, itself a healing movement, shows how the balance between meditation and movement can promote health and longevity. The harmony between spirit and matter, between mind and body, between breathing and the rhythms of life, between the energy of Heaven and Earth, between the gods of the macrocosm and the inner gods of the body – all these find their way into present practices of acupuncture and acupressure, *feng-shui* and T'ai Chi.

Subtle influences in belief and praxis came from wider cultural dimensions that have interacted over the centuries. The ancient indigenous nature of Confucianism and Taoism meant that there was much of mutual interest to both. Ko Hung/Ge Hong, for example, seemed both a Taoist and a Confucian, and the moral virtues of Confucianism were accepted by most Taoists. It was in such a way that the three strands of belief emerged in China, each interacting with and influencing the others. Confucianism donated an emphasis on ethics, personal and societal morality and the practicalities of life, and a deep sense of the need for order and meticulous ritual. Buddhism has encouraged concepts of rebirth and compassion, and the influence of Ch'an/Chan Buddhism (the Chinese term for Zen Buddhism) has also encouraged simplicity and a strong tendency towards exactitude of ritual praxis. Taoism has instilled attention to nature and the cyclical phases of life, and the practices of breathing, exercise, diet, inner alchemy and meditation to promote health, longevity and immortality. Saso describes this intermingling of essential ideas rather well:

> Confucianism is called the warp, and Taoism the woof of Chinese religion. It is precisely in the Taoist woof that creativity, color, and variable meaning are woven. The golden threads of Buddhism are blended into this tapestry . . . the Confucian threads, which run in a perpendicular manner from the top to the bottom of Chinese society, define the ethical norms of Chinese behaviour.[24]

T'ai Chi Ch'üan/Taijiquan

A familiar sight in China today is the communal practice of some form of exercise. It may be simply walking or jogging, or the practice of a martial art, and in the latter case this may be some form of *chi-kung/qigong* or T'ai Chi Ch'üan/Taijiquan. This last has been termed "China's cultural ambassador to the world" by Douglas Wile. He writes, too: "Touching the lives of more Westerners, and perhaps more deeply, than books, films, museums, or college courses, T'ai-chi Ch'üan is often the entrée to Chinese philosophy, medicine, meditation, and even language."[25] Those who know nothing of Chinese thought will almost certainly be familiar with the symbol of *yin* and *yang* and with the graceful movements of the T'ai Chi *form*. In fact, in Britain today, the BBC is currently using a brief caption of the movements as the interlude between some of its programmes. Paul Crompton's words, written long before the adoption of such, describe rather well what BBC viewers now witness: "Moving slowly, under the trees, breathing, it seems, in time with a gentle breeze; merging with Nature itself in a healing rhythm. Head, shoulders, arms, trunk, legs and feet moving as one; continuously, smoothly and restfully; as if swimming into a new, all pervading element; a different time, a different space . . . ".[26] So what does T'ai Chi Ch'üan/Taijiquan mean? We need to look at each of the individual Chinese words more deeply, in order to gain a greater understanding of the ideas that underpin its name and the practice of it.

T'ai/Tai

The word *t'ai/tai* in Chinese has a number of meanings. It can mean "high", "great", "supreme" or "remote", and in Taoism the highest or greatest level of achievement is to be in complete balance with *Tao*. Thus, the word *t'ai/tai* incorporates ideas that represent the highest goal of Taoists.

Chi/ji

Chi/ji in Chinese means the "ultimate", the "utmost point", "ridge-pole", this last as in the highest point of a building. In Taoism it is *Tao* that becomes the ridge-pole; *Tao* is the central point to which everything connects and from which everything comes. In the human body, the ridge-pole is the spinal column through which passes the essential energy of the body. Understanding the workings of *yin* and *yang* and reproducing their cosmic balance in the inner self helps to achieve that "supreme" goal of harmony with *Tao*. *Yin* and *yang* are the balancing agents that keep opposites in harmony, and T'ai Chi aims to create the kind of harmony of them – their perfect balance – that results in experience of the supreme ultimate *Tao*. Philosophically, *T'ai-chi/Taiji* is a unifying principle, a oneness, and the totality and unity of all principles – a concept that we shall take up for further examination in chapter 3. But, in this metaphysical sense, *T'ai-chi/Taiji* is the undifferentiated natural energy that comes from the Void, *Wu-chi/Wuji*. It is the source of *yin* and *yang*, and when static and unmoving is an undifferentiated whole. But, when it activates, the principles of *yin* and *yang* come into play and opposites occur through differentiation and separation causing the whole of creation. *T'ai-chi/Taiji*, then, is the force that makes this happen. Before beginning the sequence of movements that make up the practice of T'ai Chi, the practitioner stands still, feet apart, motionlessly poised, representing the undifferentiated universe before *yin* and *yang* movement begins.

Ch'üan/quan

The word *ch'üan/quan* in Chinese means "fist", or "boxing". It is a word normally associated with more aggressive martial arts such as Shaolin Ch'üan/Quan, the boxing of the Shaolin tradition. The relationship between T'ai Chi and the more aggressive martial arts will be examined in more detail below, for when we witness its practice, the measured grace and beauty of movement seem far removed from defensive martial art practice. Perhaps, as Sophia Delza interprets the term, *ch'üan/quan* is a metaphor for action, a symbol of the power and control over one's own mind and movements.[27] Putting the words together, then, we have a meaning of "Supreme Ultimate boxing" or "Supreme Ultimate fist". However, the whole term T'ai Chi Ch'üan/Taijiquan is a late one, and its practice was probably not known by this name until as late as the early twentieth century.[28] Hitherto, and preferable, was the term *Nei-chia Ch'üan/Neijiaquan*, "Internal Family Boxing". T'ai Chi is also grounded in the wider praxis that is termed *chi-kung/qigong*, the movement of energy, *ch'i/qi*, in the body.

Origins of T'ai Chi Ch'üan/Taijiquan in gymnastic exercises

To study the history of something is to seek a deeper understanding of it. In the words of Yang Jwing Ming: "History is experience. If you do not know the past, you will be lost in the future. The past gives spiritual stimulation. From the past, you know your source and root. Knowing the history of Tai Chi is the obligation of every practitioner who is willing to carry the responsibility of continuing the long tradition of the art."[29] Yet, the roots of T'ai Chi are obscure, to say the least, and to find a definitive beginning is impossible. There are a variety of traditions, each with its own view of the real origin. But it is hazardous to place its origins on the shoulders of any particular figure. Just as there is no one way of practice, so there is no one route back to a particular foundational figure as its source.

What we can say is that T'ai Chi has its roots in many practices of the ancient past. Gymnastic exercises were popular, for example, in the time of Chuang-tzu/Zhuangzi, and we have evidence for their existence in chapter 15 of his text. It seems, too, that gymnastic exercises were widely used for therapy in the third and second centuries BCE.[30] Throughout the following centuries many variations on these exercises, postures and movements developed. But we can go back even earlier than these gymnastic exercises, to the dances of the shamans. These dances were important to remedy lack of rain, illnesses, aberrations of climate and the like. The dances facilitated the flow of energy on Earth as much as in the human body. Despeux writes: "The dances are therefore conceived of as a means of resolving the congestion and stagnation of vital energy, to ensure its healthy circulation within human beings, as much as they are used to help the flow of the rivers on the earth."[31] The idea of harmonizing energies, of creating the correct balances in nature and in the human self, are clear from these words. So the idea of movement to create harmony is a very old one in Chinese culture. Then, too, shamanic dances often imitated the movements of creatures, a feature that has also inspired some of the movements in T'ai Chi.

If we move forward to the third century CE, the most popular of the gymnastic exercises were based on what was called the *Five Animals Pattern*. Here, the movements resembled those of the tiger, deer, bear, monkey and bird. Each had its respective movement that could eliminate specific diseases of the body. Thus, the *Chuang-tzu/Zhuangzi* speaks of hanging like a bear (more like swaying, judging by pictorial evidence[32]) and stretching like a bird. The crane, especially, attracted the attention of those who wished to emulate the movements of creatures for health and longevity. In particular, such movements were believed to enhance the flow of energy in the body. The movements served to guide the breath in the body, facilitating the circulation of other breaths as well as the blood. Guiding energy in such a way is an important function of T'ai Chi. The discovery of ancient Han burial tombs at Ma-wang-tui/Mawangdui, which date back to about the second century BCE, brought forth a number of silk manuscripts. On some of these there were drawings of people of all ages and both sexes engaged in physical exercises, rather like today's practices of T'ai Chi.

Taoist liturgy still contains a ritual called the *Steps of Yü/Yu*. It is a dance or pattern of steps based on a legend about Yü/Yu the Great, a legendary ancestor of the Chinese. He walked through nine regions of the earth, preventing floods and creating order in nature – so much so, that he became lame. His "dance" took on astral significance and was linked with the nine associative stars of the Big Dipper. By stepping out the pattern of these stars, energy is derived for the individual and the community. Thus, we can see that rhythmic, patterned movements have been part of Chinese practices since ancient times. But they were not simply movements *per se*, for they were aligned with breathing, with inner energy fields (*ch'i/qi*) and with Taoist alchemy. Thus, Despeux points out that "gymnastics are almost always presented in connection with breathing techniques and the circulation of *qi*. One may practice each one in isolation, but they have a far better effect when they are harmoniously joined together into one sequence of exercises".[33] This is certainly true of the practice of T'ai Chi. The whole issue of energy, *ch'i/qi*, is important enough to be taken up in a separate chapter. What needs to be said here is that its unimpeded circulation through the body is essential to the ultimate aim of return to the natural state of *Tao*, and for health and cure of illnesses, as more proximate aims. Again, Despeux pertinently writes of pre-T'ai Chi practices:

> All movements should be executed carefully and rhythmically so that all tensions will be eliminated. Gradually the movements affect the inside of the body more and more, so that the outer practice of gymnastics is gradually replaced by the inner practice of the qi. The latter is a slow guiding, a circulation done at every individual's own speed. Eventually the entire body is moved by the inner circulation of qi, a technique vitally important in the entire process of gymnastics.[34]

Again, too, these words are fully applicable to the practice of T'ai Chi today, where breathing regulates the speed and harmony of the movements and the circulation of energy within. When we come to look later at the alchemical aspects of Taoism, we shall see how the energy within works to create longevity – and, as many Taoists believe, immortality. All these exercises were given the term "guiding and pulling" or *tao-yin/daoyin*. And what was being guided or pulled, then, was the energy within, *ch'i/qi*.

All these practices were seen as having great medical advantages, and were therefore featured in medical texts. They were not originally Taoist, but came to be accepted by, and incorporated in, Taoist beliefs and practices. Literature relating to *tao-yin/daoyin* can be found in the Taoist Canon,[35] but if we want to look specifically for texts concerning T'ai Chi, it is to the much later time of the eighteenth to twentieth centuries that the major literature belongs. Clearly, however, the traditions of the early gymnastic practices, the *Tao Te Ching/Daodejing*, the *I Ching/Yijing*, the theory of *yin* and *yang*, and the Five Elements or

Agents – all of which await us in later chapters – have informed the practice of T'ai Chi Ch'üan/Taijiquan.

The T'ai Chi *Classics*, the texts that relate specifically to T'ai Chi Ch'üan/Taijiquan, are not especially helpful in establishing the origins of the art. The *Discourse on T'ai Chi Ch'üan/Taijiquan*, for example, claimed to have been written by the Ming dynasty Chang San-feng/Zhang Sanfeng, may not, indeed, have been written by him despite an appended verse attaching his name to it. The *Classic on T'ai Chi Ch'üan/Taijiquan* is more definitively written by Wang Tsung-yüeh/Wang Zongyue, who lived in the eighteenth century, and to whom a number of other texts amongst the *Classics* are assigned. Dating and authorship of the texts in the *Classics* are very problematic and generally unhelpful in establishing chronology and lineages. The *Thirteen Postures* included in the *Discourse on T'ai Chi Ch'üan/Taijiquan* are pivotal to all martial arts and to the type of boxing practised by a family known as Ch'en/Chen, with whom Wang Tsung-yüeh/Wang Zongyue had much contact, as we shall see. This text, like so many others in the *Classics*, is clearly a martial art one, and associated with more aggressive practice. Indeed, it would have to be said from an examination of these *Classics* that there is a heavy influence on the martial art side. Lo, Inn, Amacker and Foe are adamant that, while the *Classics* have a good deal to do with both the martial art side as well as cultivation of inner energy, it is the former that predominates:

> Yet since the framework of T'ai Chi Ch'uan is that of the martial arts, everything in T'ai Chi must stand up to the most rigorous martial analysis. The T'ai Chi Ch'uan *Classics* is an attempt to state (selectively, even arbitrarily, and by no means exhaustively) the irrevocable principles of Taoism in terms of martial arts. No one can truly say they understand the *Classics* until they can not only offer some interpretation of the statements, but can defend their significance in the specifics of *ch'uan* or boxing.[36]

From the texts, then, it would have to be claimed that T'ai Chi is in origins a martial art. Pas makes the point that monks in China were not permitted to carry arms, and thus monastic communities needed to be trained in self-defence.[37] A similar kind of thinking sees the origins of T'ai Chi in the Shaolin traditions of the sixth to seventh centuries in China. The Indian Buddhist Bodhidharma is said to have travelled to China in the sixth century and stayed at the Shaolin monastery. He was the founder of Ch'an/Chan (Japanese Zen) Buddhism in China. While teaching the monks at the monastery he noted their weak and degenerate state. So he introduced a martial art, *Shaolin Kung-fu/Shaolin Gongfu*, that would strengthen them. Bodhidharma became known by the Chinese name of Ta-mo/Damo. In the eighth century Ta-mo/Damo's practice was adapted by Hsü Hsüan-p'ing/Xu Xuanping into what was called the *Long Boxing Exercise*. Some of the names of the movements here, such as *White Crane Spreads Wings* and *Single Whip*, are the same as those in today's T'ai Chi Ch'üan/Taijiquan. Yet, even for these early monastic practices, the martial exercises were also seen as promoting spiritual health. Indeed, it would have been a radical departure from earlier *tao-yin/daoyin* had the health and spiritual benefits been discarded. The Buddhist emphasis would have been as much on control of the mind and meditation as strengthening of the body: the inner control of the mind was essential to the outward performance of the movement. But the movements introduced by Ta-mo/Damo were particularly muscular and forceful, quite different from the graceful performance of T'ai Chi that we know today. However, the influence of the Shaolin martial art practices and the styles that came from them should not be underestimated. Olson refers to them as "the apex of martial arts for many centuries in China".[38]

We would have to conclude, then, that T'ai Chi is fundamentally a martial art. Indeed, Yang Jwing Ming is of the opinion that the martial art perspective is essential to the wholeness of T'ai Chi.[39] Moreover, while names of movements might seem outwardly quite innocuous, their more aggressive martial connotation is often hidden within them. According to Yang Jwing Ming: "An example is "Pick up Needle from Sea Bottom". In Chinese, the perineum is called the Sea Bottom (Hai Di), and so a main application of the form is to attack the groin."[40] Similarly *Grasp the Sparrow's Tail* is a movement that demands sensitivity and caution rather than muscular strength in dealing with an opponent – exactly the kind of movement that would be needed if one wanted to catch a sparrow by the tail.[41] A movement like *Ward Off*, however, where the arms are raised in such a manner that it seems as if one is repelling an attacker, has more of an overt connection with the martial nature.

Over the centuries, the Shaolin form developed into five styles, each given an animal name – Crane, Snake, Leopard, Tiger and Dragon. From these, too, came other styled branches. Shaolin Boxing spread not only throughout China, but also to other countries. In Korea it is called Tai Kuan Do, and in Japan, the well-known name Karate. All these styles that stem from the original Shaolin practice are *hard* styles: they are *yang* in their energy, and are called *external, hard* styles. By contrast, T'ai Chi is a *yin*, *internal* and *soft* style, as are similar practices like Hsing-i/Xingyi and Pa-kua/Ba-gua. To watch, T'ai Chi is clearly the softest of all. Hard styles increase muscle, limb, sinew and tendon strength, whereas the soft styles promote circulation of energy, breath and inner vitality. T'ai Chi, especially, is meditative in nature.

Chang San-feng/Zhang Sanfeng

Having looked at the origins of T'ai Chi Ch'üan/Taijiquan in the wider context of Chinese culture and tradition, we now need to look at the traditional founder of T'ai Chi, Chang San-feng/Zhang Sanfeng, "Chang of the Three Abundances".[42] He is a highly elusive figure, of whom Anna Seidel wrote, "he is an especially rich and famous example of the cult of the immortal and well suited to reveal the multiple facets of the hagiography of a Taoist saint".[43] So, as an immortal and a saint, there have been woven into his elusive life all kinds of legends. It is also possible that stories associated with others by the name of Chang/Zhang have found their way into the life of this traditional founder of T'ai Chi.[44]

The elusive character of Chang San-feng/Zhang Sanfeng is epitomized well in his dating. Some say he lived in the Sung/Song dynasty (tenth to thirteenth centuries), some in the Chin/Qin dynasty (twelfth to thirteenth centuries), some in the Yüan/Yuan dynasty (thirteenth to fourteenth centuries), and some in the Ming (fourteenth to seventeenth centuries). And tradition has it that, since he was an immortal, he spanned all of them. We know that the Chinese liked to have a strong lineage for their kingdoms, schools of thought and traditions, and to have immortals as the founders would have bestowed on them considerable status. While it was also prestigious to have a lineage that was ancient, a late Yüan/Yuan and early Ming date for him is, however, the most likely, despite tradition. We know, too, that a certain Chang San-feng/Zhang Sanfeng was summoned to the emperor's court in the fifteenth century, but whether this was our Chang San-feng/Zhang Sanfeng is impossible to say. And as far as his link with T'ai Chi is concerned, this appears to be late – in the nineteenth or twentieth centuries.[45]

Needless to say, the life of Chang San-feng/Zhang Sanfeng is equally shrouded in elusive mystery. His strange appearance is portrayed in each of the four sixteenth-century biographies of him. Anna Seidel summarized these:

> Each of his biographies describes him as exceedingly tall (seven feet); looking as if he had the longevity of a turtle and the immortality of a crane. He had enormous eyes and ears, a beard bristling like the blades of halberds, and hair tied into a knot at the back of his head. Summer and winter he wore only one garment and a bamboo hat; he could sleep in the snow without catching cold, could eat huge quantities of food at one sitting or fast for months, and could climb mountains as if flying.[46]

He was also a magician, it seems, and taught internal alchemy – the refining of inner energies in order to become enlightened. Early in the Ming dynasty he journeyed to the Wu-tang/Wudang Mountains where he set up his retreats, as did a few of his eminent disciples who became immortals. War disturbed the peace of the mountain retreats, and Chang San-feng/Zhang Sanfeng left. There are accounts of his meetings with a few individuals, and an important account of his supposed death towards the close of the fourteenth century. At the Monastery of Pao-chi/Baoji he is recorded as having said farewell to his followers, given them some hymns, and then died. But as they were about to bury him, they heard knocking from inside the coffin. When they opened it, they found Chang San-feng/Zhang Sanfeng alive. From this time on, he appeared to Taoist hermits, but eluded the envoys of those emperors who wished to invite him to court. Nevertheless, his fame was sufficient for the sanctuaries on the Wu-tang/Wudang Mountains to be extravagantly restored early in the fifteenth century, and for him to be canonized in 1459 by the Emperor Ying-tsun/Yingzun, and given the name of Immortal Penetrating Mystery and Revealing Transformation. During the centuries that followed his pseudo death, many claimed to have seen him, met with him, or identified a stranger as him. It seems he was an unwashed phenomenon, dressed in rags, eccentric, but capable of curing illnesses and attracted to temples. His dreadful appearance earned him the title of "Dirty Immortal", but apparently the filth on his body could be rolled up into pills that would cure disease![47]

Many legends have been associated with Chang San-feng/Zhang Sanfeng. One tells of a friend who fell into misfortune. Chang had foreseen such an event, and after trying to persuade his friend to leave society and take up the hermit's life, gave him the gift of a portrait of himself, a gourd and a box. When misfortune arose and his family was near starvation, the friend sowed the seeds he found in the gourd and they sprouted sufficient cereal to feed all his family. The Emperor was impressed and restored the family to favour. In the box was Chang San-feng/Zhang Sanfeng's cloak, which proved to be able to cure illnesses. The self-portrait of Chang San-feng/Zhang Sanfeng became the focus of a cult of followers dedicated to him. Another legend places him meditating in the garden of a family. One day he planted the branches of a plum tree there, whereupon they immediately produced flowers.

Of the writings about Chang San-feng/Zhang Sanfeng, many are embroidered by later traditions. They need not concern us here, but it is important to note that any historical fact is overlaid considerably with hagiographical legend. As to Chang San-feng/Zhang Sanfeng himself, a number of texts have been attributed to him. Three texts – the *Summary of the Golden Elixir*, *Secret Principles of Gathering the True Essence* and the *Rootless Tree* – appear in a nineteenth-century text.[48] There are also others, but to establish exact dating and authorship is a formidable task, and it could well be that there are no real writings of the old immortal. Nevertheless, there are so-called "Complete Works", probably the result of later disciples and the cult that surrounded Chang San-feng/Zhang Sanfeng. He was supposed to have written a commentary on a text called *The Hundred Character Tablet* by Ancestor Lü/Lu and essays on the teaching of Wang Che/Wang Zhe, who founded an important school of religious Taoism, as well as a number of other essays.[49] Since many in the T'ai Chi tradition accept Chang San-feng/Zhang Sanfeng as the founder of the practice, some of these writings will be used to elucidate aspects of practice and belief in later chapters of this book. If nothing else, they serve to illustrate ideas that inform T'ai Chi. At the end of the *Thirteen Postures* in the *Discourse on T'ai Chi Ch'üan/Taijiquan*, as noted above, is an appended verse that associates Chang Sang-feng/Zhang Sanfeng with the practice of T'ai Chi as a martial art. The appended verse reads: "This treatise has been handed down by Ancestor Chang San-feng of Wu-T'ang Mountain so that heroes and worthy men everywhere can lengthen their lives and attain longevity, not merely as a means to martial skill."[50] It is unlikely, however, that the text can be attributed to the immortal, for it is a late text.[51] Thus, we are left with a large body of works allegedly written by Chang San-feng/Zhang Sanfeng but very little possibility that he was the author of them. Clearly, however, what emerges is a tradition of practices that amalgamate both inner meditational focus of the mind, with outward bodily movement, a factor that accords well with the long Chinese tradition of the inseparable nature of body and soul, or body and mind. The process is one of steady refining of the mind and the whole self.

To accept the evidence of the writings attributed to Chang San-feng/Zhang Sanfeng is to accept also that he practised internal and sexual alchemy. Internal alchemy will be examined below in the chapter 6, *Energy*. Here, it needs to be noted that it was a process by which the adept refined internal energy in order to transmute it into the kind of pure energy that was *Tao*. Whoever Chang San-feng/Zhang Sanfeng was, he was perhaps an alchemist of this kind. The *Summary of the Golden Elixir*, though unlikely to have been his work, combines alchemical practices with movement, advocating a "moving method".[52] Internal alchemy also characterizes the text *Secret Principles of Gathering the True Essence*. In *The Rootless Tree*, we find a strongly Buddhist ring to the text, but not one so distant from Taoist thought. Here is its first verse:

> The rootless tree,
> Its flowers secluded.
> Who among those attached to the red dust of the world
> would cultivate it?
> The affairs of this floating life;
> A ship on a sea of bitterness.
> Driven hither and thither, out of control.
> No sight of land or shore, how difficult to find a safe mooring.
> We drift forever in a sea of cruel sea monsters.
> If you will but turn your head,
> And look back at this shore.
> Do not wait for the wind and waves to wreck your ship.[53]

Many Taoist principles are to be found in the depth of these words. Cultivating the inner return to harmony in the midst of the sea of the world's constant turmoil is the aim of T'ai Chi.

Not only is Chang San-feng/Zhang Sanfeng reputed to have been an inner alchemist, he was also adept at sexual alchemy. Sexual energy, evident as coarse semen, is *yang* and Taoists who practised sexual alchemy believed it essential to store sexual energy or coarse semen rather than emit it, and therefore lose it, in intercourse. Since it is a natural energy that usually decreases with age, Taoists reasoned that maintaining semen yet, also, "gathering" it from a sexual partner, would preserve energy and enhance longevity. The coarse energy was then purified through inner alchemy into a highly refined state. A text like *Secret Principles of Gathering the True Essence* is clearly devoted to the practice of sexual alchemy.[54] But not all Taoists followed such practices though there may well have been secret transmission of the arts related to the practices for generations. When the texts supposedly written by Chang San-feng/Zhang Sanfeng were collected together in the nineteenth century by Li Hsi-yüeh/Li Xiyue he made sure that Chang San-feng/Zhang Sanfeng was removed from any connection with the practices of sexual alchemy.[55]

Despite the confusion surrounding the life and nature of Chang San-feng/Zhang Sanfeng, he became the figurehead adopted by many sects of Taoists. His cult was further popularized when his *Collected Works* were published by Li Hsi-yüeh/Li Xiyue. Those who adopted him as their patriarch did so for a variety of reasons, and practitioners of T'ai Chi Chüan/Taijiquan focused on his brand of martial art. There is little that we have seen so far to connect Chang San-feng/Zhang Sanfeng with any kind of physical exercises or martial arts. How, then, did this connection occur? Many think that there must have been some link with the Shaolin tradition that began with Ta-mo/Damo and spread through China. Some traditions accept that Chang San-feng/Zhang Sanfeng travelled to Mount Pao-chi/Baoji where he learned Shaolin *kung-fu/gongfu* of the Five Animal Form.[56] In one of his biographies he is said to have become disenchanted with Shaolin practices and to have infused ideas from the *Tao Te Ching/Daodejing* and the *I Ching/Yijing* into them, creating a different style. Those who accept Chang/Zhang as the founder of T'ai Chi vary in the degree to which they accept Shaolin influence on the practice, but it seems reasonable to assume some influence on its beginnings, given the enormous prestige and widespread practice of the Shaolin styles. Perhaps this explains why texts specific to T'ai Chi are wholly martial in emphasis rather than stressing health, meditation and longevity.

In the biography of sixteenth-century Chang Sung-ch'i/Zhang Songqi, who was a famous martial art practitioner, it is said that he was a student of the alchemist Chang San-feng/Zhang Sanfeng, and that the latter was living as a recluse in the Wu-tang/Wudang Mountains. Chang Sung-ch'i/Zhang Songqi's biography states that he adopted a different style of boxing than the Shaolin traditions. His was "esoteric", softer and more yielding, practised by mindfulness rather than outward strength like the "exoteric" style of Shaolin.[57] The transmission of this esoteric style has been linked to T'ai Chi, but there is little similarity between them.[58]

A popular story linking Chang San-feng/Zhang Sanfeng with T'ai Chi tells of his witnessing a conflict between a snake and a crane. The snake wove its head to and fro hissing at the crane in a tree above. The crane flew down to attack the snake with its beak. The snake turned its head to the side and made to strike the crane's neck with its tail end, but the crane lifted its right wing to protect its neck. In like manner the battle went on, the snake always weaving out of the crane's way and the crane always able to protect itself by the right movement. Thus, tradition holds that Chang/Zhang used the movements of animals and ordinary scenes to create movements. And in the T'ai Chi movements today we find *White Crane Spreads Wings* and *Snake Creeps Down.*

Another connection of Chang/Zhang with martial arts may have come about through his habitat on the Wu-tang/Wudang Mountains. For Mount Wu-tang/Wudang was home to the God of War, the Dark Warrior, Chen-wu/Zhenwu, from whom Chang/Zhang is said to have learned his boxing form in a dream. Chang San-feng/Zhang Sanfeng is also accepted by some as the God of Wealth, a tradition that arose from his being the master of a popular god of riches in the seventeenth century.[59] Textual statements accepting Chang San-feng/Zhang Sanfeng as the founder of T'ai Chi are related to the major traditions of the present day, but do not provide substantial evidence for the connection.[60] However tenuous the link between Chang/Zhang and T'ai Chi may be, he certainly enjoyed a large number of followers both past and present. Of the schools of T'ai Chi today that accept Chang/Zhang as the founder, the major ones are the Yang, Wu, Sun, Sung Shu-ming and Tu Yüan-hua/Du Yuanhua.[61] It is to the development of some of these schools that we must now turn our attention.

The origins of the styles

We need not dwell on the intricacies and abundant contradictions of lineages and chronologies, which will always defy attempts at accuracy. Traditions are wholly blurred on the lineage of T'ai Chi/Taiji Masters.[62] Indeed, Dan Docherty describes such traditions as "a minefield situated in a maze".[63] Nevertheless, a few points need to be explored. The immediate successor of Chang San-feng/Zhang Sanfeng is variously given as Ch'en Tung-chou/Chen Dongzhou, and Wang Tsung/Wang Zong – an individual not to be confused with the later Wang Tsung-yüeh/Wang Zongyue. Another successor is said to be the sixteenth century Chang Sung-ch'i/Zhang Songqi, who taught the internal, soft style (*nei-chia/neijia*), in contrast to Shaolin techniques. The most important character in the lineage from Chang Sung-ch'i/Zhang Songqi is Wang Tsung-yüeh/Wang Zongyue, for it is he that is credited with authorship of the T'ai Chi *Classics*. Some believe it was Wang Tsung-yüeh/Wang Zongyue who brought the martial art to the Ch'en/Chen village, others that he was a student of the Ch'en/Chens and recorded the material he learnt there in the *Classics*.[64] Most accept his authorship. Apparently, he was passing through the Ch'en/Chen village where the villagers were practising their particular martial art. Having watched them for a while he passed on, and later got into conversation with some of them at the local inn, to the effect that their art was not so good. Inevitably he was asked to prove his point. At this, he showed the superiority of his soft, internal style by defeating them all. As a result, he remained in the village to teach what became the Ch'en/Chen style of T'ai Chi. While there are no certain criteria to date him, a tentative date of the late eighteenth century is possible.

The official Chinese view, however, is that Ch'en Wang-t'ing taught the Ch'en family in the seventeenth century, and Wang Tsung-yüeh/Wang Zongyue learned the art from the Ch'en/Chens rather than transmitting it to them. Ch'en Wang-t'ing/Chen Wangting, dated somewhere in the mid-seventeenth century, introduced the Ch'en/Chen family to a new style of martial art. While he was deeply involved with martial art skills, he introduced breathing techniques and stressed concentration of the mind in practice. Like so many practitioners before him, he used animal movements in the sequences of his style, and was especially concerned with promoting the circulation of energy in the body. It is he who is said to have introduced the *Pushing Hands* exercise, and he was also concerned to incorporate alternating *yin* and *yang* movements.

The social and historical backdrop against which the development of T'ai Chi Chüan/Taijiquan took place was one of great social unrest, sectarian rebellion and natural disasters. Douglas Wile is one writer that presents this backdrop rather well. He notes that there were a number of militant sects during the nineteenth century that took up martial arts as a means of active rebellion as well as defensive protection. This was so particularly in the North. Wile writes: "That major style founders, Wu Yü-hsiang, Yang Lu-ch'an, Hao Wei-chen, Wu Chien-ch'üan, and Sun Lu-t'ang, all hailed from Hebei, China's most fertile breeding ground for martial arts, must be more than coincidence."[65] Clearly, Wile's words are another indicator of the martial art origin of T'ai Chi Chüan/Taijiquan.

It is with the Ch'en/Chen family that we find the origins of the many styles of T'ai Chi used today. Their tradition of boxing reaches back several centuries.[66] The Ch'en/Chen style is, thus, the basis from which other styles emerged. But while it is a soft style, it is more geared to martial practice than many of the styles derived from it: the martial art tradition of the Ch'en/Chen family was never completely abandoned.

Yang Lu-ch'an/Yang Luchan adapted it for his Yang style in the nineteenth century and Wu Chien-ch'üan/Wu Jianquan adapted the Yang style to create the Wu style early in the twentieth century. Another member of the Wu family taught his nephew Li I-yü/Li Yiyu (1832–92) from where we get the Li style, and this line reached Sun Lu-t'ang/ Sun Lutang in the late nineteenth century. It was he who developed the Sun style. Yet all these styles began as boxing techniques and were little like the soft T'ai Chi practice that we know today. The soft, internal forms have similar movements, but there is far more emphasis on the cultivation of the inner self, the stillness of the mind and inner spiritual development. Thus, Schipper describes T'ai Chi as "a martial art for the defense of the inner world".[67] Yang Cheng-fu/Yang Zhengfu of the Yang school wrote:

> **Seek stillness in movement**. The external schools assume jumping about is good and they use all their energy. That is why after practice everyone pants. T'ai Chi Ch'uan uses stillness to control movement. Although one moves, there is also stillness.[68]

The external boxing forms are primarily concerned with attack and defence – the crane and the snake. But we should not see the soft styles as a radical break from tradition, since stillness in movement is a foundational aspect of Taoist philosophy from the ancient past. While it is impossible to gain a true lineage of tradition, Wile makes the point that: "An unbroken master–disciple transmission might not in fact be necessary if we consider that soft-style theory is permanently embedded in the culture and perennially available to any art, or that it is a universal kinesthetic possibility that can be rediscovered at any time through praxis."[69] The soft styles of T'ai Chi practised today are the Ch'en/Chen, Yang, Li, Sun and Hao.

The Yang style

The most popular form of T'ai Chi Chüan/Taijiquan today, and the style adopted in the subsequent chapters of this book, is the Yang style. The founder of the Yang style was Yang Lu-ch'an/Yang Luchan, reputed to have been born in 1799, and an important figure in the history of T'ai Chi. He is said to have learned the Ch'en/Chen family skills by spying on them for a period of ten years while they practised, pretending that he was a deaf mute. Then, one day, he was caught, and ordered to demonstrate what he had learned. Such was his skill, however, that he was accepted as a student by the family. On the other hand, some traditions claim that he was a servant of the Ch'en/Chen family and was taught by them as such. Later, he adapted the Old Style of the Ch'en/Chens into a new method that was less focused on the martial aspect, and travelled to Beijing in the mid-nineteenth century in order to teach it. He was responsible for making T'ai Chi popular in China by adapting it for a wider audience. He died in 1872, and such was his prestige that his body was returned to the Ch'en/Chen family village for burial. His third son Yang Chien-hou/Yang Jianhou taught this Yang *Middle Style* as it was called, but it was one of his sons, Yang Cheng-fu/Yang Zengfu, who developed the *Big Style*, the slow movements that we know today.

Yang Cheng-fu/Yang Zengfu was born in 1883 and died in 1936. Apparently, he was not too keen on martial arts, and only began to follow in his father's footsteps in his twenties. His approach was still very much martial, with kicking and other fast movements. Then, he took the decision to design a much more modified style, creating the slow, controlled series of movements that were combined into one whole *form*. Such a change, he felt, would be beneficial to health and fitness, cure chronic diseases, and would promote a longer life. Yang Cheng-fu/Yang Zengfu was an accomplished practitioner of Chinese medicine. He was also expert at poetry, calligraphy and painting, and founded the first college for Chinese medicine in Taiwan.

Yang Cheng-fu/Yang Zengfu taught Cheng Man-ch'ing/Zheng Manqing, who was born in 1905 and died in 1975. In his youth, the disciple Cheng had been seriously ill, but had been cured through practising T'ai Chi. He modified the *Big Style* by taking out some of its repetitiveness, adding softer and smaller movements, and so adapted it for the West. It was he who took T'ai Chi to New York, just after the mid-twentieth century, and it was he who introduced a *Short Form* of the Yang style that would be more acceptable in the West. While the *Long Form* of his teacher is still practised, it is the *Short Form* that is learned in most classes of T'ai Chi in the West, and that is featured in this book. Most of the T'ai Chi styles that we see in the West have been adapted from the *Big Style* of Yang Cheng-fu/Yang Zengfu. And variations are prolific: in Docherty's words, "if the reader were to visit a hundred schools of Yang-style Tai Chi, he would find a hundred variations of this style, and from the writings of his students it is evident that Yang Cheng-fu changed his style at least three times".[70] It is no wonder that the Yang style is the most popular in the West, given the Yang family's dedication to extending T'ai Chi to a wide audience.

The Wu style

The Wu style is associated with two brothers, Wu Yü-hsiang/Wu Yuxiang (1812–80?) and Wu Ch'eng-ch'ing/Wu Chengqing. They also had two other brothers, Wu Ju-ching/Wu Rujing and Wu Ch'iu-ying/Wu Qiuying, who both wrote papers on, and taught T'ai Chi. There were also two nephews, Li I-yü/Li Yiyu and Li Ch'i-hsüan/Li Qixuan. The family was wealthy, scholastic, and outwardly a successful orthodox Confucian family, and in the biographies of the men, there is nothing to suggest that they were linked with T'ai Chi. Perhaps they engaged in it in secret.[71] If the family were outwardly Confucian it was inwardly Taoist. Wile makes the point here that:

> The oft-repeated aphorism that a Chinese gentleman is a Confucianist at the office and a Taoist at home seems appropriate in relation to Wu and Li activities. T'ai-chi ch'üan accomplishes the harmonization of Confucian and Taoist tendencies by being externally active but internally quiescent. The times demanded that men of learning not only serve society but save the nation. T'ai-chi may have allowed them to satisfy Taoist yearning for self-cultivation without withdrawing to the mountains.[72]

Wile's point is an interesting one given that T'ai Chi seems to have Confucian formality and preciseness, alongside a deeper and more meaningful Taoist inner process. It was Wu Yü-hsiang/Wu Yuxiang who edited the T'ai Chi *Classics*, and his brother is said to have found the T'ai Chi *Classics* in Wu-yang. Wu Yü-hsiang/Wu Yuxiang was a student of Ch'en Ch'ing-p'ing/Chen Qingping and, thus, began his martial art experience in the Ch'en/Chen family. It was he who was taught also by the founder of the Yang style, Yang Lu-ch'an/Yang Luchan. One of the latter's other pupils in the Wu family, Wu Yu-seong, began his own Wu style, after studying with both Yang Lu-ch'an/Yang Luchan and Ch'en Ch'ing-p'ing/Chen Qingping. His style is known as the *Old Wu Style*. Later, a different form of the Wu style, known as the *New Wu Style*, was founded by Wu Chien-ch'üan/Wu Jianquan, and is practised mainly in Singapore. Yang Lu-ch'an/Yang Luchan himself passed his teaching to his son Yang Pan-hou/Yang Banhou, who in turn taught Wu Ch'üan-yü/Wu Quanyu.

Since the biographies of the Wu and Li families mention nothing about martial arts, it is difficult to link the family with T'ai Chi. Was it, as Wile suggests, just indulged in for escapism?[73] Or were they interested in developing a spiritual grounding in a time of political vicissitudes? Then, again, they might have been interested purely in self-protection, by using a strictly martial art that could enable them to protect property, crops and a wealthy position.[74] But in many ways, T'ai Chi preserves much of the heritage and culture of Taoism past and present, and this must have been an important factor. Since China in their time was under foreign rule, the open practice of a martial art might have incurred the suspicion of the ruling parties. Wile thus comments: "T'ai-ch ch'üan may have represented for them a way of infusing a martial art with the most subtle spiritual values of the culture and thus synthesizing the civil and the martial. As a ritual or psycho-physical performance of this synthesis T'ai-chi ch'üan could serve as a vehicle for promoting transformation without arousing Manchu fears of sedition."[75] It is Wile's thesis that T'ai Chi Ch'üan/Taijiquan was a means of self-control that balanced the political, social and economic constraints of the ailing Manchu Empire, and the incursion of Western power, with traditional Chinese and Taoist values.[76] It was a means of inner Chinese identity during difficult times.

The Li and Sun styles

The founder of the Li style was Li I-yü/Li Yiyu, who was born in 1834 and died in 1902. He was the nephew of the Wu brothers and so learned his art from them. One of Li I-yü/Li Yiyu's pupils was Hao Wei-chen/Hao Weizhen (1842–1920), who taught the founder of the Sun style, Sun Lu-t'ang/Sun Lutang (1861–1932). Sun Lu-t'ang/Sun Lutang retained a deep interest in the other two main martial arts of Hsing-i/Xingyi and Pa-kua/Bagua, and these have influenced his particular style of T'ai Chi considerably. While in the past, the Sun style has not been as widespread as the others, currently it is experiencing considerable popularity and growth.

Such are the major traditions of T'ai Chi Ch'üan/Taijiquan. Today, there is a diversity of styles based originally on the Ch'en/Chen, Yang, Wu and Li traditions with admixtures from all of them. It may seem from the profusion of styles that no particular one can be authentic and of value, and that the true tradition is lost. But each has its value if pursued in earnest. In the wise words of Yang Jwing Ming:

> In order to become a real master, you need to know not only yourself, but also others. When you understand other styles you can understand your own style better, and evaluate it more objectively. You can evaluate how good it is, and where its limitations are. Every style has its own specialities, so if you think some style is not as good as yours, it might be just that your knowledge of that style is shallow. Also, when you see a style which seems better than yours, don't give up your style for it. That

would be throwing away all the time and effort you have spent on it. After all, once you have invested a lot of time in this new style, you may find that there is nothing beneath the surface glitter that initially attracted you. If you believe that your style and your personal level of ability are superior to others, you must beware of losing your humility, for this may cause you to lose your enthusiasm for learning.[77]

T'ai Chi Ch'üan/Taijiquan texts

The T'ai Chi Ch'üan *Classics* do not supply us with sufficient historical information to answer once and for all the problems surrounding the origin and growth of T'ai Chi, as we have seen above. This is mainly because historical information was outside the terms of reference of the texts, which were primarily concerned with the practice of the martial art. It is from the Yang family that the central texts have emerged, and they were considered important enough to acquire the status of *Classics*. The texts came to light in a salt shop in the middle of the nineteenth century and were discovered by one of the Wu brothers. However, the basic texts were later altered, added to, and edited, to the extent that it is difficult to extract the original material. And somewhere in this process, Chang San-feng/Zhang Sanfeng's name seems to have been associated with the texts. For others, Wang Tsung-yüeh/Wang Zongyue is considered to be the author. But, despite difficulties of authorship and historicity, the *Classics* did much to heighten the prestige of T'ai Chi. Wile writes of this:

> Nevertheless, the existence, and certainly the quality, of the classics has contributed greatly to the respect for and image of the art of t'ai-chi ch'üan. They have the force of scriptural authority and are a teaching tool, a standard for competition judging, and a core for the accumulation of countless commentaries. As much as the art itself, the classics have raised the dignity of t'ai-chi ch'üan by demonstrating the intense involvement of subtle minds and alignment with the culture's highest spiritual values. The classics closely document the marriage of meditation, medicine, and movement to form a ch'i-kung and the overlay of *ch'i-kung* on the body mechanics of a martial art.[78]

Wile's final words here demonstrate well the different strands that inform the practice of T'ai Chi, as well as the interrelation of those strands into a unified practice. It is the texts stemming from the Yang family in particular which have drawn on the wider context of medicine, meditation and spiritual alchemy, and which reflect so much of Taoist philosophy.

Space does not permit a lengthy discussion of the T'ai Chi texts, but, setting technicalities of dating and authorship aside, one or two examples might suffice. We have chosen the *Song of Sparring* since it exemplifies balance, soft and hard (*yin* and *yang*), and the martial art component of the texts. It also exemplifies the teaching of verse 78 of the ancient *Tao Te Ching/Daodejing*, which says that what is weak can overcome the strong, and what is supple can overcome what is rigid or stiff.

Song of Sparring

Be serious in the practice of ward-off, roll-back, press and push,
And in pull-down, split, elbow-stroke mind your bending and extending.
In advance, retreat, gaze-left, look-right, and central equilibrium,
You must stick, connect, adhere, and follow, distinguishing full and empty.
The hands and feet follow each other, and the waist and legs act in unison;
Drawing the opponent in so that his energy lands on nothing is a marvelous technique.
Let him attack with great force,
While I deflect a thousand pounds with four ounces.[79]

The other example is taken from the *Song of the Essence and Application of T'ai-chi Ch'üan*. What follows is the opening section, and the words provide a good introduction to the chapters that follow in this book:

How wonderful is t'ai-chi ch'üan,
Whose movements follow nature!
Continuous like a jade bracelet,
Every movement expresses the t'ai-chi symbol.
The whole body is filled with one unbroken ch'i,
Above and below are without imbalance.
Place the feet with cat steps,
Moving the ch'i like coiling silk.
In movement everything moves;
In stillness, all is still.[80]

T'ai Chi Ch'üan/Taijiquan today

From all that has been said about T'ai Chi Ch'üan/Taijiquan so far, it would have to be said that many different strands of belief and practice inform its practice in today's world. So there are great variations in the movements, in their nature, their speed, the degree to which the martial side is evident, and the extent to which Taoist philosophy underpins practice. Moreover, the mutual influence between the different styles has meant that today's practice must inevitably lack any really pure tradition. Such a comment is not meant pejoratively, for changes in tradition have mostly been undertaken for the right reasons, producing a refined practice. At the same time, however, there are those who set themselves up as teachers of T'ai Chi without the necessary skills and long, dedicated years of study that produce a Master in the art.

Whether the emphasis is on the martial aspect or not, the underlying philosophy of Taoism is clearly evident. In one of the Yang family texts we find the words: "Finally, we can speak of the martial and the spiritual, sagehood and immortality. If one speaks of the body and mind from the point of view of the martial arts and applies these principles to the cultivation of power, it must be in the context of the essence of the *tao*. It is a mistake to focus exclusively on physical skills."[81] The best practitioners of T'ai Chi do not neglect the spiritual for the sake of the physical. It is a holistic practice that combines meditation with movement, mind with body, the spiritual with the physical. The circulation of energy in the body, as we shall see in chapter 6, is essential for sound health. But in T'ai Chi as a martial art it is the awareness of that energy in one's own and an opponent's body, and how an opponent is about to use it, which is at the root of each movement. An exercise like *Pushing Hands* helps develop such skill. Here, two people face each other with their palms joined. Experiencing the energy of each other in the lightest possible connection of their palms, they are able to mirror each other's movements.

Whether the style is internal (*nei-chia ch'üan fa/neijia quanfa*) and soft, or external (*wai-chia ch'üan fa/waijia quanfa*) and hard, the same principles of energy will apply. But many of those in the West who practise the soft styles – and it is this style that will be the emphasis in the chapters that follow – are not interested in self-defence. They are interested in promoting sound health and personal harmony in a complex and fast-paced world. On the other hand a practitioner like Lawrence Galante demonstrates throughout his text *Tai Chi: The Supreme Ultimate* how each posture of the soft-style T'ai Chi is used in the martial style.[82] As a more martial art definition of the practice, Galante defines it as "a choreographed series of refined and coordinated techniques (blocks and attacks), which simulate actual fighting".[83]

The movements in a particular style of T'ai Chi are called the *form*, and it is this term that we shall be using throughout the book to refer to the continuity of postures. If the postures were once separated from each other, the continuity and particular pattern of them, the *form*, is now standard practice for T'ai Chi. All the martial arts will have a *form*. In Crompton's words: "The postures can be thought of as places on a map that one passes through, and the movements as the roads that connect the postures together. So a form is a kind of moving map."[84] While the postures may have the same names, there are variations in how they appear in the different styles, traditions or schools. As noted earlier, the postures in this book will be those of the Yang school.[85] The names of the postures are ancient and are taken from nature, from observance of actions, and from the movements of birds and animals, or the interaction of human and animal. Thus we have postures called *High Pat on Horse*, *Play the Lute*, *White Crane Spreads Wings*, *Snake Creeps Down*, *Rooster Stands on One Leg*, for example.

The links to Taoist ideas are numerous. The *form* is based on circular patterns that reflect the rhythmic cycles of *Tao*, rather like the well-known *yin/yang* symbol. Sophia Delza of the Wu tradition puts this point superbly when she writes: "The body in action is a small universe of multiple movements and synchronized Forms, moving on itself and in space, duplicating, as it were, the composite rotation of the planets, where each, turning in its own rhythm, is in perfect co-ordination with the others in orbit."[86] The movements of T'ai Chi reflect the fact that nothing in nature has straight lines, only arcs and curves, and that everything is subject to change. So in the *form*, as Delza puts it: "You are sensitized to the dynamics of change, to intricacies of pattern, to the weaving of space. You can experience the moment of synchronized stillness and the dovetailing process of movement."[87] Ultimately, the aim is to create the same kind of harmony that obtained at the beginning of the universe. The links with Taoism are too numerous to avoid seeing T'ai Chi as embedded in the long tradition of Taoism. In Docherty's words: "This art has all the elements of Taoistic practice, including physiological alchemy, ritual initiation, oral formulas and tradition, Taoistic terminology, and a theoretical and symbolic element drawn largely, though not exclusively, from Taoist philosophy and religion. All these elements exist in Tai Chi Chuan and existed in the heyday of Chang Sanfeng."[88]

There are strong links, too, between T'ai Chi and philosophical Taoism. Philosophical Taoism is a topic that will be taken up in chapter 3. Here we simply need to bear in mind some of the similarities, such as the idea of the soft and weak overcoming the hard and seemingly strong, in the same way that water wears away the hardest surface as it bends around it. The concepts of balance, the goal of equilibrium, and the need for harmony in the self are also very akin to philosophical Taoism. One profound feature of early philosophical Taoism was the idea of returning to the origin, returning to the source of all, *Tao*, and that is the ultimate aim of serious students of T'ai Chi. In all life there is an ebb and flow, a fullness and emptiness – a rhythmic swing between two polar opposites. Indeed, a *form* is designed on the rhythmic alterations of the ancient concept of *yin* and *yang*. The ideas of naturalness, of "going with the flow", of yielding, are also common to ancient, philosophical Taoism and T'ai Chi. All these are ideas that will be explored in subsequent chapters. But though T'ai Chi is rooted in Taoism, at the same time it has become part of the wider Chinese tradition.

The benefits to be gained from the practice of T'ai Chi are considerable, both in the long term and the short term. Physiologically, the blood circulation is improved, leading to greater energy and alertness of mind. Breathing is altered: it becomes deeper, and this, too, stimulates energy. Muscles are more relaxed and supple and the skeleton is more flexible. Mentally, the mind becomes more focused, is able to concentrate better, and the balance between body and mind is heightened, so relieving stress and tension and creating a more harmonious and calm state of being that begins to pervade all aspects of life. So the balance between mind, emotions and body becomes harmonized, promoting an integrated, unified personality. An individual does not have to be young and strong to practise T'ai Chi: it can be taken up in any state of health, at any age. It can assist in the cure of physical illnesses and it can enable the mind to use energy in the right way, without causing anxiety, stress, tension, and nervousness. Every part of the body is exercised in the practice of T'ai Chi, but in such a way that no part is repetitively under stress: the carefully choreographed movements ensure that the whole body is equally used, softening muscles, stretching tendons and articulating joints. Even in China today, where religious practice had long been suppressed, the practice of T'ai Chi is compulsory in schools, and is now a national way of exercise. As a soft form, it has mainly dropped its martial-art emphasis and become a means to restore and nurture sound health of body and mind. According to Galante, "for the body it is an exercise; for the mind it is a study in concentration, will power and visualization; and for the soul, it is a system of spiritual meditation".[89]

To learn T'ai Chi one needs the same kind of self-discipline and dedicated approach as in anything else in life that one wishes to master. The T'ai Chi *Classics* list five mental keys to diligent study:

1. Study wide and deep.
2. Investigate, ask.
3. Ponder carefully.
4. Clearly discriminate.
5. Work perseveringly.[90]

Yang Jwing Ming has the following words for approaching T'ai Chi as a student, but they are thoroughly applicable to whatever one wishes to achieve in life:

> Whether or not a person learns something depends upon his attitude and seriousness. First he must make a firm decision to learn it, and then he must have a strong will to fulfill his intention. He needs perseverance and patience to last to the end. Even if a person has all these virtues, his achievement might still be different from that of another person who has the same qualities and personality. The difference is due to their manner of learning. If a person practices and then ponders every new thing he has learned, and keeps going back to research and master it, he will naturally be better than the person who never explores what he has learned.[91]

The secret lies in internalized reflection. Stuart Olson makes the pertinent point that in the West we treat our bodies like a car, not bothering with it too much until it breaks down, and then we see a mechanic. We wait until we get ill before we help our bodies. The Chinese, he says, treat the body more like a garden, weeding it, nourishing it, caring for it, and strengthening it against illness from the inside.[92] We shall see in the chapter on *The Way* that *Tao*, which is at the heart of Taoism and of T'ai Chi, is something that cannot be explained. Neither, ultimately, can T'ai Chi. It is only by practice, and reflection on that practice, that its inexplicable subtleties can be experienced.

2 Harmony

Yin and *yang*

Our understanding of the world around us is generated by relationships between opposites. We know what darkness is, because we know what light is; we know what heat is, because of its opposite of cold. And between such opposites we have the variables of shade, dusk, brightness, dullness, as well as coolness, iciness, burning heat or gentle warmth. The Chinese view of the cosmos, from the heavens to human beings, the seasons and the hours of the day, was one based on the interplay of such bipolarities. Generically, they were called *yin* and *yang*. So important was this fundamental principle in the Chinese understanding of the universe that one author describes it as "one of the most fruitful and useful ever devised by the mind of man for making sense out of the infinite multitude of diverse facts in the universe".[1] The theory of *yin* and *yang* is not only a philosophical perspective of reality but is also a theory of inherent power in all phenomena – a changing, dynamic power that alters from one polarity to another. It was adopted by the Chinese from ancient times onwards, and came to be accepted by both Confucians and Taoists.

The *yin* and *yang* theory arose naturally from a people that felt deeply about the rhythm of the seasons, the expression of nature in rhythmic patterns, and the need to harmonize societal, agricultural and religious life with those natural rhythms. Even Chinese history seemed to follow the natural swing of the pendulum from one polarity to its opposite. Allan notes this in the early history of China. The Hsia/Xia, she writes, "were originally the mythical inverse of the Shang, associated with water, dragons, the moons, darkness and death, as opposed to the fire, birds, suns, light and life, with which the Shang were associated".[2] The waning and waxing of dynastic rule, of war and peace, of upheaval and stability are the *yin* and *yang* of Chinese historical patterns.

The theory of *yin* and *yang* provided an abstract conceptual framework that could be applied to the world of matter in the form of essences that informed all things. It arose from the descriptors given to the sunny side of a mountain or river as *yang* and the shady side as *yin*. The sunny side is warm and dry. It is bright and encourages growth activity in plant life. The warmth of the sun also encourages the evaporation of water to provide moisturizing mists to nourish the ground. The *yin* side of a mountain, on the other hand, is cool, shady, dark, cloudy and overcast. There is nothing to lift the moisture so it moves downwards into the earth, making it damp. The roots of plants are fed by the moisture but their growth is passive without the warmth of the sun. These, then, are the origins of the terms *yin* and *yang*, but we must search further back in time for the roots of the theory that the two terms came to embody.

The origins of *yin* and *yang*

Traditionally, the origins of *yin* and *yang* have been cast back to the time of Fu Hsi/Fu Xi, the mythical founder of the Hsia/Xia dynasty and of the *pa-kua/bagua*, the eight trigrams. While this is certainly not true, the simplicity of the idea of two fundamental forces operating in nature suggests an ancient origin, even if the terms *yin* and *yang* were not applied to it until later. The ancient need to understand life in terms of the balance and harmony of nature, as opposed to imbalance and disharmony, is ingrained in the Chinese psyche, as we saw in chapter 1. Indeed, according to Allan: "Within the Shang myth system, there was also a dualism, the antecedent of later *yin–yang* theory, in which the suns, sky, birds, east, life, the Lord on High were opposed to the moons, watery underworld, dragons, west, death, the Lord below".[3] Allan thus believes that the origins of the *yin* and *yang* theory lie in Shang times.[4]

The dual aspects witnessed in nature were reflected in divination practices with the use of long and short yarrow stalks. These represented the dualities of a firm and yielding nature respectively. Later, the firm line became *yang* ——, and the shorter or broken line *yin* — — . The correlation between the rhythms of nature and the dualities of *yin* and *yang* were put particularly well by Maspero in his description of ancient Chou/Zhou times:

> If life contracted in winter, if one was not to work in the fields, it was because that was the time dominated by the *yin*, repose; if life expanded in summer, if all was opened in that season, if one laboured in the fields, it was because that was the time when the *yang*, activity, was predominant. The *yang* was indeed in the ascendent and the *yin* on the decline until the summer solstice, after which they waxed and waned inversely until the winter solstice. The equinoxes were their times of equality. If the Son of Heaven [the king] had to dwell each season in a different pavilion of the Sacred Palace, he did this in order to follow the movements of the *yin* and the *yang* across the seasons: he punished in autumn (*yin*) and rewarded in spring (*yang*).[5]

Pas suggests that the first usage of *yin* and *yang* was, as their characters suppose, and as noted above, as descriptors of the shady and dark sides of a mountain, valley or river bank. Such usage might then have been extended to Heaven and Earth; to male and female; father and mother; ruler and subjects; summer and activity and winter and passivity; and so on.[6] Graham, too, thinks that while there is no evidence of *yin* and *yang* dualism *per se* prior to the school that developed the concept to its full, the *concept* itself is deeply rooted in earlier times.[7] Yet it has to be admitted that there is only scant reference to *yin* and *yang* prior to the school of Tsou Yen/Zou Yan that developed it. All later references also seem to be a product of the school itself.[8] It was probably not until early Han times that the *yin–yang* concept was applied to the famous divination text, the *I Ching/Yijing*, which we shall look at in chapter 4. Suffice it to say here, that the firm lines of the *I Ching/Yijing's* trigrams and hexagrams became *yang* ——, and the broken, yielding ones *yin* — —.

It was in the Warring States period of the fifth to third centuries BCE that the so-called One hundred Schools of Philosophy arose. It was as one of these schools that the *Yin–Yang chia/jia*, "*Yin–Yang* school" came about, at a time when circling ideas and theories were being gathered together as more organized philosophies. Another school had developed the cosmological theory of the Five Elements or Agents, to be examined in chapter 3, and while the Five Elements school was originally separate from the *Yin–Yang* school, in the melting pot of the following Han dynasty, they were coalesced.

The *Yin–Yang* school probably originated in the ranks of the practitioners of magical arts, those who later became the *fang-shih/fangshi*, who practised divination, medicine and magic in their early history, but who branched out into music, astronomy and other specialist areas in their later history. The founder of the school was Tsou Yen/Zou Yan, who seems to have organized some of the beliefs of the divergent groups of his time into a coherent and systematic cosmology. Certainly, the efforts of the school were sufficient to give Taoism and Confucianism their later allegiance to the theories of *yin* and *yang*. Tsou Yen/Zou Yan is dated somewhere in the third century BCE. He came from the state of Ch'i/Qi, but was also influential in the state of Yen/Yan. He seems to have been on the fringe of the established philosophers, perhaps because of his attachments to the popular practices of magicians and diviners, or because he was a newcomer in making his mark in court circles.[9] But he is mentioned by Ssu-ma Ch'ien/Sima Qian in his historical *Shih Chi/Shiji* about the end of the second and beginning of the first century BCE. He is likely to have been a Confucian, and this is perhaps one reason why his theory of *yin* and *yang* was wholeheartedly accepted by Confucians.[10] The *Shih Chi/Shiji* says of him:

> Thereupon he examined deeply into the phenomena of increase and decrease of the *yin* and the *yang*, and wrote essays totalling more than one hundred thousand words about strange permutations, and about the cycles of the great Sages from beginning to end. His words were grandiose and fanciful. He had first to examine small objects, and extended this to large ones until he reached what was without limit. . . . Moreover, he followed the great events in the rise and fall of ages, and by means of their omens and (an examination into their) institutions, extended his survey backward to the time when Heaven and Earth had not yet been born, to what was profound and abstruse and not to be examined.[11]

It is particularly the abstruse and non-examinable nature of that which existed prior to Heaven and Earth that would have been attractive to the Taoists, and their belief in the indescribable *Tao*.

The cosmology of the *Yin–Yang* school accepted the whole of the universe being the result of the intermingling of the two essences of *yin* and *yang* and, as we shall see in chapter 3, of Five Elements, Agents or Phases. The basis of the cosmogony was one of nature. Since the Chinese lived in the northern hemisphere, the South was connected with heat and summer. Its opposite of North was associated with cold and winter. The sun rose in the East and was correlated with springtime, while sunset in the West correlated with autumn. The day, too, could be divided in the same way, morning as spring, noon as summer, evening as autumn and night as winter. In fact, the *Yin–Yang* school correlated the two forces of *yin* and *yang*, with the Five Elements, four compass points, four seasons, five notes in a scale, twelve months, twelve pitch-pipes in music, colours and numbers, for example. The influence of the *Yin–Yang* school was considerable and was widespread in the Ch'in/Qin and Han dynasties. Its views were taken up by others and expanded considerably, for example, by Hsün Tzu/Xun Zi, who lived not long after Tsou Yen/Zou Yan, and by the twelfth-century Confucian, Chu Hsi/Ju Xi.

Yin

Yin, often referred to as "white tiger", is the yielding, receptive aspect in life. Thus it is the feminine essence, is gentle and beautiful, but also negative, cold and dark. It is autumn and winter time, from which its opposite emerges in the spring. Thus, cosmologically, it is the chaos of darkness from whence the light of creation was born: in some schools, it therefore precedes *yang* as the eternally creative element from which *yang* emerges. *Yin* is the mother aspect, passive, soft, wet, the flesh of the body, the shady, cool side of a valley, mountain, river bank or garden. Yet such general passivity and receptivity are not weaknesses, for they can be more enduring than their opposite of *yang*. Taoism, indeed, teaches that strength is often to be found in apparent weakness. Ultimately, it is *yin* that allows *yang* to rise out of its quiescence.

Yin is the valley and the womb; it is depth and descent, receiving and accepting; yet from it, all emerges. Cooper writes: "It is because it is the lowest, humblest place that the valley receives the full force of the waters which fall into it from high *yang* places. Majestic waterfalls and turbulent mountain torrents, for all their power, come down to the lowly and are absorbed by it and converted into the deep-flowing, broad, quiet and irresistible forces of the rivers, lakes and oceans, the *yin* principle."[12] *Yin* is also square, its strict sides symbolizing immobility and passivity. The moon is *yin*, as is silver, the colour connected with the moon. Pearls, since they are obtained from water, are also *yin*. The physical spirits that survive after death are called *kuei/gui* and since they return into the earth are also *yin*. In the human being, instinct, emotion and intuition are *yin*, as well as flexibility, openness and calmness. *Yin* is everything that is esoteric. The eighteenth century Taoist Liu I-ming/Liu Yiming had the following to say about the flexibility of character that is the nature of *yin* in a person:

> Flexibility is docility, yielding, self-mastery, self-restraint, self-effacement, humility, selflessness, consideration of others, absence of arbitrariness, pure simplicity, genuineness. Those who use flexibility well appear to lack what they are in fact endowed with, appear to be empty when they are in fact fulfilled. They do not take revenge when offended.

> They seek spiritual riches and are aloof of mundane riches; they do not contend with people of the world.[13]

Negatively, however, *yin* can be weakness and stasis, pettiness and small-mindedness.

Yang

Yang emerges from *yin* as the light that arises from darkness. It is the spirit, the intellect, the father, and thus male, and is the active principle in life. It is aggressive, hard, heat, dryness, the bone of the body, the hard, dry stone of the home, the south, sunny side of a valley or river bank, and the spring and summer time of the year. It is symbolized by the sun and is sometimes known as "blue dragon". It is round, indicative of its active ability to move. Roundness is also the symbol of Heaven, which is also *yang*. Gold, associated with the sun, is *yang* as is jade. The *shen* spirits that rise from the body at death into new life are *yang* unlike their *kuei/gui* and *yin* counterparts that are held in death. *Yang* is the right side of the body, the side that holds the sword, hence its aggression. *Yang* is experienced in the transcendence that sometimes floods the mind at odd times in life. The Taoist Huang-ch'i/Huangqi from Yüan/Yuan dynasty times explained this well:

> It may also happen that while you are reading books or reciting poetry, personal desires suddenly vanish and a unified awareness is alone present – this too is one aspect of the arising of yang.
>
> Also, sometimes when friends gather and talk, they reach a communion of the inner mind, and suddenly yang energy soars up and the true potential bursts forth – this is also one way in which yang arises.
>
> Furthermore, even when playing music, playing games, drawing, fishing, cutting wood, plowing fields, reading books, if you can harmonize spontaneously based on the natural essence, without seeking or desiring anything, there will be a serenity and contentment, clearing the mind so that you forget about feelings – this is in each case a form of arising of yang.[14]

However, despite the positivity of such transcendent experience, over-excitement, overdoing the experience, transforms into negativity. Similarly, firmness that becomes overbearing can become self-destructive. Cultivating the firmness of *yang* is the goal, but it has to be in the right ways. Liu I-ming/Liu Yiming explained what this means:

> To establish firmness, first get rid of covetousness. Once covetousness is gone, firmness is established, and the pillars of the spiritual house are firmly stationed. Once the basis is firm and stable, there is hope for the great Tao.
>
> What is firmness? Cutting through sentiment and clearing the senses is firmness. Not fearing obstacles and difficulties is firmness. Putting the spirit in order and going boldly forward is firmness. Being harmonious but not imitative, gregarious yet nonpartisan, is firmness. Not doing anything bad, doing whatever is good, is firmness. Being inwardly and outwardly unified, working without ceasing, is firmness.[15]

Here, then, the characteristic of *yang* as the rising principle in life is applied to the spiritual evolution of the human being, and the goal of harmony of the inner and outer self. Liu I-ming/Liu Yiming's words show clearly how *yang* implies progress and growth in the best possible dimensions of living.

The interplay of *yin* and *yang*

Yin and *yang* are complementary essences or forces. Just as we cannot understand darkness without light or *vice versa*, and just as we need the variances of dark, light and shadow to see well, so *yin* and *yang* cannot exist without each other. So in being mutually dependent, *yin* and *yang*, like all opposites in Chinese thought, are complementary rather than oppositional. *Yin* and *yang* are *alternating* creative forces representing the interplay between physical and spiritual, emotion and intellect, passivity and activity, the yielding and the firm, resistance and generation. Rather than opposition between the two there is polarity in unity, like two sides of one coin – a harmonized unity of opposites. There is tension between them and a mutual play and interaction that makes them too close to be outright opposites. And in that interaction there is never a state of perfect *yang* or *yin*. The goal may be balance between the two, but whatever exists is simply dominated by one or the other; it is the varying degree of *yin* or *yang* present in an entity, or in a period of time, that makes them what they are. Such mutual dependency is called *hsiang sheng/xiang sheng*. Lao-tzu/Laozi spoke of it thus:

> Everyone sees beauty as beauty only because there is ugliness.
> Everyone knows good as good only because there is evil.
>
> Therefore having and not having arise together.
> The difficult and the easy complement one another.

Long and short contrast with each other;
High and low depend upon each other;
Sound and silence harmonize with each other;
Before and after follow one another.[16]

Not only, then, is our understanding of the world based on the interplay of polarities but, in the Chinese view of things, nothing can ever be wholly one polarity as opposed to its opposite. All males have a certain amount of the female within their physical and psychic make-up, as do women have a degree of masculinity. Quite contrary to most western thought it is not the triumph of good over evil, of light over darkness, of the divine over the demonic that is the Chinese goal, but the perfect balance between *yin* and *yang* polarities that enables the self to transcend them in activity. Evil is but temporary disharmony, just as night is the temporary suspension of day.

The continuous transformation and rhythmic patterns of *yin* and *yang*, their waxing and waning, coming and going, rising and falling, are related to all phenomena in the universe. The degrees of balance and tension created by *yin* and *yang* account for all things. Thus, *yin* and *yang* are the qualitative essences found in all entities in the universe, constantly reacting with each other. The energy they generate in doing so is the activity of *ch'i/qi*, the energy that is necessary for life, and for things to come into being. Their interaction controls the cycle of seasons, *yin* being the passive, cold seasons of autumn and winter, spring and summer being *yang*. So when winter is at its deepest – the time of maximum *yin* – *yang* begins to ascend once again, as far as the height of summer. But *yin* and *yang* affect all aspects of life, not just the seasons: the temperament of an individual, the nature of a society, war, religion – every aspect of life. They make life possible, their interaction creating the relativity necessary for existence. Rest and motion, contraction and expansion, advance and retreat are the dynamics of the universe.

The idea of the relativity of opposites, reflected so much in nature and life, made sense to the Chinese psyche. As we saw in the introduction to this chapter, the world that we experience is one of multiplicity and plurality in which we differentiate between all things through a system of categorization by language and experience. In order to exist in the world we have to know what things are and what their properties are. We need to know that if something is hot, that it can hurt, or that if music is beautiful, we may enjoy it. These perspectives that we have in life are *relative*: that is to say, we can only know what one thing is or means in relation to something else, usually its opposite. Thus, we know what is hot because of its relation to what is cold, of beauty because of ugliness and so on. These are the dualities of life that help us to make sense of it. In much eastern religion, and certainly in classical Taoism, the ultimate goal in life is one that is involved with transcending these dualities. This is not to say that such dualities do not exist, that they are not there, but that we need to overcome the desires for, and aversions to, one thing rather than its opposite. To the Taoist, the perfect balance between *yin* and *yang* brings this about. Indeed, the enlightened being in much eastern thought is at the point of equilibrium between all opposites, and is able to flow in any direction in life without losing that equilibrium.

Since the relativity of opposites forms a considerable part of our space–time understanding of the world, if we focus on one thing too much we automatically highlight its opposite. If, for example, we concentrate on the good in life, we become even more aware of its opposite. If we imagine any pair of opposites pictorially as connected by a straight line, they become, as Capra described them, "extreme parts of a single whole".[17] The interdependence of polar opposites is what is behind the *yin* and *yang* principle. Their relativity means that nothing can exist in its own right. Lao-tzu/Laozi put this simply:

> That which contracts
> Must first expand.
> That which is weak
> Must first be strong.
> That which is cast down
> Must first be raised up.
> Before something is taken away
> It must first be given.
>
> This is called discernment of things.
> The soft and weak overcome the hard and strong.
> Fish should not leave deep water,
> A country's weapons should not be revealed.[18]

Human beings are constantly at some point other than the central equilibrium between all kinds of polarities. Only when dualities are transcended can the true perspective of reality be known. Jean Cooper pertinently points out: "No observation in the realm of duality can see the whole and therefore cannot be absolutely right. It is little wonder that so many of our judgements, both individual and social, produce such unfortunate results when they are based on the erroneous assumption that we can see the whole."[19]

While it is difficult to deny the complementary nature of opposites, the Chinese took the concept a stage further and, as noted earlier, accepted the *alternation* of opposites, *yin* becoming *yang* and *yang* becoming *yin* in endless cycles. As noted above, nothing is entirely *yin* or *yang* for each contains an element of its opposite. When one reaches its maximum, the other begins to increase until it, too, reaches its maximum point. Such a concept makes life like a pendulum swinging between multiple polarities. Metaphysically, the belief points to the perpetual flux of all life; it also highlights the point that anything taken to its extreme will automatically produce its opposite. Again, Lao-tzu/Laozi said:

> Yield then overcome;
> Bend and become straight;
> Empty and become full;
> Wear out and become new;
> Have little and gain much;
> Have much and be confused.[20]

Since all opposites are relative to, and interdependent on, each other, one can never be victor over another. Indeed, recognizing the dynamic balance between opposites, between the *yin* and *yang* of things, and "flowing with them" is what Taoism is all about. *Yin* and *yang* are never static. They are not two irreconcilable, opposing forces, but are different, interdependent aspects of one whole, two parts of a unity, two sides of a coin. Their rhythm, to use Bodde's expression, is one of "eternal oscillation".[21]

Taking the gains and losses in our stride is the moral of a story told by the Taoist Lieh-tzu/Liezi. An old man and his son lived together at the top of a hill. They were very poor. One day their horse strayed away. The neighbours came to express how sorry they were. But the old man said: "Why would you see this as misfortune?" Not long afterwards the horse returned bringing with it many other wild horses. This seemed good fortune indeed, so the neighbours all came to congratulate the old man. But the old man asked: "Why would you see this as good luck?" Having so many horses, the old man's son took to riding, but he fell off a horse and broke his leg. The accident left him lame. Once again, the neighbours gathered round to commiserate with the old man, but again he said: "Why would you see this as misfortune?" Some time later, war broke out and, of course, his young son was not able to go because he was lame.

Diversity in unity

The natural, non-differentiated state of the universe, then, is a dynamic one. It is a spontaneous flow of experiences bound within the natural order of the expression of *Tao* in the universe, the cyclical ebb and flow of all life and all in it. Things are always subject to change and extremes of one kind or another, but must always revert to their opposites. Ultimate Reality in Taoism, then, is at once the voidness of *Tao*, and the spontaneity of its essence, or *Te*, within existence – the contiual flow and flux of all life. Separateness in manifest existence is an illusion brought about by the continued interplay between *yin* and *yang*.

The unity of polarities and the interrelation of *yin* and *yang* are graphically displayed in the well-known *yin–yang* symbol of more modern times:

Here, *yin* and *yang* are enclosed in a circle representing their unity – the source of the two is One, though the One is not *Tao* as we shall see in chapter 3, for *Tao* is beyond even the One. The circle surrounding *yin* and *yang* symbolizes perfection, and in enclosing them it encloses all the possibilities and potentialities of the cosmos, at the same time indicating their interrelation. Since neither *yin*, represented by the black area, nor *yang*, represented by the light, are able to exist without each other, a particle of each is present in its opposite. This rather neatly shows how good always contains the seed or potential for evil, the masculine for the feminine, and so on. In the symbol, too, *yin* and *yang* are intimately wrapped around each other, showing their mutual dependency and that one can never entirely dominate the other. The symbol is indicative of the vital energy forces that provide the rhythm of life, for between them *yin* and *yang* are the products of *ch'i*/*qi*, the essential energy that makes material existence possible.

The *yin* characteristics of contraction, condensing, inertia and retreat are balanced with *yang* expansion, dispersion and advance. *Yin* and *yang* wane and wax, retreat and advance, go and come, close and open as the pendulum of creative rhythms swings between one and the other. The *yin–yang* symbol shows that, though dualities are evident in all existence, wholeness and completeness underpins the universe. The symbol of *yin* and *yang*, then, suggests the existence both of manifest dualities and of the unity of all opposites. Ultimately, Reality is a unity not a plurality, and *Tao* and *ch'i/qi* are its unifying principles. It is because of the unity of the cosmos that disturbance in one aspect of it is presumed to affect the whole.

The possibility of transcending the dualities of *yin* and *yang* in order to enter the sage-like state of immortal enlightenment was particularly attractive to Taoists. Stephen Teiser notes that some characters with unusual, numinous spirituality were thought to be impossible to characterize as *yin* or *yang*.[22] But it is the sage in whom the balance of *yin* and *yang* becomes such that *yin* and *yang* are transcended in the perfection that lies at the mid-point between all polarities. In being at this unperturbed point of equilibrium, experience of *Tao* as the ultimate source from which *yin* and *yang* originate is possible. Cooper writes, "it is the 'perfectly balanced union' which establishes an inner harmony in man and the universe, so that man becomes at peace with himself and the world about him, with the world within and the world without. It renders him harmless both to others and to himself. It produces the Perfect Man of Confucianism and the Sage of Taoism."[23]

Creation

Most religions and cultures have ancient creation myths to explain how the universe began and how humankind came into being. China, however, had no such creation myths in its ancient stratum. It was only towards the end of the classical age of China that a developed cosmology occurred. In the second century BCE a group of master philosophers at the court of a prince or king of Huia-nan combined a number of prevailing ideologies into a composite cosmology. They were an eclectic group of men, but their overall thought seems to have been Taoist. In the *Huai-nan-tzu/Huainanzi* that they compiled the root of all creation is *Tao*, depicted as a nebulous Void, tenuous and transparent, indescribable and beyond all Space and Time. From *Tao* emerge Space and Time, and from these, *ch'i/qi*, "Breath" or "Vital Energy", the unitary essence necessary for all things. From *ch'i/qi* first comes Heaven, *yang*, and then Earth, *yin*, the two polar forces of all life, the light and spiritual aspects of *ch'i/qi* becoming Heaven and the grosser and heavier material becoming Earth. From the interchange of *yin* and *yang* come the four seasons and all things in existence. And since all things in existence are underpinned by *Tao*, *ch'i/qi*, Heaven and Earth, all is interrelated with correspondences and resonances that mutually affect each other.

The text describes how furry and feathered creatures are *yang*, while shelled and scaly ones, and ones that hibernate, are *yin*. Birds fly upwards and are *yang*; fish swim downwards and are *yin*. In short, the natural world is divided between the two essences of *yin* and *yang*, according to their respective natures. It was the *Huai-nan-tzu/Huainanzi* that set out the pattern of annual rhythms for *yin* and *yang* that became the generally accepted theory, though there were variations. The cycle begins with the arising of *yang* in the north-east, when *yin* is at its height, and it reaches its zenith in the south-west, at which point, *yin* begins to arise again.

Ch'i/qi is especially important in this cosmological profile. It is the basic stuff of the universe, the source of *yin* and *yang*. Yet it is neither matter nor spirit, for it is primordial to both and yet at the same time transforms into both. *Ch'i/qi* informs all things in the universe from matter to thought and emotion. The human being, whether physical or psychological, is *ch'i/qi*, as is the whole universe. Thus, *ch'i/qi* is the "Breath" of the universe, its "Vital Energy". While it was mainly conceived of as a "oneness", a unifying principle, *yin* and *yang* were the dualities by which it operated. It is self-perpetuating in its transformations into the myriad forms of phenomenal existence, constantly regenerating itself in all that exists in the universe. Robinet depicted it as "condensing" itself to greater or lesser extents; the more condensed it becomes the grosser the matter, the less condensed it is, the more it becomes "indefinite potential".[24] Robinet's descriptions of *ch'i/qi* are particularly attractive. She wrote of it as "a force that expands and animates the world in a turning motion by which it spreads and distributes itself into every corner of space and time", and as "both a principle of unity and coherence that connects all things and a potential, an immanent life force in the world that is knowable only in the various changing aspects it assumes".[25]

Absent from this scheme of things is a creator god or goddess. The rhythms of the cosmos are natural ones, self-perpetuating and regulating. The Taoist goal was not to emulate either a transcendent or an anthropomorphic deity, but to regulate personal life in conformity with cosmic patterns. Just as on the macrocosmic level the interplay and harmony between *yin*, the white tiger, and *yang*, the blue dragon, are believed to create the rhythms of the cosmos, so, on the microcosmic level, male and female are the living manifestations of the two forces. As miniatures of the cosmos, they need to be mediators of *Tao*. The natural society also blends the *yin* and *yang* – the intuitive, religious, gentle and mystical aspects of the female *yin* with the active, competitive, aggressive and rational aspects of the male. Taoism accepts the cyclical regeneration of the macrocosm and microcosm in the same way that the seasons follow each other in rhythmic renewal. And just as all birth must contain the potential for death, so death contains the potential for regeneration; the beginning contains the end, and the end the beginning.

One of the important concepts of philosophical Taoism was the nature of the unity of opposites – a theory that was a legacy to much Taoist thought and practice down to present times. To view the world only from its manifest dualities is to miss the calm that is experienced from the point of balance between them, the point where things neither are nor are not. Poised between opposites, everything is as it is; there is total equanimity between life and death, sickness and health, good and evil, gain and loss. Such a state is experience of the tranquillity and stillness of *Tao*. Emptying the mind so that it is devoid of differentiation between opposites allows it to "go with" the flow of life that is *Tao*. It is not opting out of life but viewing the world from, as it were, the centre of a revolving circle where the world is active but the centre is still. Yet the centre is the only point from which all other parts of the circle can be understood, the only still point from which the active dynamism of the interchanges between *yin* and *yang* can be known. Movement rooted in stillness is the result, and is the end product of a practice such as T'ai Chi Ch'üan/Taijiquan.

It is the emergence of all things in the universe – not only forms, but attitudes, concepts, emotions and so on – that gives rise to differentiation between this and that and the ensuing desires and aversions that involve the individual with one polarity rather than another. Thus we kick against the traces of what happens in life, wishing this or that were the case instead of dealing with the matter in hand and focusing on the moment in hand. The sophisticated interaction of *yin* and *yang* brings about the complexities of ideas – religious, philosophical, linguistic – and causes us to differentiate in abstract or ideological ways, as much as to differentiate between physical phenomena in existence. The more humankind identifies with these differentiated polarities, the more *Tao* is lost: the world of senses becomes important and ultimate Reality and its oneness is blurred. Sense-based consciousness interferes with the natural order of things in the self and is inimical to harmony. Moreover, the continued interplay of *yin* and *yang* makes all life subject to change and impermanence. Everything emerges from *Tao* like waves arising in the ocean, only to be submerged in the ocean that gave rise to them. Things contract and expand, fill and empty, wax and wane, without ever gaining any permanence, and with a considerable measure of spontaneity. Even at the level of subatomic physics the behaviour of particles can only be predicted with probability but never with certainty. We cannot, then, take indefinite ownership of things, people and moments. The deeper purpose of T'ai Chi Ch'üan/Taijiquan is to assist the self in creating the kind of inner harmony that facilitates natural adaptation to the environment, and expanded awareness of the unity of existence.

The wider applications of the *yin* and *yang* theory

So important was the theory of *yin* and *yang* that it pervaded astronomy, medicine, mathematics and music. But it is in its relation to human beings that the theory of *yin* and *yang* has played a particularly notable part. Taoists, especially, apply the theory to the human psyche. If the *yin–yang* balance in a person is good, then a greater degree of harmony will ensue. If perfectly balanced, then the individual will be at one with *Tao*. On the other hand, imbalance of *yin* and *yang* results in disharmony, discontent and failure physically, mentally, emotionally and spiritually. Part of the purpose of T'ai Chi is to counteract such disharmony. However, regardless of how difficult life may become when one of the *yin–yang* forces predominates, such difficulty cannot last, because its opposite must follow. The same applies on the wider scale to global events – war and peace, evil and good, the lull and the storm, famine and plenty – these are the *yin–yang* transformations of the earth itself.

In the life of any human the polarities of personality lie in the conscious and subconscious self. How close they sometimes are is revealed when we cry when we are happy, when we laugh hysterically when we are radically upset, and when we find laughter painful. In the complex web of interconnectedness and unity in manifest existence we build up from childhood a picture of dualities in existence and an egoistic desire for some things as opposed to others. Many people strive to be what they are not, and to have what they do not have, finding it difficult or impossible to be still for a moment and reflect on what is. Quiet reflection about life, and times of stillness, are all the more important when we think of the following words attributed to the Taoist philosopher Lieh-tzu/Liezi, though the allegory turns up in many cultures outside China. If we lived for a hundred years – and few of us do – then the bulk of the beginning of it is spent in immaturity, and the bulk of the end of it in senility. A third of life is spent in sleep, and another percentage in illness, anxiety, stress, and the struggle to achieve. Add to this the working world in whatever form that takes, and *life*, at least with any quality, seems rather short!

Yin and *yang* were also applied to the human body and thoroughly influence modern-day Chinese medicine, such as acupuncture. The body's liquid element is *ching/jing* and is *yin*. *Ching/jing* covers saliva, gastric juices, sweat and semen. The other element is the *yang ch'i/qi*, the vital essence essential to life. The third element comprising the human is the *yang* spirit, the *shen*, which at its best experiences *Tao* and at its worst is anxiety, worry and excessive mental activity. When *yin* or *yang* in the body become excessive or deficient, a physiological or pathological imbalance occurs that causes disease – dis-ease. Applied to the human body,

> yin corresponds to nutrient substances, and yang to functional activities. The nutrient substances remain in the interior, therefore "yin remains inside," while the functional activities manifest on the exterior, so "yang remains outside." The yang on the exterior is the manifestation of the substantial movement in the interior, so it is known as "the servant of yin." The yin in the interior is the material base for functional activities and is therefore called the "guard of yang."[26]

The whole organic structure of the human body is explained in terms of *yin* and *yang*. The body is considered the unified whole that is animated by their interplay, and all the parts, organs and tissues are assigned to one or other of these forces. However, though the upper body is generally *yang* and the lower *yin*, organs have their *yin* and *yang* functions, so the principle of nothing being totally *yin* and *yang* is not forgotten. Good health results from maintaining the *yin–yang* balance throughout the body. This can be promoted by the right balance between sleep (*yin*) and wakefulness (*yang*), rest (*yin*) and activity (*yang*), salty foods (*yin*) and bitter foods (*yang*), in other words between all aspects of life. At death the *shen* souls that are *yang* move upwards towards Heaven, while the *po/bo* or *yin* souls move down to Earth.

The physicians of ancient times explained the three major functions of the body – respiration, digestion and circulation – through *yin* and *yang* theories. Breathing is especially important in Taoist practices and in Chinese medical practice. Inhalation of breath is *yin* because it is thought to descend, and exhalation is *yang* because it ascends. This factor is crucial to the practice and understanding of the T'ai Chi *form*, as we shall see below. The descent of the intaking *yin* breath takes *ch'i/qi* via the spleen to the liver and kidneys, while the *yang* exhales it via the kidneys, heart and lungs. Organs also have their "breaths", which facilitate their appropriate functions. But it was and is as part of Taoist meditation that breathing techniques – the control of the *yin* and *yang* within the body – are particularly relevant, and are essential to the practice of martial arts and their derivative practices to the present day. The classic Chinese medical text was the *Yellow Emperor's Classic of Internal Medicine*. It was not composed by the legendary Yellow Emperor Huang-ti/Huangdi, but was a product of Han dynasty times. Apart from relating all illnesses to the imbalances of *yin* and *yang* and giving explanations for cure, the text explains how good *yin–yang* balances can promote longevity. A sample of its pragmatic advice is the following:

> Experts in examining patients judge their general appearance; they feel their pulse and determine whether it is Yin or Yang that causes the disease. . . . To determine whether Yin or Yang predominates, one must first be able to distinguish a light pulse of low tension from a hard, pounding one. With a disease of Yang, Yin predominates. With a disease of Yin, Yang predominates. When one is filled with vigor and strength, Yin and Yang are in proper harmony.[27]

The physical body of the human being thus reflects the unity of the universe, and is a microcosm of the *yin* and *yang* balances that pervade it. No divine force directs this process, and the *yin–yang* theory stands as an impersonal system that explains the phenomena of the universe without the need of a divine creator. The natural state of humankind is one of harmony with the human being uniquely placed between the *yang* of Heaven and the *yin* of Earth. To be perfectly balanced between the two is the goal of the Taoist. The position of humankind in the cosmos is, therefore, unique in the Taoist scheme of things. The tortoise has always been the symbol for the three-tiered cosmos, its domed shell being Heaven, the bottom of the shell Earth, and the tortoise itself – which can expand outward or contract inward – humankind.

In ritual the emperor was the medium of harmonizing the *yin* and *yang* of Heaven and Earth. Indeed, this was the most important ritual of all. But the theory of *yin* and *yang* pervaded all kinds of religious and non-religious ritual in Taoist practices, and is to be found in its festivals, in Taoist alchemy, its deities and demons, even in its art and calligraphy.

As noted above, it informs the movements of the T'ai Chi *form*, with the aim of creating balance and harmony in movement, in respiration and in the focus of the mind.

Yin and *yang* and Tai Chi Ch'üan/Taijiquan

The principle of *yin* and *yang*, the two opposing forces in the universe, was in use long before the development of the Taoist martial art of T'ai Chi. The ultimate good for Taoism was to be able to bring *yin* and *yang* into a state of balance or equilibrium within the self: the art of T'ai Chi combines such a theory with movement in a very holistic way. The success of such a combination is witnessed by the fact that today T'ai Chi and its *yin* and *yang* theory are still widely taught and practised. T'ai Chi is often the medium through which people come into contact with Taoism and, sometimes, with the principals of *yin* and *yang* for the first time.

To understand how *yin* and *yang* work in the practice of T'ai Chi Ch'üan/Taijiquan, then, we must know how to distinguish what is *yin* and what is *yang* when applied to the human body, and how each is expressed in the practice of the T'ai Chi art. Below are some examples of how *yin* and yang are applied in T'ai Chi. These examples will provide a sound format for analysis of *yin* and *yang* in what follows.

Yin	*Yang*
Lightness	Heaviness
Slowness	Quickness
Closing	Opening
Softness	Hardness
Inhalation	Exhalation
Left	Right
Lower	Upper
Inside	Outside
Downward	Upward
Mental	Physical
Vital energy	Strength
Defence	Attack

Once we can distinguish the difference between what is *yin* and what is *yang* in T'ai Chi, we can understand better how to bring *yin* and *yang* into a state of harmony. Ordinarily, because *yin* follows *yang* and *yang* follows *yin*, each is constantly changing and evolving into the other. Thus, at the opening of the *Treatise on T'ai Chi Ch'üan* we find the statement:

> This martial art is called "t'ai-chi" because it is based on *yin* and *yang*, full and empty. After one is clear about *yin* and *yang*, one can begin to understand advance and retreat. Although advance means to advance, it must contain an awareness of retreat; to retreat is still to retreat, but it conceals an awareness of the opportunity to advance.[28]

It is through the practice of T'ai Chi that *yin* and *yang* harmony is achieved for both health and self-defence. At a higher level, too, the application of the *yin* and *yang* principle in T'ai Chi assists in attaining *Tao*. Natural body movements are used which, after a certain level of achievement, help to develop the vital energy *ch'i/qi* that is needed for deeper Taoist meditation practices. Although many individuals will not wish to proceed to such goals, they will find T'ai Chi an excellent exercise for improving health and encouraging long life.

As the art of T'ai Chi developed into many different branches or schools over its long history, the *yin* and *yang* principle was also applied more extensively, especially when it came to the practice of T'ai Chi as a martial art. As we saw in chapter 1, T'ai Chi has its beginnings as a martial art. Today there is some distinction between the martial art aspect and T'ai Chi for health benefits alone, though both are informed by the same principles. In what follows we shall be using the *form* mainly as the term to depict T'ai Chi as a health, relaxation and meditation exercise in contrast to its expression as a martial art, though the latter also uses the same term. And most people today only practise the *form* – the sequence of slow movements linked together, which express the basic techniques of a particular style – for health and relaxation. Here, the *yin* and *yang* theory, though very important, will have more limited application than in the more aggressive martial arts. Thus, when individuals choose to practise T'ai Chi as a martial art, the *yin* and *yang* dimensions are widened to include such exercises as *Pushing Hands*, striking and kicking techniques, joint-locking methods and many more. As a martial art, T'ai Chi is really no different in its approach or methods than any other form of martial art. Like other Chinese martial arts, T'ai Chi, too, uses striking actions of the hands and arms, many kicking methods, joint-locking techniques and throws; the exception is that T'ai Chi as a martial art does not *encourage* the use of these techniques in a strength-versus-strength contest. Instead it applies techniques that use the attackers' strength against themselves. Below are some explanations of *yin* and *yang* mainly in relation to the *form* as a gentler practice for health, relaxation and meditation, though the martial art aspect will occasionally be referred to.

Lightness

In the T'ai Chi *form* lightness occurs in the movement of the whole body, giving the feeling of gentle, graceful, flowing movements. Lightness is *yin*, and gives the sensation of swimming in water. Lightness also means that the stepping movements should be light, as if floating above the ground. The steps should not be clumsy or sudden with the possible chance of losing balance, but should be skilful, controlled, light movements that are performed in four directions. Lightness can also be explained as emptiness. Being light in movements means that there is no chance of tension in the muscles, and that the whole body is relaxed.

Heaviness

Heaviness in the *form* relates to the feeling of the lower body from the waist down, which is heavy and has the sensation of sinking and connecting with the earth. At the same time the upper body, from the waist upwards, has the feeling of lightness. Heaviness is also determined by the weight-bearing leg, which is classed as *yang*, in contrast to the light non- weight-bearing leg, which is *yin*. *Yang* heaviness is also characteristic of the moving primary limb of the upper body. This is because, as the individual concentrates on the moving limb, he or she also co-ordinates the body weight to follow the movement, so more blood and energy are produced. Such a movement gives the individual the impression of heaviness or fullness in the limb. But it is in the transference of body weight through the general movement, creating the sensation of pressing, which makes the limb feel heavy. Conversely, the non-moving secondary limb is classed as *yin* because the concentration of energy into this limb is not as strong as in the moving limb. Also, there is no body weight on this side, thus creating the sensation of lightness or emptiness.

Slowness

Yin slowness is critical to the practice of the T'ai Chi *form*. The movements of the whole body are gentle and smooth and at the same speed. This helps to develop a better sense of balance and coordination of the limbs, but it also helps to develop concentration and stronger connections between the mind and the body. Learning to move slowly allows the body to use more muscle groups than would be used if the individual were moving quickly. By allowing more muscle groups to be exercised when moving slowly, muscle tone, shape and strength are developed throughout the whole body over a long period of time. Slowness of movement also helps the body to relax more, so that the individual releases tension and resistance within the whole body and mind. The circulation of both blood and the vital energy, *ch'i/qi*, will then be improved, allowing them to flow smoothly round the whole body. There are different stages of slowness from one individual to the next. The correct speed should be guided by the breathing; the deeper and longer the breath the slower the movement should be. Obviously the shallower the breath the faster the movement will be. So the speed of each individual's T'ai Chi *form* will differ from that of another because of the varying development of the respiratory system and lung capacity. Through the practice of T'ai Chi Ch'üan/Taijiquan both can be improved.

Quickness

The use of quick *yang* movements occurs mostly when T'ai Chi is practised as a martial art. Here, quick movements release or discharge the vital energy, *ch'i/qi*, out of the body, mainly through the palms, fingers and feet, which are employed in striking or kicking actions. In the *form*, too, there are striking and kicking actions, but the speed of the action is still dictated by the breathing, and does not have the speed and intensity of similar movements in martial art praxis. There are some schools of T'ai Chi that do not use any quick movements at all, choosing to keep the *form* slow. Where quicker movements occur in some versions of the *form*, as in a sudden explosive shaking action of the body, there is a rapid return to the slow movement. Thus, quick movements in T'ai Chi *forms* are relatively few. Using quick movements encourages the vital energy to arrive at the hands or feet more rapidly and powerfully than slow movements.

Closing

Closing occurs when the limbs are drawn closer to the body, and is a *yin* action. By bending or closing movements of the joints, and the contraction of the muscles, tendons and ligaments, the individual will have the feeling of drawing the vital energy back in towards the body. Bending or closing the joints has the effect of slowing down the flow of blood into the limbs. But it also has the effect of stimulating the central nervous system to release stress or tension. This occurs because most nerves accumulate in the joints of the body, and the bending or closing of the joints through the movements of the T'ai Chi *form* allows the individual to release built-up stress within the body. Such movement eases stiffness, and maintains joint flexibility and looseness – all of which help to speed up relaxation.

Opening

Opening has the *yang* quality of expanding. It happens when the individual extends the limbs away from the body. Such action allows the muscles, tendons and ligaments to stretch gently, releasing muscle tension and enhancing the feeling of relaxation. Opening will also develop blood and vital energy circulation into the furthest extremities of the limbs. Importantly, such opening, expansion or extension should not be to the full extent of locking the joints. Rather, the limbs are kept slightly bent as they move away from the body, allowing the movements of the T'ai Chi *form* to remain soft and relaxed.

Softness

The movements of the upper body of the individual performing the T'ai Chi *form* must be soft and pliable and not stiff or rigid. But the individual must be careful not to be over soft in his or her movements, so allowing the upper limbs to wave around loosely. Movements should have *yin* softness but should also be precise and accurate; the flow of the vital energy should be strong. In some schools of T'ai Chi Ch'üan/Taijiquan there is a general saying that the movements should be like a needle hidden in cotton wool. What is suggested here is that, on the outside the individual's movements look very soft and of no use. However, the inner vital energy is very strong and powerful. Softness also applies to the stepping movements of the *form*. They should be performed in a relaxed manner and should not be stiff or heavy. The principle of softness also applies to the breathing; it should be soft, deep and long. There should be no sound made while breathing and it should not be forced or heavy. Softness gives the feeling of harnessing, cultivating and storing of the vital energy.

Hardness

In performing the T'ai Chi *form*, no tension, stiffness or hardness in the movements should be evident. The only time real hardness applies is when it is practised as a martial art. Hardness is *yang* and can be used both in defence and counter-attack situations. In defence, hardness is used to destroy the opponent's attacking limb, while in counter-attack situations hardness is used when we attack the opponent's body or head with a striking or kicking action. Hardness, as defined in the practice of the T'ai Chi *form*, combines relaxation, muscular strength and a sudden explosive releasing of vital energy, alongside the physical workings of the muscles, tendons, ligaments and joints – all co-ordinated and timed precisely to release a surge of power from the whole body, after which the body quickly returns to a relaxed and calm state.

Inhalation

Inhalation is classed as *yin* and has the impression of lifting and drawing energy back into the body. True *yin* breathing in T'ai Chi occurs where the inward breath is much longer than the outward breath; *yang* breathing is where the outward breath is longer than the inward breath. Because the practice of T'ai Chi is all about being in balance or a state of equilibrium with oneself, then the breathing method used is a *yin/yang* method. The inward breath and outward breath are balanced and of equal length. When practising the *form* the inhaling of air and energy is co-ordinated with the closing of the joints and limbs towards the body, giving the feeling of contracting inwards. There should be no sound when inhaling; breathing should be soft and deep.

Exhalation

As already mentioned above, exhalation is characterized as *yang*. The outward release of breath gives the feeling of sinking downwards and of releasing or throwing energy away from the body. A true *yang* breath is where the outward breath is much longer than the inward breath, as noted above. The speed of the outward *yang* breath can be slow and gentle, or it can be quick and forceful depending on the use of T'ai Chi for health or martial art purposes respectively. When practising the T'ai Chi *form* movements the exhaling of breath is co-ordinated with the opening of the joints, and the limbs moving away from the body in a stretching and expanding action.

The left

The left side of the body is *yin*. In ordinary life the right side of the body is usually foremost in activity, but in T'ai Chi the left is developed just as much as the right. This is because T'ai Chi encourages co-ordination over the entire body. By working the left side, the muscle tone, shape, strength and joint flexibility are kept in balance with the right side. Also, through the turning and twisting movements of the *form*, the functions of the internal organs on the left side – the lung, spleen and kidney – are strengthened. Developing and working the left side of the body will also be beneficial in stimulating the right side of the brain, thus creating a stronger connection of the mind and body.

The right

The right side of the body is the *yang* side, and is co-ordinated and developed alongside the left side of the body so that the muscles, tendons, ligaments and joints are kept in tone, in shape and flexible. Neither the right side, nor the left side, move predominantly in the practice of the *form*, but are co-ordinated together. Through the turning and twisting of the torso and waist the functions of the internal organs on the right side of the body – the lung, liver and kidney – are strengthened. Developing the right side of the body will have a beneficial effect on the left side of the brain, creating stronger connections of the mind and body by stimulating the central nervous system.

The lower

The lower here means below the waist or the legs, is *yin*, and should be co-ordinated with the upper torso and limbs. Through the particular stepping action of the T'ai Chi *form*, and the transference of the weight from one leg to the other, the muscles, tendons and ligaments will be strengthened and, through the twisting and turning actions of the *form*, the ankles, knees and hips will develop flexibility. Because the practice of T'ai Chi is a standing exercise the legs, especially, take the full extent of the exercise, and individuals who have practised T'ai Chi over many years develop very strong leg muscles. As the legs become stronger the individual connects better to Mother Earth. In T'ai Chi circles this is called "rooting" and is where the individual lowers his or her centre of gravity and vital energy into the ground to develop stability. In a martial-art sense such a practice allows the individual to generate more power in his or her techniques. Chang San-feng/Zhang Sanfeng mentions this in his T'ai Chi Ch'üan/Taijiquan teachings to his students:

> The motion should be rooted in the feet,
> Released through the legs,
> Controlled by the waist,
> And manifested through the fingers.
>
> The feet, legs and waist
> Must act together simultaneously,
> So that while stepping forward or back
> The timing and position are correct.[29]

For those individuals who practise T'ai Chi for health and relaxation, the stepping actions of the *form* are an excellent workout for the heart. Because of the lifting and stepping actions in all directions, more blood flows into the muscles of the legs. The muscles in the legs have the largest muscle groups within the body, so the heart needs to pump more blood and energy into them for them to work. Hence, the stepping actions of the T'ai Chi *form* gently exercise and strengthen the heart and improve the circulation of blood and energy round the entire body.

The upper

The upper here means the upper body from the waist upwards, and is *yang*, as mentioned above. The lower and the upper must be co-ordinated together so that the whole body moves as one unit. The movements of the top half of the body must be soft, gentle and light. The torso shows flexibility and suppleness at the waist and lower back, the spine is upright as if the head is suspended from above, and the shoulders and elbows sink towards the ground. There should be a feeling of heaviness from the waist down and lightness from the waist upwards in T'ai Chi. Some teachers look at the legs as if they were the roots of a tree sinking into the earth and the upper body as the branches and stems moving freely in the wind.

Inside

Inside is classed as *yin* and corresponds to the inner side of the limbs and the front of the body. It is also indicative of the *yin* acupuncture meridians and channels that run along each of the limbs and along the front of the body. "Inside" also means to become aware of the internal sensations of the vital energy as it moves round the whole body. As the individual performs the movements of the T'ai Chi *form*, co-ordinating breathing with the movements, he or she, after a long period of time, will begin to experience the sensation of energy. These sensations differ from one individual to another but the most common are the feelings of warmth, heat, tingling and itchiness. Gradually the individual will feel the sensations through the entire body, indicating that the circulation of blood and energy are moving strongly and smoothly through the energy channels and points.

Outside

The outside of the body is characterized as *yang* and it corresponds to the outside of the limbs and the back of the body. It also relates to the *yang* acupuncture meridians, the channels that run along the outside of the limbs and back. When the individual performs the T'ai Chi *form* the outside relates to the physical workings of the body's mechanics. Movements in the *form* involving the outside of the body are related to, and have a beneficial effect on, the internal organs, nervous system and vital energy on the inside of the body.

Downward

The downward movement of the body is classed as *yin*, and has the feeling of sinking both the body weight and vital energy into the feet and ground. As Chang San-feng/Zhang Sanfeng mentions in his treatise on the teachings of T'ai Chi Ch'üan/Taijiquan:

> If there is up, there is down;
> If there is forward, then there is backward;
> If there is left, then there is right,
>
> If the mind wants to move up,
> It contains at the same time
> The downward idea.[30]

When practising T'ai Chi as a martial art, the downward action can be applied to throwing or sending an opponent to the floor, or is applied to pressing down on an opponent's limb. When the downward movement is applied to the *form*, it mainly comes from the knees sinking and not from the torso bending over from the waist. In T'ai Chi the spine is always kept upright.

Upwards

Upward movement in the *form* is characterized as *yang*. It involves the feeling of lifting or rising and encourages the energy to flow upwards into the moving limb. In the martial art aspect of T'ai Chi it may be used to lift an opponent off the floor, or it can be used to lift and control an opponent's limb. When we apply the upward movement to the *form*, the hand may pass upwards above the head, but the shoulders must not be allowed to rise, as this will make the bottom half of the body light and the top half heavy, thus affecting balance. "Uprooted" is a martial art term, which means to push or knock someone off balance, and occurs when the individual has no connection with the ground. Thus, for both martial art praxis and the *form*, it is always important to sink *ch'i/qi* into the ground, so that a better connection with the earth is achieved by lowering the centre of gravity – hence to "root", like the roots of a tree penetrating into the earth.

Mind

Through the practice of T'ai Chi, the concentration and focus of the mind is greatly developed. The mind is *yin*, and in Taoist meditation is referred to as an active and playful monkey that cannot maintain concentration for a long period of time! Most beginners of T'ai Chi have this state of mind. But with regular practice of the *form* the mind develops a state of focus and concentration. Slowly, after a period of time, and with plenty of patience and practice, the mind becomes still and quiet. This is the first step on the rung of the ladder in Taoist meditation practice. Once the mind becomes still and focused it then becomes consciously aware of the inner feelings of the physical, emotional, mental and spiritual energies of the entire body.

So through the practice of T'ai Chi Ch'üan/Taijiquan individuals will be able to relax more into their own being. Once the mind has become strong in its concentration, then intention, or *i/yi*, is used to propel the vital energy, *ch'i/qi*, to any given part of the body. In martial art it is important that the individual issues energy to the hands and feet quickly and smoothly. The *form* movements, however, are a system of Taoist moving *meditation*, where the mind must become disciplined and sensitive to the inner workings of the body. The mind must be considerably developed to be able to control the vital energy and to guide it round the whole body. The practice of T'ai Chi for complete beginners starts as a physical exercise but, gradually, as they become more and more proficient, they begin to realize that it is more a mind exercise. The connections between the body and mind are strengthened and the hidden power of the mind can be felt.

Physical

Physical strength and actions of the body are *yang* characteristics. The physical actions help to discipline and focus the concentration of the mind. Because the practice of T'ai Chi develops balance and co-ordination of the upper and lower limbs, along with the breathing, it also strengthens the connections of the mind and body, because the individual needs to concentrate on the timing of the movements working in harmony with each other. One of the great benefits of practising T'ai Chi is that it can be prolonged into old age: its slow, graceful movements help to keep the body relaxed, fit and free of tension. But it is also an excellent way to maintain a healthy mental state, since the physical movements help to stimulate the functions of the brain and help in slowing down the spread of some mental illnesses like short or long-term memory loss.

Vital energy

The development of the vital energy, *ch'i/qi*, is what every individual aims to achieve through the practice of T'ai Chi Ch'üan/Taijiquan. Vital energy is *yin* and its development is the essence behind all of the movements of the T'ai Chi *form*. As the flow of blood circulates through the veins and arteries, so the vital energy flows through the acupuncture meridians of the body. Like the arteries, the acupuncture meridians span the whole body. As noted earlier, on the inside of the limbs and front of the body, the acupuncture meridians are *yin*. The acupuncture meridians on the outside of the limbs and the back are *yang*. As the individual performs the T'ai Chi *form* he or she naturally invigorates the flow of the vital energy to circulate throughout the *yin* and *yang* energy lines of the whole body. The rhythmic actions of breathing in co-ordination with the movements of the body and the concentration of the mind, or intention, enhance such circulation. Over a period of time the individual will begin to feel the many sensations of the vital energy beginning to activate and circulate. It is only when the individual balances both the *yang* physical movements with *yin* concentration that he or she will achieve the cultivation of the vital energy.

Strength

Strength refers to the physical or muscular strength of the body. It is considered *yang* and in the T'ai Chi *form* it is not fully called upon since, here, the aim is to keep the body relaxed and free of muscular tension and stiffness. But when it comes to using T'ai Chi as a martial art then the full use of physical strength is balanced with the vital energy of the body. T'ai Chi as a martial art does not encourage the development of large muscles, but encourages the development and strengthening of the tendons and ligaments, as well as promoting circulation of the vital energy through the many solo and two-person exercises. The co-ordination of muscular strength and vital energy is used in the striking, kicking and throwing actions of T'ai Chi as a martial art.

Defence

Defence is a term used purely for the practice of T'ai Chi Ch'üan/Taijiquan as a martial art. It is *yin*, and is used to yield and absorb the opponent's force, aggression, speed and balance in such a way as to be able to use it against him or her. It requires many hours of practice to develop a high level of manipulative skill that offers no resistance to the incoming blow or kick, and then to be able to re-direct the attack into nothingness. As far as the *form* is concerned, it occurs when the limb contracts back towards the body, or when the body weight moves backwards in a rocking or stepping action. It is as if one is moving away from an attack, is offering no resistance, and is re-directing the incoming force away from the body and into emptiness. In the T'ai Chi exercise of *Pushing Hands*, *tui-shou/duishou*, which is a two-person exercise, tactile awareness, co-ordination, balance and concentration are developed. It basically brings the movements of the T'ai Chi *form* as a martial art to life. *Pushing Hands* is performed when static or by moving around. The aim of the exercise is to uproot one's partner, taking him or her off balance, through experiencing his or her inner energies.

Attack

As a martial art, T'ai Chi is non-aggressive. It incorporates the principle of blending in and turning the attackers' force and strength against themselves. Because Taoists looked closely at nature, they realized that to resist against a stronger force than oneself was futile; defeat would be inevitable. They could see this happening in nature all around them, especially when there was bad weather and a storm raged. The tree that was upright and rigid would be uprooted and blown away; yet the tree that was flexible and supple would survive because it absorbed the storm's force and yielded rather than resisted it. In today's fast and stressful life such a Taoist principle of non-resistance and going with the flow is a philosophy that many people try to emulate. Because T'ai Chi follows this principle it is viewed as a counter-attacking martial art and not just attack orientated. However, in the T'ai Chi *form* it is the opening, expanding movements, where the limbs move away from the body, which are the counter-attacking methods.

The Taoist health, meditative and martial art exercise of the T'ai Chi Ch'üan/Taijiquan system totally utilizes the Taoist philosophy of *yin* and *yang*, the two opposing forces within the universe. The above principles are only a few examples of how *yin* and *yang* are used as a guide to help the individual to the goal of skilfully performing T'ai Chi. Through the practice of T'ai Chi, and the better understanding of the *yin* and *yang* theory, many individuals achieve an enhanced state of balance and harmony in their own beings and lives. It helps them to develop a better sense of balance and co-ordination between the physical and mental, to calm the emotions, and to balance the vital energy within the whole body. Again, this will take a great amount of time and effort from each individual. When we stand in the neutral position at the beginning of the *form*, we are in a state of emptiness. As soon as we commence the movements of the T'ai Chi *form*, then *yin* and *yang* are born. As we progress through the *form* we are trying to express fully the balance of *yin* and *yang* in total harmony and achieve the level of T'ai Chi or Supreme Ultimate. Once we have finished the *form* we return back to nothingness. Clearly, however, self effort and constant practice are essential. Thus, Lao-tzu/Laozi mentions in the *Tao Te Ching/Daodejing*:

> When the best student hears of Tao
> He practises it diligently.
> When the average student hears of Tao
> He thinks of it now and again.
> When the worst student hears of Tao
> He laughs aloud.[31]

While many of the elaborate theories of Tsou Yen/Zou Yan were not to find their way into mainstream thought, and there were times when correlative thinking was not in vogue,[32] it would have to be claimed that even westerners understand the philosophy of *yin* and *yang*. This is so even if they have never heard of Taoism, and can only loosely connect the theory with China. Indeed, the two terms have now found their way into western dictionaries. The importance of the *yin–yang* system in Chinese religion cannot be overestimated. Rites of passage, festivals, the layout of temples, and even the place where a home was built, were influenced by *yin* and *yang*. The influences are still evident today in many legacies of Chinese culture to the West, in martial arts like T'ai Chi, in Chinese medicine, and in *feng-shui*, for example. The psychologist Jung was sufficiently interested in *yin* and *yang* to correlate them with the inner and outer personalities of the individual. In the West, we have only comparatively recently become aware of the way in which our daily lives have an impact on global issues – illustrating only too well the interconnectedness of the whole. Robinet described the Taoist world as "a closed whole, a sequence of nested enclosures in time and space".[33] As such it is an interconnected whole in which the interplay of dualities – the *yin* and *yang* of existence – "are lines of force, directions whose nature is to cross and mingle, to play against each other, both self-generating and self-propelling, disappearing and alternating; and their function is to define a double syntax of polarity and ambiguity".[34] As ancient theories go, that of *yin* and *yang* was a rather developed perspective of reality that seems to have stood the test of time.

3 The Way

The heartbeat of Taoism – its whole pulse and rhythm – is expressed in the thoughts of its ancient philosophers and in the seminal concepts of *Te/De*, *wu-wei*, naturalness, spontaneity, the sage and, above all, in the concept of *Tao* itself. It is these concepts, too, that are the philosophical foundation of T'ai Chi Ch'üan/Taijiquan. Living in a distant age of savage warfare, of death, disease of the body and dis-ease of the inner being, two thinkers of the ancient past stand out for the refreshing simplicity yet profundity of their thought. These men are Lao-tzu/Laozi and Chuang-tzu/Zhuangzi. The fact that their historical existence is questionable, or that much of the works bearing their names may not, indeed, have been written by them, need not concern us. Suffice it to say here that Lao-tzu/Laozi's *Tao Te Ching/Daodejing* and Chuang-tzu/Zhuangzi's book that bears his name are of such immense importance that they are the foundation of Taoist belief regardless of how it has diverged into multiple paths. Indeed, many of the teachings of the *Tao Te Ching/Daodejing* have been absorbed into the practice of T'ai Chi Ch'üan/Taijiquan. To these two philosophers, we want to add the later thinker Lieh-tzu/Liezi, who also gave his name to a book. These three thinkers were adopted by later Taoists as the "founders" of Taoism, but they did not set out to "found" a religion, and Lao-tzu/Laozi and Chuang-tzu/Zhuangzi would not have thought of themselves as "Taoists" in any way. All we can say is that those who later came to accept the teachings of the three philosopher-sages, and who called themselves Taoists, projected their beginnings back to the traditional authors of such teachings, and saw them as founders of their schools.

Except for short periods of time Confucianism was the orthodox "religion" accepted in China. It was a systematically rational, measured, moralist and conformist tradition that was expressed in exactitude, correctness and methodical practices. The thought found in the *Tao Te Ching/Daodejing*, the *Chuang-tzu/Zhuangzi* and the *Lieh-tzu/Liezi* is quite the opposite – free, spontaneous, non-conformist and challenging to orthodox thought. It was the *yin* of the feminine, receptive, yielding and mystical inner spirituality in contrast to the *yang* of the defined, rational, rigidity of Confucian existence. The choice was between roaming beyond societal constrictions and conditionings or succumbing to existence within them. Our three philosophers chose the former route.

Lao-tzu/Laozi and the *Tao Te Ching/Daodejing*

Excluding the Bible, no other book has been translated so often as the *Tao Te Ching/Daodejing*. This is so despite the brevity of the text – a mere eighty-one very short chapters, many amounting to just a few lines. It is a text well known to teachers of T'ai Chi in all its aspects. But the brevity of the text belies the difficulty in interpreting it, and many different interpretations are to be found in its many translations and commentaries. Indeed, it is almost possible to see in its words what one wills. Be that as it may, Needham referred to the book as "without exception the most profound and beautiful work in Chinese history".[1] And, indeed, it is an exquisite text, delightful in its simplicity and serenity, and yet tantalizing in its depth.

The name of its traditional author, Lao-tzu/Laozi, is a title meaning "Old Master", "Old Boy", "Old One" or "Old Fellow", where *Lao* means "old". Lao-tzu/Laozi may have been a real personage, an archivist of the state of Chou/Zhou in the latter part of the fourth century BCE. However, the *Shih Chi/Shiji, The Records of the Grand Historian*, of Ssu-ma Ch'ien/Sima Qian of the end of the second and beginning of the first century BCE, and our only source for the life of Lao-tzu/Laozi, cannot supply a clear account. We are left with different theories about Lao-tzu/Laozi's identity and life.[2]

The *Tao Te Ching/Daodejing* was originally called the *Lao-tzu/Laozi* after the Old Master. Indeed, it was not for many centuries that it was given the former title. The first two words of the later title *Tao Te Ching/Daodejing* reflect neatly the division of the book into two parts, one dealing with, or rather beginning with, the word *Tao*, translated as "Way", and the other with *Te/De*, "Virtuality" or "Power". The addition of *Ching/Jing*, meaning "prestigious book" or "classic", came later. Jacob Needleman writes of the work: "To read it is not only to see ourselves as we are but to glimpse a greatness extending far beyond our knowledge of ourselves and the universe we live in."[3] Despite its enigmatic and profound content, however, the *Tao Te Ching/Daodejing* is not removed from the practical world of statecraft, and has as much a message to rulers as it does to the hermit or the reflective individual. But it is clearly a text that aims to dislodge normal thought patterns. It challenges conventional knowledge and the narrowness of conditioned thought.

Did Lao-tzu/Laozi write the book? Traditionally, the answer is yes; academically, we would have to say that it is unlikely. Indeed, it is likely that the text is the result of multiple sources, some of which reflect ancient tradition, other parts being later additions. While being an integrated work, it is, nevertheless, a compilation, the work of several authors. Hanson describes it as "an edited accumulation of fragments and bits drawn from a wide variety of sources – conventional wisdom, popular sayings, poems, perhaps even jokes".[4] The bottom line of this is that there may, in fact, be very little connection at all between a man called Lao-tzu/Laozi and the *Tao Te Ching/Daodejing* that he is alleged to have written. Its date is also disputed. Traditionally it is believed to have been written about 500 BCE in the Spring and Autumn stage of the Chou/Zhou dynasty. This would make its author as Lao-tzu/Laozi an older contemporary of Confucius. However, a date of the fourth century BCE is likely.

Lao-tzu/Laozi later became the chief deity in an important movement that began the process of Taoism as a real religion. In many ways he became the anthropomorphic representation of *Tao*. In the seventh century the emperor gave him the title of the Great Supreme (T'ai Shang/Taishang), and in the eleventh century he gained the title Great Supreme One, the Ancient Master (T'ai-shang Lao-chün/Taishang Laojun). Religious Taoism made him the greatest god in the Taoist pantheon.

Chuang-tzu/Zhuangzi

The work of Chuang-tzu/Zhuangzi, which has the same title as his name, is a delight to read. Instead of the terse depth of the *Tao Te Ching/Daodejing*, we find a plethora of stories, amusing incidents and anecdotes on which to feed the mind. Wilhelm called Chuang-tzu/Zhuangzi "a splendid figure in Chinese intellectual and spiritual life".[5] In contrast to the vague identity of Lao-tzu/Laozi, in Chuang-tzu/Zhuangzi we have a refreshingly vivid person, with an evolved sense of humour and wit, and the ability to convey profound thoughts through simple imagery. Yet his work has a somewhat elusive nature that challenges conventional thought, particularly since he loved discourse and discussion – especially if there could be no right answer! In many ways, Chuang-tzu/Zhuangzi sought to be deliberately elusive!

As in the case of Lao-tzu/Laozi, we still know little of Chuang-tzu/Zhuangzi.[6] But while we know little about his life, it would have to be agreed, with Palmer, that "the figure who does emerge is one of the most intriguing, humorous, enjoyable personalities in the whole of Chinese thought and philosophy".[7] And if there is mockery in Chuang-tzu/Zhuangzi's words, and accounts of practical jokes and tricks, the humour that pervades the book has the purpose of breaking down the barriers of the mind, so that it becomes possible to laugh at the conventions of society.

If we turn to the authorship of the *Chuang-tzu/Zhuangzi* the first seven chapters, called the *Inner Chapters*, are fairly consistently ascribed to Chuang-tzu/Zhuangzi himself. The remaining twenty-four chapters were written by others. The whole work, then, "is a catch-bag, an anthology of stories and incidents, thought and reflections which have gathered around the name of Chuang Tzu".[8] The dates of Chuang-tzu/Zhuangzi place him somewhere in the mid-fourth and early part of the third centuries BCE, traditionally 369–286 BCE. However, the other contributors of material to the *Chuang-tzu/Zhuangzi* lived much later, and it was centuries later that the text reached a full form.

The *Inner Chapters* contain a rich mixture of tales about rich and poor, kings, sages, robbers, potters, butchers, carpenters and many others. Indeed, beggars and cripples are treated in exactly the same way as kings and sages. "It is a bag of tricks, knaves, sages, jokers, unbelievably named people and uptight Confucians! And through it strides the occasionally glimpsed figure of Chuang Tzu himself, leaving a trail of humour, bruised egos and damaged reputations."[9] It is no wonder that Maspero called Chuang-tzu/Zhuangzi the finest writer of ancient China. He wrote, too, of Chuang-tzu/Zhuangzi: "His style is brilliant, he has a marvellous sense of rhythm, and his wonderfully supple language lends itself to all sorts of nuances. His lively imagination gives to all the anecdotes with which he embroiders his tales an extraordinary colour and life. At the same time, he was probably the most profound thinker of his time."[10] Underlying all is the focus on *Tao* as that which makes possible the flight of the self to unlimited freedom in the natural spontaneity of life lived within the reality that is *Tao*.

There was much of which Chuang-tzu/Zhuangzi disapproved. In fact, he disliked anything that impeded the simple, uncomplicated awareness of nature and the expression of the cosmic power of nature in all things. He tried to free people from their conventional beliefs and ways of thinking, releasing the self from conditioned habits and behaviour – a practice not far removed from a proximate aim of the T'ai Chi *form* today. He disliked the uniformity that state law and order imposed on the country, along with the bureaucracy and officialdom that perpetrated it and that was so alien to the natural way of Heaven. He was a free spirit that despised any shackling of the spiritual evolution of all things and all nature.

Lieh-tzu/Liezi

We know very little about the life of Lieh-tzu/Liezi. He seemed to have lived his life in poverty and as a recluse. Chuang-tzu/Zhuangzi refers to him so there must have been some prior tradition about him, perhaps a collection of his sayings. Despite the portrayal of Lieh-tzu/Liezi in the *Chuang-tzu/Zhuangzi* as a real person, we have no real evidence to suggest that he existed outside legend. The book that bears his name, the *Lieh-tzu/Liezi*, was probably compiled several centuries after his supposed lifetime. Many now date the text to around 300 CE, or later. Like the *Chuang-tzu/Zhuangzi*, the *Lieh-tzu/Liezi* contains tales and legends, parables and miracles, humorous anecdotes and jokes, but also a good deal of reflective philosophy, conveyed through the medium of prose and rhythmic verse. Magic and mystery are interwoven.

Such, then, is the philosophical foundation of Taoism, retrospectively cast back to three ancient sages and the works ascribed to them. We now need to turn to the heart of their philosophy and examine the concept of *Tao* as they understood it, and as it is still mainly understood by Taoists who practise T'ai Chi Ch'üan/Taijiquan.

Tao

Something formless, yet lacking nothing
There before heaven and earth.

Silent and void,
Standing alone and unchanging,
Revolving, yet inexhaustible.
Perhaps it is the mother of the universe.
I do not know its name
So I call it *Tao*.
If pressed, I call it "Great".[11]

Such is the description – or lack of it – of *Tao* in the *Tao Te Ching/Daodejing*. The Chinese ideogram for *tao* contained the sign for moving on and a head. It indicated moving step by step, with the ideogram of walking feet, possibly in rhythmic movement.[12] The use of the character for the head combined with a foot suggests a "way", "path" "road", or even "method", with the head suggesting, perhaps, that it should be a thoughtful way forward. Thus it can be used in the sense of a political way, a social way, a religious way, or the way of Heaven. It can include the manner in which one goes along the way in the sense of "to lead" or "to guide". It can also mean "to speak", "to tell" or "to instruct".[13] It is a very old word that can obviously be used in a quite mundane sense. But from ancient times, it could be used in the sense of the way of humanity, and thus had connotations of morality, virtue and righteousness. In more abstract meanings, and in a metaphysical sense, it can mean "Way" or "Truth" in the sense of an ultimate doctrine, or principle.[14] Here, the meaning of the word is deepened, and it is in this sense that we shall need to look at the concept in Taoism, where the term was projected to its metaphysical ultimate. In Taoism, *Tao* represents ultimate Reality. Jonathan Star points out that since it can be both a noun and a verb: "It can represent the substance of the entire universe and the process by which the universe functions."[15]

The Confucians used the term *Tao* in the sense of social order, and as a foundational ethical principle. Here, it is a right way in the political, social and moral activities of life. In this sense it could be furthered through knowledge, study, discipline and excellence in living. It could be nurtured in culture and propriety, and success in pursuing the Way would bring its rewards in life. It was an anthropocentric view of the human being as thoroughly capable of winning the support of Heaven by right societal behaviour. Such a conception of *Tao* has nothing of the metaphysical connotation that the Taoists gave it. In Taoism it is used in a metaphysical sense to portray the Way of all nature, the deep naturalness that pervades all and makes everything such as it is. It is the ultimate Reality that informs all things. Yet the ultimate principle that is *Tao* in the Taoist sense is essentially *impersonal*: it cannot reward or punish. It is a unifying *principle* or *force*, not a being. The Way of the Confucians is a describable Way; the Way of the philosophical Taoists is essentially metaphysical – the still, underlying, changeless unity that is the source of all motion, change and plurality in the universe, the point at which opposites meet and the harmony between them all.

An inexpressible ultimate principle

What was there before existence of the universe began? Was there absolutely nothing or was there some kind of *potentiality* for things to be? Before all the differentiation of the extant cosmos, was there an undifferentiated Void from which all came? For Taoism, the answers to these questions are all affirmative. *Tao* is that undifferentiated Void and potentiality that underpins all creation; immutable, unchanging, without form and beyond all deities and even the idea of them. It is indescribable Reality, eternally nameless, but experience of it, and of its profound emptiness, is the goal of the Taoist. The opening of the *Tao Te Ching/Daodejing* has the words:

> The *tao* that can be spoken of is not eternal *Tao*
> The name that can be named is not the eternal Name.[16]

There are a variety of ways in which the Chinese characters can be translated here, but really they all amount to the same thing, and that is to say that if you can speak about, tell about, or express *Tao*, then you do not really know what *Tao* is.[17] *Tao* is beyond human comprehension, and the term *Tao* is the best we can do to refer to it. *Tao* is a name that is not a name. Essentially, it has no name for it is beyond all language and thought. Giving it names, then, only suggests that it is not understood, and refers to something other than *Tao*.

In the same way that potentiality has to exist before things can come into being, so *Tao* is that which begins all things. In the words of Fung Yu-lan: "The *Tao* is that by which anything and everything comes to be. Since there are always things, *Tao* never ceases to be and the name of *Tao* also never ceases to be. It is the beginning of all beginnings, and therefore it has been the beginning of all things. A name that never ceases to be is an abiding name, and such a name is in reality not a name at all. Therefore it is said: "The name that can be named is not the abiding name."[18] For Taoism, then, *Tao* is the unchanging "that" which underlies all things as their source, giving impulse, form, life and rhythm to the changing plurality of the cosmos – this last, depicted in the *Tao Te Ching/Daodejing* as the "ten-thousand things":

> Great *Tao* flows everywhere, filling all to the left and to the right.
> The ten thousand things depend upon it for existence;
> it rejects none of them.
> It accomplishes its purpose silently and claims no fame.
>
> It nourishes and protects the ten thousand things,
> And yet is not their ruler.
> It has no desire; it is very humble.
>
> The ten thousand things return to it,
> Yet it is not their ruler.
> So it is very great.
>
> It does not claim greatness,
> And is therefore really great.[19]

The inexplicable nature of *Tao*, and the inability of language to penetrate to the level that it is, is reiterated in the *Chuang-tzu/Zhuangzi*: "The great Way is not named" and "The Tao that is clear is not the Tao."[20] So we find contrasted the unchanging, unnameable absolute Reality that is *Tao* with the impermanent, changing world of names and forms, differentiation, opposites and dualities. Chang San-feng/Zhang Sanfeng, the traditional founder of T'ai Chi, is reputed to have written: "The Tao is something miraculous. Spiritual, it has an essence; empty, it has no form. It is unfathomable whether we follow after it or go forth to meet it. It cannot be found in shadow or echo. No one knows why it is as it is. Supreme sages attained it in antiquity; it has been transmitted to the present by subtle means."[21] It is such subtle functioning of *Tao* that Chuang-tzu/Zhuangzi brings out, by associating it with the ebb and flow of change in the universe. The inexplicable, rhythmic, pulsating, dynamism of *Tao* pervading life is the abstract principle with which the sage and others need to become in tune in life. For Chuang-tzu/Zhuangzi *Tao* is the means by which the soul is nourished and is able to return to its source. But while the *Chuang-tzu/Zhuangzi* emphasizes that *Tao* transcends all language and thought it sees the immanence of *Tao* in all things down to a blade of grass.

Thus, the nature of *Tao* in the *Tao Te Ching/Daodejing* and in the *Chuang-tzu/Zhuangzi* is beyond description. It is a mystical abstract that stands outside conventional thought. In essence, *Tao* is that which makes things as they are – the flying of birds, the flowing of rivers to the sea, the blowing of the wind. All that *Tao* is in life is effortlessly and naturally accomplished and that is exactly the message of the *Tao Te Ching/Daodejing* and the *Chuang-tzu/Zhuangzi* for living life – effortlessly and naturally, like *Tao*. Operating naturally in the world is working with nature rather than treating nature as something extraneous to the self. It is operating in the same way that *Tao* does in nature, and is the seminal philosophy that underpins T'ai Chi.

It is clear that the concept of *Tao* is a deeply mystical one in the *Tao Te Ching/Daodejing* and the *Chuang-tzu/Zhuangzi*. And it is only the mystical path in life by which it can be intuitively understood. While *Tao* makes things what they are it is not itself a thing, and is *no-thing*, but experience of things as they are is also experience of *Tao*. Epithets used to describe *Tao* are enigmatic ones – vast, cool, shadowy, still, tranquil, hidden, mysterious, silent. It is the ultimate mystery, and as *no-thing* it would be useless to pray or sing praises to it, for it is completely impersonal, is without wilful intention, and yet performs all things. It contains all, sustains all and permeates all and nothing can be separate from it. It is the "is-ness" of all things, all forces and all subtleties, the rhythms of existence, the patterns of nature, the order of the cosmos. The *Tao Te Ching/Daodejing* alludes to it as the eternal valley spirit. The valley is the darkness into which all must fall, just as it is the recipient of the higher waters and streams that cannot but drop into its depths. The valley and shade were always seen as *yin*, the female, the yielding, the soft, the receptive and the mysterious.

The incomprehensible *Tao* that obtained before the universe began is the Void, Emptiness, or *Wu-chi/Wuji*, *Wu* meaning "nothingness", "negation" or "absence of", and *Chi/Ji* meaning "ultimate". So we have ultimate nothingness. In the T'ai Chi *form*, the state of *Wu-chi/Wuji* is expressed in the stage before movement. Here, the individual is standing still, legs shoulder-width apart, arms hanging loosely by the sides of the body, and the spine and head are held upright but in a relaxed manner without stiffness or rigidity. No intention of movement pervades the body or mind. It is a state of nothingness, a return to *Wu-chi/Wuji*. But *Wu-chi/Wuji* is not just confined to the stillness before movement. It occurs, too, in other aspects of T'ai Chi. For example, in the *Pushing Hands* exercise noted earlier, two individuals stand opposite each other making light contact, their hands against each others. Neither person uses any strength, force or intention; both are in a state of *Wu-chi/Wuji*, nothingness. Yet another example of the state of nothingness in T'ai Chi is reflected when first entering and when leaving an empty training room. Thus, the concept of *Wu-chi/Wuji* describes not only the pre-creation of the universe, but also the stages or gaps between the dynamics of relationships with individuals, groups of people, between objects, and between people and objects.

Diagrammatically, *Wu-chi/Wuji* is represented by an empty circle, indicative of total Void. When it stirs, then the universe begins with the energy of *T'ai-chi/Taiji* "Supreme Ultimate", the life force that is manifest as the potentiality and actuality of *yin* and *yang*, and that is born out of the emptiness of *Wu-chi/Wuji*. As soon as this process takes place, nothingness is transformed into potential – the mother of *yin* and *yang*. After standing still and symbolizing *Wu-chi/Wuji* before commencing the T'ai Chi *form*, the transformation to *T'ai Chi/Taiji* is represented by slowly raising the arms. Such movement is indicative of the intention and potential to move the body in the same way that *T'ai-chi/Taiji* has the potential to bring about all things through the operation of *yin* and *yang*. Diagrammatically, this potential of *T'ai-chi/Taiji* is represented by a circle that contains concentric inner circles of rotating darkness representing *yin* and light representing *yang*.

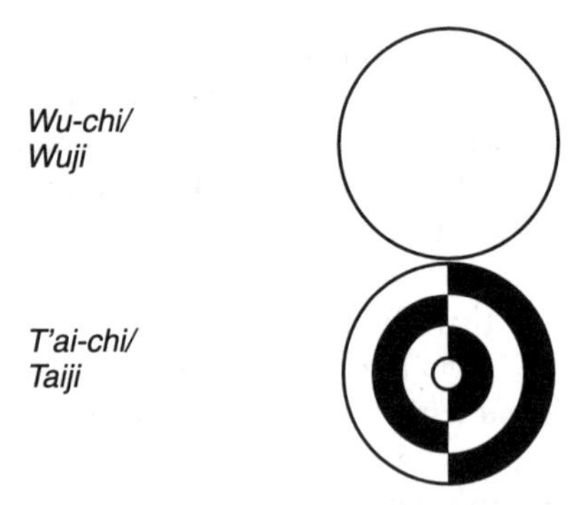

The diagram symbolizes the power behind dynamic movement and static states, in which *yin* and *yang* are combined.

Creation

The source of all creation, then, is the mysterious depth and darkness of *Tao* that is beyond name, form and conceptualization. It is the potential for all things and that to which all things will return – the utter silence of the primordial Void. In this sense *Tao* is beyond One, beyond unity, but always present throughout all creation. The relational continuity between the primordial Void and the existent present is paramount. Not to know such is to misunderstand the nature of reality. The inactive stillness of potentiality in the Void exists alongside the spontaneous activity of *Tao* in life: Thus, in chapter 37 of the *Tao Te Ching/Daodejing* it says:

> *Tao* exists in non-action,
> Yet nothing is left undone.

The inseparability of these two aspects of *Tao* is critical to the understanding of the nature of *Tao*. Pas says on this point that, "Tao is a self-transforming process. Tao is reality, but reality understood as a continuous process of becoming, changing, beginning, and ending . . . the visible and continually changing universe *is* the Tao, but if one wants to make distinctions, one can say that the universe, including our own planet earth, is the visible expression of the Tao. It is the Tao in a momentary self-manifestation. Yet the Tao is also something beyond".[22] The pervasion of *Tao* in all also includes its presence in the self – not only in the mind, but also in the body.

In Chapter 42 of the *Tao Te Ching/Daodejing* we have the words:

> *Tao* produced the One
> The One produced the Two
> Two produced Three.
> And Three produced the ten thousand things.
>
> The ten thousand things support yin and embrace *yang*.
> They achieve harmony by the interplay of these forces.[23]

It is important to note from these words that, at least from the evidence of the *Tao Te Ching/Daodejing*, *Tao* is beyond and prior to One – a factor that belies a monistic interpretation of Taoism. The primordial Void exists alone. The *Chuang-tzu/Zhuangzi* echoes the same thoughts:

> In the Grand Beginning (of all things) there was nothing in all the vacancy of space; there was nothing that could be named. It was in this state that there arose the first existence; – the first existence but still without bodily shape. From this things could then be produced, (receiving) what we call their proper character.[24]

One

From *Tao* comes One, the cosmic energy of *ch'i/qi*, a concentration of powerful creative potential. Graham described it as a "pool of energetic fluid".[25] It can be subtle, light and dissolving or heavier, inert and solidifying. Heaven has more of the former, and Earth, the latter. It is a vital energy in all things. The Chinese character for it has the symbol for rice below, while the upper radical is that for steam or air, the combined meaning indicative of the steam that rises from cooked rice.[26] As energy it circulates as the wind, and is the cycles of the planets and the rains. But it also circulates in the human body in its fluids and its breath. It is with its presence and circulation here that T'ai Chi is primarily concerned. Nothing can exist without *ch'i/qi*. It will permeate the universe in both *yin* forms and *yang* forms. Whatever expands, opens out and moves forward is *yang* and what contracts, closes up and returns to stasis is *yin*. Within the dense *ch'i/qi* that has solidified to form the human body, the breath circulates as a more subtle and light *ch'i/qi*, as does the vital energy. Each is a different manifestation of *ch'i/qi*.

Two

From *ch'i/qi* comes the two, *yin* and *yang*. The spontaneous interaction between these two forces produces all in the universe. So there is no creator deity. Nor is there a creation in time and space. Rather, the sense is of a dynamic and ongoing process underpinned by the stillness of *Tao* and pervaded by its immanence. The rhythm of *yin* and *yang* in the sense of cyclical waxing and waning, strengthening and weakening, advancing and retreating, production and loss, and so on, provides the ceaseless activity of *Tao* in the universe in its changing modes. In the human being *yin* informs the gross materiality of the body, and *yang* the spiritual subtleties of it. In the T'ai Chi *form*, as the individual begins to move his or her arms and legs in any direction, then *yin* and *yang* separate into their respective characteristics. Commenting on Wang Tsung-yüeh/Wang Zongyue's *Tai Chi Ch'üan Classic*, Yang Jwing Ming writes: "As soon as your mind leads the body into Grasp Sparrow's Tail,[27] the hands and feet differentiate into substantial and insubstantial. The interaction of substantial (*Yang*) and insubstantial (*Yin*) generates all of *Taijiquan's* fighting strategy and technique."[28] Diagrammatically, the interplay of *yin* and *yang* is depicted in the well-known symbol of the circle with the black and white interacting areas, each containing a small dot that represents its opposite (see p. 56). In the *form*, *yin* and *yang* also interchange, the one leading to the other. Thus, in the T'ai Chi classic, *Thesis of Interpreting the Origin*, we find the words:

> Those who practice Taijiquan know Yin and Yang, are able to discriminate the insubstantial and the substantial, and know advancing and retreating. When there is an advance, there is a retreating. When there is

a retreating, it is advancing. Within retreating, there is a hidden maneuver of advancing. Within this, it must have (the function) of turning and unification.[29]

The separation, interaction and alternating of *yin* and *yang* informs the whole T'ai Chi *form*.

Three

The interplay between *yin* and *yang* produces the three. There are a variety of ways in which the "three" are interpreted. Some seem to think it is *yin*, *yang*, plus the results of their combination.[30] Another way of expressing the three is as *great yin*, *great yang* and the *central harmony* that is represented by humanity. Heaven is *yang* and represents the abstract power of *Tao* in the cosmos. Earth is *yin* and the manifestation of *Tao*. Humanity is the equilibrium between the two, and is responsible for maintaining the balance and harmony of that equilibrium. The three on the microcosmic level of the human body especially are the *Three Treasures*. These are *ching/jing* "essence", *ch'i/qi* "vitality" and *shen* "spirit". It is these three energies that are the life-giving properties of all things in existence; they are the source of life and the means by which *Tao* sustains the universe. In particular, they are essential to the existence of the human life form as mind, body and spirit.

It is the more passive, receptive and still aspects of life that are closer to *Tao*. It is the feminine *yin* rather than the masculine *yang* that is associated with the naturalness necessary to attain experience of *Tao*. The feminine is the valley, where all the streams of the universe collect. It does nothing, but all pours into it. Everything in existence is in a state of flux, is changing, growing or decaying and transitory: nothing is permanent. Yet everything has *Tao*, its own way to reach its full potential. Such *Tao* is the "Mother" of all things, a concept that reinforces the feminine image surrounding *Tao*. But if *Tao* is referred to as the Mother of all things this is in no way meant to indicate anything to do with the concept of a Goddess. The figure of speech is used only in the sense of indicating *Tao* as the ultimate Source of all things. *Tao* as begetter and nurturer are feminine idioms, like the *yin* valley that nurtures things through the richness of its well-watered soil, in contrast to the bareness of the *yang* mountains. To experience *Tao* in life is to experience the tranquillity and peace of the feminine; it is to yield the self to its own naturalness, to "go with the grain", termed *li* in Chinese. *Li* is the ripples of the stream, the patterns of the waves of the ocean, the bubbles in foam, the softness of the breeze, the way pebbles are strewn on the beach – the innate and spontaneous way of nature, the order of nature. Experiencing such order in oneself is experience of *Tao*.

Ten thousand things

And so we come to the "ten thousand things" that emerge from the three. The expression is synonymous with all the phenomena that emerge in the universe. The sophisticated and complex combinations of varying degrees of *yin* and *yang* bring about the whole of the material world and all the ever-changing subtleties contained within it. It is beautifully described by Blofeld as a "perception of existence as a vast and timeless ocean of spotless purity upon which, through the interplay of dark and light, a myriad illusions play like ever-changing cloud formations or restless waves".[31] It is over-involvement with the myriad phenomena of the world that obscures the reality behind them that is *Tao*.

Thus we have the concept of on-going creation as reflected in the *Tao Te Ching/Daodejing* and the *Chuang-tzu/Zhuangzi*. While *Tao* is nameless, it is not a static state of non-manifestation. Although *Tao* has no consciousness and volition it represents all organic order – the patterns and rhythms of all cosmic existence. It is, therefore, essentially dynamic in that it informs the myriad patterns and created entities of existence, animate and inanimate, gross and subtle. It is such immanence that is experienceable to the Taoist, not by the intellect, logic or any kind of empirical knowledge, but by intuitive awareness of the essence of things. Such intuitive experience is the beginning of the return to *Tao*.

The idea of return is part of a cyclical process that is reflected in the macrocosm of the universe and the microcosm of the human realm. The unceasing activity of flux in all life is the work of *Tao* and is accepted as proceeding in orderly cycles. Thus we have the perpetual cycles of seasons, days, nights, and patterns of stars and planets; as the interplay of *yin* and *yang* these are the active patterns of *Tao* within manifest existence. The process of manifestation, therefore, is not seen as an evolutionary forward movement, but as a cyclical movement of emanation and dissolution, of being and non-being, of arising and decaying, of life and death. There is no beginning and no end, merely arising and dissolving in rhythmic patterns. Such is the state of manifest existence at both the macrocosmic and the microcosmic levels, and the human being is merely a miniature of the universe.

The path of return to the "Supreme Ultimate" involves the re-uniting of *yin* and *yang* as one energy. This means that there is stillness in movement, and movement in stillness. There is no separation of *yin* and *yang*; everything is in a state of equilibrium. In the T'ai Chi *form* the action of the hands and legs, breathing, movement, and mind and body functioning must be fully connected and operate as one energy. The aim here is to develop such strong correlation bettween the physical and mental qualities of the individual, and to such a high level, that he or she begins to become aware of the vital energy flowing strongly around the body. Then, the goal is to sink the energy into the lowest *tan-t'ien/dantian* of the body. The concept is reflected in chapter 16 of the *Tao Te Ching/Daodejing*:

> Attain to utmost emptiness,
> Let the mind become completely still.
> The ten thousand things rise together
> And the Self observes their return.
> The multitude of things flourish
> Then all return to their roots.
> To return to the root means stillness
> And stillness is the destiny of all.

The first two sentences show the importance of stilling the mind. In T'ai Chi, it means concentrating the inner energy in the lowest *tan-t'ien/dantian.* This can only come about when the mind collects itself and becomes calm; for where the mind is, the vital energy will flow. The third to sixth lines correspond to the movements of the limbs, joints, muscles, tendons, and so on, in the T'ai Chi *form*. The postures slowly rise and fall, combining and flowing, while all the time the mind watches their return from movement to stillness. The last but one sentence expresses that the body, energy and mind must return to its source of stillness in the *form*.

Bringing the actions of the body, breathing and mind functioning into harmony, allows the vital energy to return to its source in the lowest *tan-t'ien/dantian*. In the context of T'ai Chi, the final line reiterates that body, energy and mind must return to stillness, from which the cycle of movement in stillness can repeat itself, just as in nature, where life is manifested in repeated cycles. By becoming aware of the vital energy through the practice of T'ai Chi, and learning to cultivate and harness it, not only will a healthier life be ensured but, also, a gradual awareness of how to maintain a sense of balance between mind, body and emotions is developed. Such experience, acquired in the practice of T'ai Chi, will then inform everyday life and, ultimately, lead to discovery of *Tao*.

Chang San-feng/Zhang Sanfeng is reputed to have written in the *Preface* to the *Summary of the Golden Elixir*:

> Moreover, this illustrious *tao* of mysterious heaven precedes the emergence of the 10,000 phenomena. Taking heaven as warp and earth as woof, it originates from the Single Source. Therefore, if a man can fully realize this art, entering upon the path with sincerity, maintaining it in silence, using it with gentleness, and practicing it with faithfulness, he can then be restored to life and revived from death, revert to the state of primal unity, enter sagehood and transcend the mundane, seize the sun and moon, and recover the lustre of lost beauty.[32]

Unity

From all that has been said above, it is clear that unity underpins the cosmos through the essence of *Tao*. Every entity has its own innate nature, but *Tao* unites all those natures into one. The multiplicity of the world is held in potentiality in the unformed *Tao*, and it makes no difference to the unity of all things whether they are in potential or realized form or part one and part other. In the end, all is *Tao*; multiplicity exists in unity, a unity that is itself beyond all duality yet that underpins all change. The search for unity is the goal of the sage, the Taoist adept, and the T'ai Chi Master. Graham wrote: "In detaching himself from the many he is returning to the 'root' or 'trunk' or 'seed' from which they grow, into the 'ancestor' from which they descend, the 'gate' out of which they emerge, the 'axis' round which they revolve. It is at the common point from which all start that they are found to merge together and with oneself in a single whole."[33] Being anchored in the self is the key to experience of such unity and the way by which all things are achieved. Those who practise T'ai Chi Ch'üan/Taijiquan solely for its health and relaxation benefits are mainly unaware of these deeper facets of its connection with Taoism, especially the spiritual following of the Way that leads to *Tao*.

The world of multiple phenomena is real, interconnected, and relational. To operate in it successfully, the Old Masters saw the necessity of blending with its complex rhythms and patterns, rather than flying in the face of them. The more we become involved with this and that, with the myriad phenomena in life, the more we shift attention from awareness of the deeper currents that inform life. In the words of the *Tao Te Ching/Daodejing*:

> Once unity is divided, the divisions need names.
> When there are names

One should know it is time to stop.
Knowing when to stop frees one from fear.
Tao is to the world what the ocean and seas are to rivers and streams.[34]

Within the world there are many patterns, many different rhythms. While *Tao* underpins them all, it still permits the differences that make reality multifaceted and spontaneously expressed. There is a difference in the self-expression of all things, a "naturalness" (*tzu-jan/ziran*) in the way that things spontaneously are and act. Yet, the fact that *Tao* produces One, One, two and so on, means that the reverse process is possible: multiplicity ultimately returns to its common denominator that is One, and One returns to *Tao* as well as emerging from it. But the reality of external differences is not denied; it is just that their separateness is not as deep as we think. It is when we are involved with the dualities of life and forget the unity that informs them, that we have an incorrect perspective of reality. Chuang-tzu/Zhuangzi, especially, brings this point to the fore, with his challenges to the ways in which people normally think.

Our understanding of the world is based on the perception of opposites. If we imagine a circle in which extreme opposites are either end of diameters that cut through the centre, then it is only at the centre that opposites cancel each other out. And it is the energy of that central point as *Tao* that makes possible the dualities or opposites in life by which we come to know what things are. At the same time it is that point to which all returns, in the same way as a circle cannot exist without its centre. Opposites and dualities can only exist away from the centre, and the aim of the Taoist and the T'ai Chi adept is to return to that still, central point where opposites cease to exist. The *Chuang-tzu/Zhuangzi* states: "The universe is the unity of all things. If we attain this unity and identify ourselves with it, then the members of our body are but so much dust and dirt, while life and death, end and beginning, are but as the succession of day and night, which cannot disturb our inner peace. How much less shall we be troubled by worldly gain and loss, good luck and bad luck!"[35] The moment we name something we differentiate it from everything else and, by so doing, place limitations on it. But at that point where opposites meet, which is neither this nor that, no limitations can be set at all because it is unnameable, indescribable and beyond the dualities and opposites that constitute normal knowledge. *Tao* is that centre point of rest, tranquillity, stillness. Perhaps this is what the *Tao Te Ching/Daodejing* means when it says that: "Stillness and tranquillity establish order in the universe."[36] It is the sage standing at the centre of the circle between all opposites, who has the correct view of things as neither this nor that, but as *Tao*. Experiencing *Tao* in this way is experiencing the essence and harmony of all the myriad things within existence – something that can be done only at that central point of *Tao* around which all revolves, and from which all emanates. In words attributed to Chang San-feng/Zhang Sanfeng: "Calm your body and mind in perfect silence so that you are at peace within and undisturbed without."[37]

The central point of *Tao*, then, is the point of equilibrium between all opposites. It is a point of egolessness from which it is possible to respond naturally, from the point of *Tao* itself, to any of the multiplicity of situations that occur in life. To use an analogy of Chuang-tzu/Zhuangzi's the sage at this central point of equilibrium is like a mirror that reflects all things but does not hang on to them when the image is gone. It is exactly in this way that T'ai Chi should be performed. To cite words attributed to Chang San-feng/Zhang Sanfeng, again: "To be in the midst of things without being affected, to deal with affairs without being disturbed, is truly great, truly wonderful."[38] So must the mind become: the "I" of the self has to lose its "me". In such a state, or lack of one, rational forms of knowledge are left behind, emotions are stilled, definitions are abandoned, classifications are forgotten: "Fully at one with the flow of existence, with the Tao, one is able to enjoy everything as it is. This is 'free and easy wandering'; this is 'perfect happiness.' Attaining this, the true person fully realizes the spontaneity of the Tao."[39] The more complicated life becomes, the more one abandons simplicity, and the more involvement there is with the dualities presented by the "ten-thousand things", the further one is from *Tao*. So in the *Chuang-tzu/Zhuangzi* we find the words:

> The heart of the wise man is tranquil
> It is the mirror of heaven and earth
> The glass of everything.
> Emptiness, stillness, tranquillity, tastelessness,
> Silence, non-action: this is the level of heaven and earth.
> This is perfect Tao. Wise men find here
> Their resting place.
> Resting, they are empty.[40]

The performance of T'ai Chi reflects such balance. It is movement that is natural without overstraining this way or that. Commenting on a line of a text attributed to Chang San-feng/Zhang Sanfeng, Yang Jwing Ming states: "*Taijiquan* emphasizes balance, efficiency, and precision.

No posture or part of the body should stretch out too far or be pulled in too much. Every motion should be smooth, always just right; every force just enough to do the job. Each posture should be rounded and should involve the whole body in a smooth, continuous, flowing motion."[41] Such perfection is achieved through the state of inner balance and equilibrium. If desires creep into the mind, then that balance is lost. Similarly, in general life, according to Chang San-feng/Zhang Sanfeng:

> Yet even though we work and strive, we should not think of gain and loss. Let the mind be always calm and steady, whether or not there is anything of concern. Seek the same as other people, but do not be greedy like other people; get what others get, but do not hoard like others do. Without greed, there is no anxiety; not hoarding, there is no loss. One is then like others in outward appearance, but the inner mind is always different from that of worldlings.[42]

In a condition of equilibrium there is no urge to interfere with the way things are in the natural order of the world. The tranquillity of stillness is the happiness of utter peace. And it has been beautifully depicted. Blofeld wrote: "The illusory ego falls away, yet nothing real is lost. Spirit, freed from its bonds, returns to Spirit, not as a dew-drop destined to form an insignificant particle of a vast ocean, but as the boundless returning to the boundless. The liberated consciousness expands to contain – to *be* – the entire universe! Could there ever, ever be a more glorious endeavour?"[43] While the ultimate goal may be distant, Lao-tzu/Laozi said that a journey of a thousand miles begins with a single step. T'ai Chi should be seen in the same way. Its beauty and depth come from the Taoist philosophy that guides its principles and practice. It is only by studying over a long period of time that an individual can begin to understand how deeply beneficial the practice of T'ai Chi can be.

In the practice of T'ai Chi Ch'üan/Taijiquan there are three levels of development through which each individual must progress in order to become closer to understanding, or returning to *Tao*. The levels correspond to Humanity, Earth and Heaven, each level having another three sub-levels, adding up to a total of nine levels or stages of development.

The Human level

At this particular stage or level the individual is learning the mechanical actions of the T'ai Chi *form*. It is the stage of the beginner who is learning the order of the postures that make up the particular style of T'ai Chi. The three sub-levels or stages of the human level comprise learning the skills of relaxation of the ligaments, tendons, joints and muscles of the whole body from head to toe. By learning to relax fully the individual allows the blood and vital energy to flow freely around the body without any restriction.

The Earth level

The three sub-levels or stages in the Earth level are concerned with sinking the *ch'i/qi* to the lowest *tan-t'ien/dantian* and, then, circulating the *ch'i/qi* to the four limbs. Finally, the ability is acquired to circulate energy in such a way that it opens up the two energy orbits in the body, the microcosmic or small orbit, and the macrocosmic large orbit. We shall be looking at these in more detail in the chapter on *Energy*. Here it needs to be noted that, at this level, the individual learns to flow smoothly through the *form* without any pauses or loss of balance. The ability to combine the movements with deep breathing is also acquired. Through concentration, the vital energy is guided around the whole body.

The Heavenly level

Like the Human and Earth levels, there are three sub-levels or stages that make up the Heavenly level. These levels are about learning to listen and feel for the power of the vital energy, not being guided by the *ch'i/qi*, breath, but using the mind and spirit as guides of the *ch'i/qi*. It is said that when the vital energy reaches its highest level it becomes pure mental energy – spiritual power. At this level the T'ai Chi *form* becomes personal to the individual and changes from large movements to smaller actions that are now generated by the mental and spiritual development of the individual. Many never achieve such a level, for it takes many years of refinement to reach this stage.

Te/De

The Chinese character for *Te/De* consists of three symbols: ten eyes and a curve, suggesting perfection (since ten eyes failed to see a curve), the heart, and a foot going forward. Combined, as Star comments, "Te is not so much 'perfect-heartedness' but its *expression* and the action that gives rise to it".[44] This leaves us with a meaning of something like "perfect-hearted action", or "straightness of heart in action". Waley noted, too, the earlier connection of *te/de* with the idea of planting and potentiality, as in the planting of seeds. In this sense, it is the "latent power" or "virtue" in an entity.[45] Confucius used the term to signify virtue in the sense of correct living according to *Tao*, the right way. Later Confucians came to emphasize *te/de* as moral rectitude in living one's life, especially in relation to the community, both politically and socially.

The usual translations of *te/de* have retained the notion of "virtue", though it is sometimes translated as "power", or even as "nature" or "essence". But the Confucian sense of moral living is not the way in which we should see the word virtue. It is more like "virtuality", if ungrammatical, because in the Taoist sense of the word it is that power and potential in things that makes them what they are. It is the *Taoness* within, the true nature of something, that is activated exteriorly. As Needleman aptly depicts it: "*Te* refers to nothing less than the quality of human action that allows the central, creative power of the universe to manifest through it."[46] But that "central creative power" is not something that an entity may or may not have, for it is the force of life that flows from *Tao*. This is certainly the way in which Lao-tzu/Laozi understood the word – "something spontaneous, original or primal, that which is timeless and infinite in every individual living being".[47]

Te/De is the functioning of *Tao*. And it functions in the wind that blows, the soil that nurtures, the growth of the seed, the growth, and even the decomposition, of the human. It is the potential inherent in all things that makes them what they are and dictates how that nature is manifested. Essentially, however, it is a *natural* and *spontaneous* potential, not a forced innate drive. Nor can such a potential be acquired from without; it exists naturally, instinctively and is primal in all things. It is by means of *Te/De* that *Tao* can be experienced. The ability to be at one with the innate virtuality of what one is, is the ability to "go with" the flow and essence of things. It is the ability to experience *Tao* emanating out into the universe, and it will also be the means of experience of returning to *Tao*. Needleman writes:

> The picture before us is of a cosmic force or principle that expands or flows outward or, more precisely perhaps, descends into the creation of the universe, "the ten thousand things." Together with this, we are told of a force or movement of return. All of creation returns to the source. But the initial coming-into-being of creation is to be understood as a receiving of that which flows downward and outward from the center. Every created entity ultimately is what it is and does what it does owing to its specific reception of the energy radiating from the ultimate, formless reality. This movement from the nameless Source to the ten thousand things is *Te*.[48]

Te/De, then, is the threads outward from *Tao* that allow experience of the ultimate Source. Being able to experience the virtuality of something is connecting with the Source in different dimensions; it is experience of *Tao* in human, animal, plant and inanimate objects. It is an inward, mystical experience of the natural essences of things, a simple and natural experience that can be accomplished by "forgetting" conventional standards and conditioned ways of thinking and acting. Listening to the innate virtuality of the self, rather than directing energies to the outward ten thousand things makes such "forgetting" possible. It will lead to a greater understanding of what life is and a concomitant freedom and happiness. Again, this is at the heart of the philosophy informing the practice of T'ai Chi.

Outward perfection is not an indicator of *Te/De*. In chapter 4 of the *Chuang-tzu/Zhuangzi* it is pointed out that the crooked and gnarled tree is the one that is left standing, not the one whose straight trunk is useful for timber or whose fruit is plucked. Similarly, it is the hunchback who is too misshapen to be sent to war who escapes the misery of being a soldier. The particularization of *Tao* as *Te/De* in any thing does not suggest that it has to be perfect or even good. It is simply such as it is. And if we transfer such thought to the world of today, it is full of people who have always wished to develop a skill and potential that they know they have, but who have forced themselves, or have been forced, into doing other things at which they are not happy. In the *Chuang-tzu/Zhuangzi* we read so much of the craftsmanship of the highly skilled worker, whose skill is based on the naturalness that comes from inner experience. Similarly, it is often emptiness rather than materiality that reveals the *Te/De* of something:

> Thirty spokes unite at the wheel's hollow hub;
> It is this centre hole that makes it useful.
> Mould clay to make a vessel;
> It is the space within that makes it useful.
> Cut out doors and windows to make a room;
> It is these holes that make it useful.
> Therefore gain comes from something;
> Usefulness from nothing.[49]

People are happy being what they are best fitted to be and doing what they are best suited to do; things are as they should be, when allowed to be what they are.

Virtue, then, is naturalness, as seen in everything in nature, in the blackness of a raven's wing and the whiteness of the swan, in the beauty of the tiger's and leopard's skin, or the length of the stork's legs. To the Taoist these were the visible signs of the invisible *Te* that should not be tampered with in any way. As with creatures, so it is with humankind: there should be no interference with the virtue in man or woman—with his or her soul or spirit. Through the practice of the T'ai Chi *form*, virtue or power is achieved by an individual through relaxed, soft, gentle movements. It is performed in a non-aggressive attitude where the mind, body, emotions and spirit are connected, and the individual's "power" can be felt, though not seen. The T'ai Chi *form* should never be performed in a self-display of aggressive, forceful movement, where the individual's ego is in control; to the Taoist this would be going against the natural way. A chance encounter with someone, or a group of people, performing the T'ai Chi *form* is usually accompanied by amazement at the effortless way the performer moves, and at the softness of the movement, but there would be no awareness of the invisible signs of power. This is the true virtue of T'ai Chi Ch'üan/Taijiquan. The Taoist is reminded again and again that the apparent weakness of *Tao* is its strength, and so it is with T'ai Chi. The apparent soft, relaxed, weak movements are its true strength; through the soft, gentle, flowing movements, an inner strength is developed.

Change

Tao and its manifestation as *Te/De* underpin the processes of change and transformation in all things. Everything is subject to impermanence, every moment passes forever into the next. Transience is the nature of all life. Things flourish and die, fill and empty, wax and wane, proceed and return. Such cyclical process has been described as "an endless spiral that evidences, on the one hand, persistent and continuing patterns and, on the other, novelty, with each moment having its own particular orbit and character".[50] This is an important point, because the change and transformation do not revert to old patterns but to new, unique formulations. Reality is an ever-changing one in which no two moments can ever be the same. This is why Chuang-tzu/Zhuangzi, for one, despised the fixed conventions that suggested there could always be one answer, one right way, in all situations of *x* or *y*. Going with the flow of life means understanding the shifting and dynamic nature of reality and moving with it, not against it. While cyclical change is orderly and predictable in that day follows night, and the seasons follow each other with regularity, the particular character of each day, each night, each spring-time, is never the same.

The cyclic, rhythmic patterns of existence revert in pendulum-like fashion from one extreme to the other. Such reversal is an important feature of philosophical Taoism. The higher we climb the further we have to fall. The lower we are, the further we are able to climb. The imperfect often conceals perfection, and the unassertive and humble person, great wisdom. So in the *Tao Te Ching/Daodejing* we find the following advice:

> Bow down then overcome;
> Bend then be straight;
> Empty then be full;
> Worn out then new;
> Have little and gain;
> Have much and be confused.
> Therefore the sage embraces the One
> And is a model to all.
> Not showing off,
> He shines forth.
> Not considering himself right,
> He is distinguished.
> Not boasting,
> He receives recognition.
> Not bragging,
> His fame endures.
> Because he does not contend,
> No one contends with him.[51]

For something to shrink, it must first expand, to fail it must first be strong, to be cast down it must first be raised, and for someone to receive, someone has to give.[52] If anything, however, Lao-tzu/Laozi seems to favour humility, softness, weakness and the feminine. Similarly, the *Chuang-tzu/Zhuangzi* raises the crippled and the crooked to importance. Lao-tzu/Laozi's advice to political and social problems, therefore, is one of reversal of conventional norms of political and social praxis. But such advice is not just an attempt to redress the imbalances in society, it is a statement of what is believed to be an invariable law of nature: reversal is the way things must be, just as hurricanes don't last forever or rain for eternity. So if we want to be strong we have to begin by recognizing that we are weak; whatever we want, we begin with its opposite – a point made very clear in the words above from the *Tao Te Ching/Daodejing*, and echoed again and again throughout the text. While the *Tao Te Ching/Daodejing* barely uses the term *yin* and *yang*, the same principle of reversal, of the swing of the pendulum between opposites, is embodied in the *yin* and *yang* principle – the "two" that underpin all creation – and in the processes of change in the ancient *I Ching/Yijing*.

The ability to understand death alongside its opposite of life, and as part of the process of transformation and change, occupies considerable space in both the *Chuang-tzu/Zhuangzi* and the *Lieh-tzu/Liezi*. The latter is realistic about death: "That which is born is that which in principle must come to an end. Whatever ends cannot escape its end, just as whatever is born cannot escape birth; and to wish to live forever, and have no more of ending, is to be deluded about our lot."[53] Later, in the same chapter, Lieh-tzu/Liezi says: "Death is a return to where we set out from when we were born. So how do I know that when I die here I shall not be born somewhere else? How do I know that life and death are not as good as each other? How do I know that it is not a delusion to crave anxiously for life? How do I know that present death would not be better than my past life?"[54] To these words we might add the beautiful statement, again in the same chapter: "Dying is the virtue in us going to its destination."[55] The *Chuang-tzu/Zhuangzi*, too, accepts death as a necessary part of the natural processes of change, and an occasion when true belief in the natural laws must allow the passing away of one's closest without the usual lamenting and wailing. Like the *Lieh-tzu/Liezi*, Chuang-tzu/Zhuangzi is pragmatic about death: "That hugest of clumps of soil loads me with a body, has me toiling through a life, eases me with old age, rests me with death; therefore that I find it good to live is the very reason why I find it good to die."[56]

The relationship between *Tao* and *Te/De* is one of transcendent passivity of the former that becomes the immanent dynamism of the latter. *Tao* manifested in particulars is *Te/De*, and the universal behind the particulars is *Tao*. When the *Tao Te Ching/Daodejing* says that: "The greatest Virtue is to follow *Tao* and only *Tao*",[57] it means that *Te/De* as the natural dynamism of change and transformation is the only real path that one can follow; all else is illusory virtue. The intimacy between *Tao* and *Te/De* is invariable: "All things come from Tao. They are nourished by Virtue."[58] Nothing can exist without either *Tao* or *Te/De*. It is by *Te/De* that the Taoist lives life in order to be rooted in *Tao*.

Wu-wei

Broadly speaking, *wu-wei* means not acting, though its specific meanings are wide and a little ambiguous. The word *wei* means "To be; to do;

to make; to practise; to act out; to cause".[59] It can also have the nuance of meaning of acting out, as if on a stage, or to pose, make a show of. The addition of the negative *wu* means not to do these things. Paul Carus, therefore, suggested that *wu-wei* means "to do without ado", "to act without acting", "acting with non-assertion".[60] Such suggestions indicate admirably the sense in which the *Tao Te Ching/Daodejing* uses the term to mean acting without inner egoistic involvement with the action. It is action carried out externally from the still *inactivity* of the ego within. It is thus an unforced and natural action of the kind that has no ulterior drives and motives behind it. It is the art of accomplishing much with the minimum of activity, so wonderfully expressed in the movements of the T'ai Chi *form*. It is such natural action with the mind focused on the movement and breathing rather than the usual day-to-day activities and thoughts that is central to T'ai Chi. *Wu-wei* is the ability to act with minimum forced effort by going with the natural flow of things, in short, being in tune with *Tao* and its expression as *Te/De*. When heavy snow covers the branches of trees, the branch that can bend, like the willow, does not break. Just so, the art of taking the natural and softest path through life, with the minimum of show, force, assertion or parading of oneself, is acting according to *wu-wei*, and incurs less wear and tear. Just so are the movements of T'ai Chi Ch'üan/Taijiquan.

Thus, *wu-wei* is the kind of inactivity that is characterized by non-interference in forceful ways with the natural flow of *Tao*. Clearly, the *Tao Te Ching/Daodejing* does not suggest that *wu-wei* as inaction should be no action at all, total *laissez-faire*, since it states that nothing is left undone by *wu-wei*:

> Pursuing learning, one gains every day.
> Pursuing *Tao* one does less every day.
> Do less and less
> Until non-action is gained.
> When nothing is done, nothing is not done.
> The world is ruled when things are not meddled with,
> If you meddle, you are not fit for ruling.[61]

Interference is the egoistic imposition of the will of a human being or human groups in a matter that can be better solved by more natural, moderate means. Water, for example, is weaker than stone, but in time will wear it away. *Wu-wei*, to quote Liu Xiaogan, is "the balance between minimal effort and best result".[62] If one is in tune with *Tao* then actions are undertaken naturally, appropriately, harmoniously, with a certain spontaneity, and in line with the laws of nature. Given the interconnection and fine ecological balances that exist in the world, it is all too easy to create disharmony on a wide scale.[63]

In today's existence, little is done dispassionately, unplanned and without being motivated by some kind of desire for an end product. Then, too, our actions are mostly conditioned by the societies in which we live, by education, religion, politics, and social, familial and peer groups. It is much the same in any age and any culture, and the Old Masters pointed out the folly of becoming entrapped in such life-patterns to the extent that naturalness in life was replaced with artifice, rigidity of thought and unnatural attitudes to life and its real meaning. In the words attributed to Chang San-feng/Zhang Sanfeng: "The mind is like an eye – if even a tiny hair gets in an eye, the eye is uncomfortable. Similarly, if even a small matter concerns the mind, the mind will be disturbed. Once afflicted by disturbance, it is hard to concentrate."[64] The very movements of T'ai Chi, while requiring observance of pattern and order, like *Tao*, break down normal mind functioning and replace it with focused, meditative concentration. Human beings get caught up in the multiple pressures of the challenging, postmodern world of home, work, family, finance, material improvement, and the host of proximate goals that propel people through a day's existence. *Wu-wei* today, no less than in the times of the *Tao Te Ching/Daodejing*, asks for a reassessment of the way things have become, and a return to the way they should be. T'ai Chi assists in this process.

When actions are carried out in the *wu-wei* sense, they are harmoniously aligned to natural laws. They are not aggressive or forceful, violent or ego-motivated. Thus, they are usually right actions, and should reap harmonious results, even though they are not done with moral intent. Moreover, liberated from the constraints and conditionings of usual patterns of thought, there is a sense of freedom in natural, effortless action that is devoid of concern for selfish end products. Spectators of T'ai Chi, therefore, witness its effortless movements and the ability to perform them in easy freedom. Such freedom involves the letting go of normal response patterns, the ability to give way, yield, and be receptive. In general life, *wu-wei* is an ability not to go against the grain of things in the multiple situations life presents. And it is an ability to use the natural potential of one's own self, one's own *Te/De*, to fulfilment. Such living is far from passivity. The *Tao Te Ching/Daodejing* expected rulers to operate according to *wu-wei*, with sage-like qualities, but not to abrogate all activity: *wu-wei* is not a recipe for idleness. Much of the *Tao Te Ching/Daodejing* is a manual of how to govern well, how to maintain order amongst subjects, how to organize farming, trade, and the army. But to govern well the laws of nature cannot be disregarded, and the natural path – the more subtle way to look at things – is the way of *wu-wei*. *Wu-wei* is knowing, too, just the right amount to act and when to withdraw without being over-involved. It is relaxing into the action without the intensity of force, volition and tension – an essential facet of T'ai Chi practice. Most of us can do this when we drive a car, or ride a bicycle, for example. Chapter 19 of the *Chuang-tzu/Zhuangzi* includes the tale of a drunken man who falls off a cart. Because he is so relaxed he has no consciousness of falling out of the cart, any more than he knew he was riding in it! He is not worried about anything and so is not tense, rigid and fearful as he falls, which is exactly what would be expected had he had no wine. If wine can give this much security, the *Chuang-tzu/Zhuangzi* states, how much more is to be got from spontaneity?

While the principle of *wu-wei* underlies the practice of the T'ai Chi Ch'üan/Taijiquan *form*, it is particularly effective in martial-art praxis. Here, it is by yielding that strength is overcome. Benjamin Hoff gives the example of trying to strike a cork floating in water. The harder it is struck, the more it yields, and the more it yields, the harder it bounces back. The moral here is that it is better to neutralize force than use violence against it.[65] So the *Tao Te Ching/Daodejing* tells us that the softest thing in the universe will overcome the hardest (chapter 43). It is wiser to temper aggressive action, particularly when others suffer as a result. And it is wiser to temper the inner desires that lead to aggressive achievements of goals – both on personal levels, and on national levels as in the case of aggressive war. The *Tao Te Ching/Daodejing* speaks of three treasures in life:

> The first is compassion; the second is frugality;
> The third is daring not to lead ahead of others.[66]

The word "compassion" here is sometimes translated as "love", "mercy", "gentleness" or similar. Frugality means a certain economy and moderation in the way one lives, that is to say, curbing the materialistic desires that drive the self for more and more possessions. Most importantly, there must be that inner inactivity of the egoistic self, of the competitive drives and passions, the desires and aversions, which are the usual motivators for action. The root of the understanding of *wu-wei* comes from this inner stillness of the ego.

The ultimate level of humanity is that of the sage. Much is said of the sage in the *Tao Te Ching/Daodejing*, especially in connection with *wu-wei*. The sage keeps in the background, but is always ahead, is detached, but at one with everything, acts selflessly, but is fulfilled (chapter 7). If kings and lords could act in this way, the *Tao Te Ching/Daodejing* says, then the ten thousand things would be able to evolve naturally, and everything would be peaceful (chapter 37). The foolish person is always busy, always doing things, always active, and the more he or she does, the more there will be to do. The sage refrains from acting and people are reformed. He enjoys peace and finds that people around him become honest. He does nothing and people become rich, and when he has no desires people revert to a more natural life (chapter 57). So the advice of the *Tao Te Ching/Daodejing* is:

> Act through non-action.
> Do things without working.
> Find tasteful that which is tasteless.
> Treat few things as though many.
> Reward injury with goodness.
>
> See simplicity in what is complicated.
> Find greatness in little things.[67]

According to the *Chuang-tzu/Zhuangzi*, we pursue results, money, friends, changes, and become hopelessly caught up in complex activity:

> Those who are caught in the machinery of power take no joy except in activity and change – the whirring of the machine! Whenever an occasion for action presents itself, they are compelled to act; they cannot help themselves. They are inexorably moved, like the machine of which they are a part. Prisoners in the world of objects, they have no choice but to submit to the demands of matter! They are pressed down and crushed by external forces, fashion, the market, events, public opinion. Never in a whole lifetime do they recover their right mind! What a pity![68]

As far as the *Chuang-tzu/Zhuangzi* is concerned nature works perfectly without boasting, and its brilliant laws proceed without discourse. It simply operates naturally and spontaneously – a perfect model for humanity. And when at one with *Tao*, a sage like Lieh-tzu/Liezi, unobstructed by conventional goals, desires and ego, rode on the winds, totally liberated in every dimension of being, not knowing whether it was the wind that he rode or whether the wind rode him. In the *Lieh-tzu/Liezi*, *wu-wei* is extended to non-ownership. The *Lieh-tzu/Liezi* has a beautiful passage that speaks against the desire for subtle possessions. In discussing who owns one's body, it says:

> It is the shape lent to you by heaven and earth. Your life is not your possession; it is harmony between your forces, granted for a time by

> heaven and earth. Your nature and destiny are not your possessions; they are the course laid down for you by heaven and earth. Your children and grandchildren are not your possessions; heaven and earth lend them to you to cast off from your body as an insect sheds its skin. Therefore you travel without knowing where you go, stay without knowing what you cling to, are fed without knowing how. You are the breath of heaven and earth which goes to and fro; how can you ever possess it?[69]

And by extension, the *Lieh-tzu/Liezi* states, we should not steal from the land or sea. Living life according to the principle of *wu-wei* is to live it in spontaneous alertness to the vitality of nature. It is having one's finger on the pulse of the universe. In Hoff's words: "The efficacy of *Wu Wei* is like that of water flowing over and around the rocks in its path – not the mechanical, straight-line approach that usually ends up short-circuiting natural laws, but one that evolves from an inner sensitivity to the natural rhythm of things."[70]

Attaining the highest level of *wu-wei* in the performance of the T'ai Chi *form* takes the individual many years. Reaching this level of achievement is only by progressing through the three levels of development, Human, Earth and Heaven. It is only when the Heavenly level of enlightenment is reached that the true experience of total *wu-wei* is really attained. To the Taoist to "act in inaction" (*wei-wu-wei)* includes both a positive and a negative element and this also corresponds to the individual as he or she performs the T'ai Chi *form*; the meaning is the same. To act, and to act but at the same time not act, are two very different concepts. The former is the positive meaning of *wu-wei.* It corresponds to the early stages of perfecting the *form*, when the individual is still thinking about the movements. Thus, the movements are large and the *form* is guided by the physical and mental nature of the individual. There is a feeling of forcing, or the desire to complete the *form* by design – in other words of resisting the natural way because of the emphasis on "action". Of course, everyone has to start from the same point, so we are all going to be at this stage of development at some point of time in our journey of returning to *Tao*. Sadly, most people will only ever reach this level and go no further, because in today's T'ai Chi world community, most people only know of T'ai Chi as a relaxation exercise: too few associate it with Taoism and its philosophy.

The negative meaning of *wu-wei*, or non-action, refers to acting but not acting. In relation to T'ai Chi it occurs where the individual's movements are effortless and the mind is no longer involved in the toils of positive action, of remembering the correct sequence of movements.

Instead the self is abandoned in the negative state of allowing the body to "let go". At such a level the T'ai Chi *form* changes in its shape and nature. It now becomes a personal, unique form of movement that has been refined and has become compact over a long period of time. The individual is now guided by the feeling of energy and of *Tao,* or true action, where "doing nothing" is the master of everything. This is the highest level to achieve in T'ai Chi Ch'üan/Taijiquan, and is the rationale of the practice for students. To be able to achieve return to *Tao* through the moving meditation of T'ai Chi Ch'üan/Taijiquan is the supreme goal of the practice.

Naturalness and spontaneity (tzu-jan/ziran)

Anyone watching the practice of the T'ai Chi *form* cannot but be impressed by the gracefulness and naturalness of the movements. Because *Tao* operates naturally and spontaneously everything is accomplished with simplicity, softness, peacefulness and tranquillity. T'ai Chi movements encapsulate such belief. Everything has its own natural way, given to it by *Tao* and sustained by *Tao*. If things are permitted to follow their own path, their own *li,* then harmony and balance in life ensues. Too much interference will upset the natural balance and harmony of creation. Such naturalism was deeply rooted in the Chinese temperament long before the Old Masters took up the theme, and long before the beginnings of Taoism proper. It is being at one with the cosmic force of *Tao* that is tantamount to naturalness in every aspect of life. And the more we strive in life, the further away we are from the naturalness that offers calm and quietude.

The example most cited in nature as a symbol of naturalness, called *tzu-jan/ziran* in Chinese, is water. In the words of the *Tao Te Ching/Daodejing*:

> Nothing in the world is more soft and yielding than water.
> Yet for attacking the solid and strong, nothing is equal to it.
> Nothing can triumph so easily.
> Softness overcomes what is strong;
> The supple overcomes the unyielding.[71]

While water is a humble element, giving way to that which blocks its path, nothing can exist without it:

> The highest good is like water.
> Water benefits the ten thousand things without contending.
> It flows in places people avoid, just like *Tao*.[72]

Chapter 76 of the *Tao Te Ching/Daodejing* points out that at birth we are weak and gentle, soft and supple. At death we are brittle and stiff. The same can be said of young tender plants that become withered and dry at death. So, to be stiff and unbending is to encourage death, but to be soft, yielding and flexible is to encourage life. To be flexible, adaptable, and to find ways around force and confrontation is to embody naturalness.

It is overdoing things, forcing life, lacking moderation in life, which are against naturalness. The *Tao Te Ching/Daodejing* advises one to stop short before filling things to the brim, over-sharpening the blade, amassing so much wealth that it cannot be protected, claiming great wealth and titles. It advises that it is better to retire when work is done rather than attempt to do that bit more. We can see this concept in the T'ai Chi *form*, for example, where limbs are never extended to the point where they are straightened and stiff. Such is naturalness and the way of *Tao* the *Tao Te Ching/Daodejing* tells us (chapter 9). But this can only be achieved by appreciating simplicity, realizing one's true nature and curbing selfishness and desire (chapter 19). It is not wrong occasionally to drift like the waves on the sea, or like the breeze and the wind (chapter 20). And it is essential to respect the naturalness that is part of the created universe:

> If you think you can take over the universe and work on it
> You won't be able to.
>
> The universe is spiritual.
> You cannot work on it.
> Whoever wants to change it, will ruin it.
> Whoever tries to grasp it will lose it.[73]

To gain naturalness in life, the *Tao Te Ching/Daodejing* tells us that we need to nourish *Te/De* in the body, the family, village, nation and the universe (chapter 54). Naturalness and *Te/De* go hand in hand.

The *Chuang-tzu/Zhuangzi*, too, endorses naturalness as the way to experience life. By getting rid of the conventional goals and drives of conditioned life, as Graham put it, "the focus of attention roams freely over the endless changing panorama, and responses spring directly from the energies inside us . . . this is an immense liberation, a launching out of the confines of self into a realm without limits".[74] So Chuang-tzu/Zhuangzi advises:

> Go side by side with the sun and moon,
> Do the rounds of Space and Time.

Act out their neat conjunctions,
Stay aloof from their convulsions.
Dependents each on each, let us honour one another.
Common people fuss and fret,
The sage is a dullard and a sluggard.
Be aligned along a myriad years, in oneness, wholeness, simplicity.
All the myriad things are as they are,
And as what they are make up totality.[75]

For Chuang-tzu/Zhuangzi, excess in living inhibited the experience of naturalness. A simple life engendered awareness and openness to the natural way of things. The *Lieh-tzu/Liezi*, too, extols naturalness:

If nothing within you stays rigid,
Outward things will disclose themselves.
Moving, be like a mirror.
Respond like an echo.[76]

For some, naturalness led to the reclusive life, the simple life of the hermit, others became like the child, uninhibited by life's constraints and the conventions of society – an analogy that the *Tao Te Ching/Daodejing* frequently expresses. The simplicity of the child's knowledge, desires, and even breathing, are commended, and the sage is said to treat all like children. The breathing of the sage, the *Chuang-tzu/Zhuangzi* (6:2) tells us, is not like that of ordinary human beings because the sage breathes right down to his heels – a point often raised by teachers of T'ai Chi.

Naturalness, then, is that hidden undercurrent in life that we find when we set aside for a short time the normal constraints of living, the stresses and strains, the things for which we strive in long-term and short-term goals, and just stop. It is only when we are still, caught perhaps in a moment of warm sunshine, a smile, the song of a blackbird, a midnight sky full of stars, that the pendulum passes through the still point and permits a glimpse of another way of life:

Be a valley to the world.
For being a valley to the world
Te will never leave you.
Turn back and be an infant[77]

If *Tao* were to be given qualities, then spontaneity would be its essential nature in terms of its functioning in the world as *Te/De*. And spontaneity is indicative of no pre-set plans, no rigid determinatives.

Chuang-tzu/Zhuangzi, especially, gives examples of those highly skilled craftspeople who carry out their tasks spontaneously from innate skill within; they do not have to think about what they do, they simply do it naturally, being completely absorbed in the activity. So often in life we have to have *reasons* for doing things and we have to deliberate about what we do. Spontaneity is acceptance of the moment as it is, and response and adaptation to that moment that is completely natural. Such, in fact, is the way the universe is, the way night follows day, and the seasons follow each other. Being assertive and purposeful about everything are inimical to balance and harmony in life.

The delicate balance between humanity and nature is a particular feature that has always been stressed by Taoism. In nature, the acorn grows to the oak tree without the need of an agent. It grows in its own manner, out of its innate "self-so-ness". Both naturalness and spontaneity are encompassed by the Chinese term *tzu-jan/ziran*, a term that really means "self-so" or "naturalness", but which is often translated as nature.[78] Importantly, nature functions in itself, by itself. There is no agent, no divine being, which is responsible for its operation. Needham described such functioning as a "naturalistic pantheism, which emphasises the unity and spontaneity of the operations of nature", [79] a concept that reinforces the importance of human harmony with the interconnected universe, since there is no divine responsibility for it. Encouraging such harmony, effortlessly modelling one's life on it in the little things of life as well as the greater issues of state and social living, is what it means to experience *Tao* in life. Nature, then, has its own natural and spontaneous course in the universe. Graham depicted this superbly when he wrote: "This course, which meanders, shifting direction with varying conditions like water finding its own channel, is the *Tao*, the 'Way' . . . it is what patterns the seeming disorder of change and multiplicity, and all things unerringly follow where it tends except that inveterate analyser and wordmonger man, who misuses it by sticking rigidly to the verbally formulated codes."[80] Such, indeed, was the message of the *Chuang-tzu/Zhuangzi*. Human beings have within them the natural spontaneity of *Tao* that they submerge, overshadow and forget, through conditioned conventions. Instead of living harmoniously and accepting the gifts nature offers, nature is harnessed, conquered and dominated, without anything being given back. Ultimately, however, nothing can be taken from the universe without having to be given back.

The *Tao Te Ching/Daodejing* says little about nature *per se* but, like the *Chuang-tzu/Zhuangzi*, the emphasis on naturalness and spontaneity – the functioning of *Tao* in the ten thousand things – is synonymous with nature. But it is the *Chuang-tzu/Zhuangzi* that highlights strongly the differences between conventional life that lacks spontaneity of being, and the more harmonious responses to life that spontaneity permits. As human beings we are shrouded in the multiple decisions that have to be made in day-to-day living in a complex world. What can an individual do to recapture some of the sparkle of spontaneity in life? Graham answered such a question with the following words: "To recover and educate his knack he must learn to reflect his situation with the unclouded clarity of a mirror, and respond to it with the immediacy of an echo to a sound or a shadow to a shape."[81] In a beautiful rendering of *Chuang-tzu/Zhuangzi* 19:12, Merton captures the simplicity and essence of spontaneity in the following:

> Ch'ui the draftsman
> Could draw more perfect circles freehand
> Than with a compass.
>
> His fingers brought forth
> Spontaneous forms from nowhere. His mind
> Was meanwhile free and without concern
> With what he was doing.
>
> No application was needed
> His mind was perfectly simple
> And knew no obstacle.
>
> So, when the shoe fits
> The foot is forgotten,
> When the belt fits
> The belly is forgotten,
> When the heart is right
> "For" and "against" are forgotten.
>
> No drives, no compulsions,
> No needs, no attractions:
> Then your affairs
> Are under control.
> You are a free man.
>
> Easy is right. Begin right
> And you are easy.
> Continue easy and you are right.
> The right way to go easy
> Is to forget the right way
> And forget that the going is easy.[82]

Such words encapsulate the heart of the *Chuang-tzu/Zhuangzi* very well. The search for happiness that characterizes human living is a frenetic one built into the complexities of socio-economic drives. The urge to avoid death – albeit something that later Taoism adopted in the search for longevity – is a wish to avoid the natural processes of birth and decay in all things. The natural current of harmony runs through all things; few pause to experience it.

But harmony is the key to life in all its manifestations. The spontaneous character of nature is indicative that there cannot be fixed principles in approaching life. Each moment is different, and it is the ability to correlate the self with the situational moment that is the key to spontaneous living. In achieving inner harmony through taking the softer paths by way of experience with minimum effort, then maximum health, strength and benefit to others are achieved. For the individual acquires the ability to adjust in mutual response to the forces operating at a particular moment of time and space. The secret is the stillness within. T'ai Chi is devoted to establishing just that – stillness within while movement takes place. Movement, action, speech, thought should stem from the silence and stillness of *Tao* within the self. Such is *wu-wei*; such is the source from which naturalness and spontaneity should spring. The mind is allowed to turn meditatively inwards on itself to *Tao* and away from the anxieties and stresses that normal sense-stimuli bring. While we cannot turn our backs on the world as did the sage, we can acquire wisdom that comes through patience. We do not have to know or say something on every subject, meddle in the affairs of others, have reasoned answers for all that we do. We intuitively know when we are doing too much, when we need to step back and be still. The *Tao Te Ching/Daodejing* tells its rulers to ease off, lessen aggression and ruling, and let people develop their own natural responses to life. But if we cannot control our own impulses to action, and we have no stillness and silence within, how can we expect governments to function with restraint, non-aggression and a more yielding politic? The answers, Lao-tzu/Laozi would have said, come from within, not from more injunctions from outside. The truly free person is liberated from the confines of over-activity and manipulative living and achieves goals naturally.

The functioning of *Tao* in life

As we have seen, according to the *Chuang-tzu/Zhuangzi*, *Tao* is experienced by the skilled craftsperson that is able to perform action with that extra ingredient that comes from within. This is how the T'ai Chi *form* also needs to be performed. It is that intuitive relaxation into the activity that takes place when the individual is at one with the action. Then, no matter how complicated the activity is, it seems to happen naturally, effortlessly and smoothly. It is suggestive of experience of *Tao* in daily life, when we are at one with what we do. Conversely, according to the *Tao Te Ching/Daodejing*, when we become over-excited about things, over-desirous, over-emotional, because our senses are over-stimulated, we are unable to experience *Tao*. Whereas the craftsperson is open to the flow of *Tao* in life, the sense-bound person is only open to the stimuli of the material world. The goal of the Taoist and the adept of T'ai Chi is to experience the flow of *Tao* increasingly until it pervades all life, and when this happens, the individual is able to live life in the fullness of the moment. Happy, contended, serene, moderate and in harmony with all, those who achieve such a life-style attain to *Tao*. According to Chang San-feng/Zhang Sanfeng:

> In the mountains there is a kind of jade that keeps plants and trees from withering. Similarly, if people embrace the Tao it will keep their physical bodies strong. By steeping oneself in the Tao for a long time, one can transform substance so that it is the same as spirit, refine the body into something subtle, and merge with the Tao. Then the illumination of knowledge is boundless, and the body is infinitely transcendent. One makes totality of matter and emptiness one's function, one sets aside creation in achieving realization, one adapts from reality without convention – this is the power of the Tao.[83]

What the practice of T'ai Chi facilitates is the ability to lose the ego, to empty the mind, and begin the process of refinement of the inner self. In Sophia Delza's words: "Personal moods and distracting emotions evaporate as one is taken out of oneself by attention to motions and forms that are completely objective and impersonal. In this way, one understands oneself without subjective interference."[84]

The desireless state when all dualities are transcended is the highest state: friends and enemies, good and harm, honour and disgrace, the *Tao Te Ching/Daodejing* tells us, are all the same (chapter 56). In a sensitively written passage Paul Wildish describes the enlightenment and immortality that are the ultimate state of the Taoist sage:

> At the moment of death the ego dies with the physical body and becomes pure spirit. Freed from all constraints the liberated consciousness then expands to encompass the universe. This is not a merging with the One as a mere rain droplet is returned to the ocean; one molecule amongst

> millions of molecules. This is to become the immense consciousness of the ocean itself, which simultaneously feels its waves beating on the shores of a thousand coasts and the pulsating rhythm of myriad organisms moving within its depths. *This* is the transcendent immortality that the adept seeks.[85]

The release of the self from the world of desire brings about the highest gain of all – emergence into the energy of the stars, the suns, the moons, the earth and the whole universe.

4 Change

The *Book of Changes*: the *I Ching/Yijing*

The *I Ching/Yijing* is probably one of the oldest known books, some parts of it being perhaps about three thousand years old. Yet, despite its antiquity, the *I Ching/Yijing* has been in constant use over the millennia right up to the present day. Its prestige in China has been unsurpassed by any other text, and its easy availability in bookshops in the West is a measure of its continued popularity. Adopted widely in Korea, Vietnam and Japan, it was essential reading for Japanese militarists down to the last century, and the psychologist Carl Jung was sufficiently impressed by the book to endorse its contents in the *Foreword* to Richard Wilhelm's translation of it.[1] It is certainly the oldest of the Chinese *Classics*, itself being incorporated into the Chinese Confucian *Classics* during the Han dynasty. Not only does the *I Ching/Yijing* predate Confucius; it is also antecedent to formative Taoism by a long period. In its beginnings, it was more of a Chinese phenomenon than the prerogative of any particular school of religious or socio-political thought. And yet, there is much in it that was to appeal to Confucianism and Taoism in such a way as to make the *I Ching/Yijing* an essential text to both and, even more, to contain the seeds out of which Confucianism and Taoism grew. Taoism, especially, was to become closely involved with the philosophy underpinning the *I Ching/Yijing*, appropriating its ideas to render a Taoist view of the cosmos. Taoists were also particularly attracted by the divinatory and mystical characteristics of the text. In his seminal work on the *I Ching/Yijing*, Richard Wilhelm referred to the "seasoned wisdom of thousands of years" that comprise the *I*

Ching/Yijing we have today. He wrote: "Nearly all that is greatest and most significant in the three thousand years of Chinese cultural history has either taken its inspiration from this book, or has exerted an influence on the interpretation of its text."[2]

So what exactly is the *I Ching/Yijing*? Many scholars argue extensively that it is not a fortune-telling oracle – even if it began, as we shall see, as a divinatory text. The main reason for such an objection is that, while one has to *consult* the text in the same way as one might a fortune teller, the response the text gives describes the state of things as they are and as they are becoming. But there is no suggestion that something *must* happen in the future, or that things cannot change. It is a matter of actively changing course not of sitting back to await unavoidable results. It is more a response to "How can I handle the situation in which I find myself?" rather than "What is going to happen in the future?" And the response allows freedom to choose the appropriate path, not, as in fortune telling, acceptance of fate to come about which one can do nothing. Then, too, the other objection to depicting the *I Ching/Yijing* as a fortune-telling oracle is the fact that its responses are believed to be *morally* geared to the evolution of the self and of society. The need to develop virtue is presupposed by the *I Ching/Yijing*. Thus, it is concerned with the best directions for shaping life, and the pathways that conform best to the changing patterns of the universe. The messages it gives are cryptic, leaving the reader to relate the words to his or her particular life-condition in time. But the advice given will essentially be concerned with establishing the right balance and harmony in life.

Despite such views, in its origins the *I Ching/Yijing*, as we shall see, was clearly a divination text and, equally clearly, there are many easterners that today use it in much the same way. But between these extremes of time, the *I Ching/Yijing* developed into a text that was believed to encapsulate the patterns and transformations of life itself. It became on the one hand a philosophical text and, on the other, a pseudo-scientific one that professed to explain the law of the existence, interrelation and interaction of all things in the universe. It is in this sense that it is fundamental to the practice of T'ai Chi. It served to relate the individual, familial or societal situation to what was happening in the cosmos, and to suggest how co-operation with the prevailing cosmic forces might best be achieved. In Blofeld's words:

> From this it is clear that, could we but analyse the pattern of changes governed by this Law and could we but relate our affairs to the right point in the everlasting process of ebb and flow, increase and decrease, rising and falling, we should be able to determine the best action to be taken in

each case. Then, by peacefully according with the necessity to advance, remain stationary awhile or retreat, by cheerfully accepting the promise of gain or loss when each is due, we could come close to being masters of our lives![3]

But while the divinatory nature of the text may have been rejected by many in favour of a more philosophical conception,[4] it is likely that the text has maintained its complementary, divinatory character alongside its deeper associations. Those who preferred the latter saw the *I Ching/Yijing* as a book of wisdom and, as such, it acted as an inspiration to a number of eminent philosophers and thinkers like Confucius and Lao-tzu/Laozi.

Perhaps one of the reasons for the *I Ching/Yijing's* timeless survival is its uniqueness in not being associated with a particular religion or, for that matter, any religion at all. Indeed, it is a very humanistic text, centring on the interrelation of the human being with a changing universe. Deborah Sommer aptly writes: "Human action is not circumscribed by dualities of good and evil but is guided by the principles of appropriateness and timeliness, qualities that mirror the seasonal periodicity of the natural world."[5] If there are hints of divine dispensation in the *I Ching/Yijing*, they are minimal. It is preoccupation with the reality of nature that is the essence of the developed concepts of the *I Ching/Yijing*. The work represents Heaven and Earth constantly in states of transformation through their alternation and interaction with each other, and represents each and all the possible results of their interaction – the "cosmic archetypes", as one writer calls them[6] – in dynamic images. The *I Ching/Yijng* is believed to guide the individual who consults it according to the cosmic principles of the universe. Every individual or entity in the universe has its own vital essence and its own path that brings it into line with the cosmic laws. The *I Ching/Yijing* states the way things are at the moment, in what ways one has deviated from this norm, and points out the changes necessary to return to that norm. Such changes might demand passivity or activity, withdrawal or advance, and so on – all dependent on the nature of the moment. In Jung's *Foreword* to Wilhelm's work on the *I Ching/Yijing*, noted above, he suggested that at any moment in time we are caught up in the particular conditions that obtain in the universe; we are like a series of connected atoms in a cosmic whole. How we are in one moment is not isolated from the rest of the universe but reflects our degree of harmony or disharmony with the cosmic norms. The *I Ching/Yijing* points to this condition and, if necessary, how it can be improved, because it connects the moment of time of the individual with the moment of time of the cosmic process. It is, to use Fung Yu-lan's words, "a reflection in miniature of the entire universe".[7] Such an idea presupposes that the individual subconscious affects the moment as much as the conscious inquirer. Perhaps this is what fascinated Jung about the *I Ching/Yijing*. In closing his *Foreword* to Wilhelm's book, Jung wrote of the *I Ching/Yijing*: "To one person its spirit appears as clear as day; to another, shadowy as twilight; to a third, dark as night. He who is not pleased by it does not have to use it, and he who is against it is not obliged to find it true. Let it go forth into the world for the benefit of those who can discern its meaning."[8]

Historical development of the *I Ching/Yijing*

What we now know as the *I Ching/Yijing* is the result of a development in content and philosophy that evolved over thousands of years. Its beginnings are veiled in mystery and legend. Traditionally, the ancient sages attempted an explanation of life in terms of their own experience of the patterns and cycles of earthly and heavenly phenomena that existed in time. As Jou comments: 'They looked at the world around them and sought to understand why and how change occurs. They did not look beyond reality or ascribe all events to the "hand of God." Instead, they found enlightenment through the very practical process of examining the concepts of space and time.'[9] In the words of the *Ta-chuan/Dazhuan*, *The Great Treatise* appended to the *I Ching/Yijing*: "The holy sages were able to survey all the confused diversities under heaven. They observed forms and phenomena, and made representations of things and their attributes. These were called the Images."[10] But it was particularly the changing patterns of the phenomena of the universe that interested the sages, and such change was replicated in the archetypal images they used. These representations will be examined below. But we must go back earlier than the sages, for the origins of the *I Ching/Yijing* are to be found in the ancient practices of divination that were prolific in Shang and early Chou/Zhou times as discussed in chapter 1. Early divinatory practices were an attempt to understand future events in the context of a particular need of the moment. By heating the shoulder blades of deceased animals or the under-surface of tortoise and turtle shells, cracks appeared, which were interpreted by skilled diviners. Such a system had obvious limitations, and by Chou/Zhou times it found disfavour at court.

Oracle bones and bronzes of the late Shang and early Chou/Zhou dynasties have been discovered, revealing counting in groups of three and six.[11] But though the origins of the trigrams and hexagrams are obscure, it makes sense to suppose that divining by cracks on bones and shells was replaced by the trigrams and hexagrams of a more systematic system of divination. Such a system was in place well before the time of Confucius, comprising a basic *I Cing/Yijing*, with sixty-four hexagrams, a brief statement of the image each represents, and some explanation of those images. This early *I Ching* was known as the *Chou I/Zhouyi*, *The Changes of the Chou/Zhou*, which, after the short reign of China's first emperor, was added to the four Chinese *Classics*. It dates perhaps to the late second or early first millennium BCE, though there is no certainty of its age. There may, indeed, have been an oral transmission of some of its contents in the prognostications and sayings of the divinators before these were committed to written form.

Today, the academic view is that the *Chou I/Zhouyi* was an early divination text that served the purely pragmatic need for prognostication at the Shang and Chou/Zhou royal courts. It is likely that it was a guide for official royal diviners. This original system was developed to provide greater philosophical and moral content in what we know as the *I Ching/Yijing*. The original *Chou I/Zhouyi* contained no developed philosophy at all.[12] The current academic view, then, is that the *Chou I/Zhouyi* evolved through the collective skills of many diviners.[13]

The *Shuo-kua/Shuogua*, the *Discussion of Trigrams*, one of the appendices to the book, gives the traditional view of the authorship:

> In ancient times the holy sages made the Book of Changes thus:
>
> They invented the yarrow-stalk oracle in order to lend aid in a mysterious way to the light of the gods. To heaven they assigned the number three and to earth the number two; from these they computed the other numbers.
>
> They contemplated the changes in the dark and the light and established the hexagrams in accordance with them. They brought about movements in the firm and the yielding, and thus produced individual lines.
>
> They put themselves in accord with tao and its power, and in conformity with this laid down the order of what is right. By thinking through the order of the outer world to the end, and by exploring the law of nature to the deepest core, they arrived at an understanding of fate.[14]

From these words it can be seen that the original text, and the changes from a simple divinatory text to a more philosophical one, were accredited to the ancient sages. While the authorship of the *I Ching/Yijing* that we know today is much more complex than this suggests, the traditional accounts need some consideration here, for it is the traditional view of the *I Ching/Yijing* with which the philosophy of T'ai Chi is concerned.

The Chinese have long regarded the *I Ching/Yijing* to have been compiled by Fu Hsi/Fu Xi, King Wen, the Duke of Chou/Zhou, and Confucius. The first of these, Fu Hsi/Fu Xi, is probably completely legendary. Fu Hsi/Fu Xi was credited with introducing crafts to humankind, as well as the eight trigrams that form the basis of the *I Ching/Yijing* images. Then, traditionally, came the contributions of King Wen and the Duke of Chou/Zhou in the early Chou/Zhou dynasty. King Wen was responsible for the addition of explanations to the hexagrams – the so-called *Judgements*. Tan/Dan, the Duke of Chou/Zhou, and son of King Wen is believed to have added comments on the individual lines of the hexagrams.[15] These later contributions were highly important. They shifted the emphasis from primarily a divinatory purpose, to one that was far more philosophical, one that proffered freedom of choice, and one that could offer the possibility of evading the negativities of the future by recourse to correct actions. Wilhelm wrote of this change:

> They endowed the hitherto mute hexagrams and lines, from which the future had to be divined as an individual matter in each case, with definite counsels for correct conduct. Thus the individual came to share in shaping fate. For his actions intervened as determining factors in world events, the more decisively so, the earlier he was able with the aid of the Book of Changes to recognize situations in their germinal phases. The germinal phase is the crux. As long as things are in their beginnings they can be controlled, but once they have grown to their full consequences they acquire a power so overwhelming that man stands impotent before them.[16]

It is to Confucius and his later followers that the appendices of the *I Ching/Yijing* are credited. He is believed to have edited and annotated the *Chou I/Zhouyi*, producing what are called the *Ten Wings* (*Shih-i/Shiyi*), the ten sections and *Appendices* to the work. These consist of seven texts, three of which are divided into two, resulting in ten texts. Although his authorship of this complementary material is questionable, Confucius had a great respect for the *Chou I/Zhouyi*, and it was probably a number of his followers that accredited him with the authorship of the important extraneous material.

While the ancient nature of the *I Ching/Yijing* makes it a difficult text to understand at times, Cleary believes that the *I Ching/Yijing* can be applied to any system of organization – the family, a societal group, a political group, a culture, for example. He writes: "The *I Ching* analyzes the interplay of relations as functions of qualities, roles, and relative standing. It is therefore extremely versatile in handling both individual and collective perspectives; and since all standing is relative, it can be applied internally to any system of human organization, regardless of scale or configuration."[17] Such a view suggests a basic, pragmatic purpose for the *I Ching/Yijing*. But from a more philosophical point of view, Blofeld had the following to say about the purpose of the *I Ching/Yijing*:

> It is the function of the *Book of Change* so to interpret the various interlocking cycles of change that the progress of individual transformations can be deduced from them and the enquirer thereby receive a firm support which will help him to avoid being swept through the vortex like a leaf carried by angry waters. Though we cannot, by holding up our hand and using Words of Power, bid the winds and waves to cease, we can learn to navigate the treacherous currents by conducting ourselves in harmony with the prevailing processes of transformation; thus we can safely weather successive storms in this life and in all lives to come until that probably remote time when, having penetrated to the heart of change, we enter the immutable, undifferentiated stillness which is at once the womb and the crown of being.[18]

Blofeld's words suggest an inner role for the *I Ching/Yijing* in the context of today's world, a role that might promote inner harmony, and it is this kind of thought that is so much in line with Taoist thought and with the practice of T'ai Chi Ch'üan/Taijiquan. Taoists accepted the philosophy underpinning the *I Ching/Yijing*, particularly the need for harmony with the incessant interplay of complementary and opposing forces on the canvas of change and flux that characterizes the universe. Cleary writes: "For Taoists, to harmonize with the celestial in human life means to deal with each 'time', each combination of relations and potentials, in such a way as to achieve an appropriate balance of relevant forces and their modes of manifestation."[19] This is living life with one's finger on the pulse of the universe, and is the goal of the serious T'ai Chi practitioner.

For Taoists, too, there is a cosmogonic message underlying the *I Ching/Yijing*. Time is not linear but cyclical in the sense that the universe is constantly regenerating itself. It is a universe that is dynamically changing in its process of generation and regeneration, and it is with that backdrop in mind that the inquirer of the *I Ching/Yijing* seeks to harmonize the condition of the moment with the macrocosm of the universe. The *I Ching/Yijing* presents options, opens the mind to different perspectives and possibilities, and expects the inquirer to use reason to apply its contents to the moment in life. What we have today in the *I Ching/Yijing* is a composite, though heterogeneous, collection of Chinese wisdom throughout the ages. The resultant *I Ching/Yijing* is thus built up of many strata. In Hellmut Wilhelm's words: "Archaic wisdom from the dawn of time, detached and systematic reflections of the Confucian school in the Chou era, pithy sayings from the heart of the people, subtle thoughts of the leading minds: all these disparate elements have harmonized to create the structure of the book as we know it."[20]

Reality as perpetual flux and change[21]

The view of reality underlying the *I Ching/Yijing* is that everything in the universe is subject to change. Nothing can ever be static, but is dynamically and perpetually changing. Hellmut Wilhelm put this point forcefully when he wrote: "The world of this book is a changing world; every static expression, every binding form appears here as a frozen image that is opposed to life."[22] Such change, as we have already seen in other contexts, is not haphazard but rhythmic, and the rhythms of the universe are subject to certain fundamental laws that ensure its change conforms to certain patterns. It is the word *I/Yi* of the *I Ching/Yijing* that means "change" or "transformation". In the Chinese character for the word the upper part means "sun" and the lower "moon", thus reflecting the passage of time in the perpetual contrasts and opposing interplay of day and night.[23] But just as day and night have their own particular pattern, so the patterns of the whole universe resonate and interact in an organic whole according to their respective laws of change. So acorns become oak trees according to their specific patterns of change, just as season follows season, old age follows youth, and so on. That all reality is flux and change is the fundamental law of the *I Ching/Yijing*. And if there *is* anything that is changeless in the cosmos, it is the very fact that all is subject to change. The *I Ching/Yijing* is believed to reflect the resonating cosmos. If individuals are able to align themselves with that resonance, then they will have the potential to bring harmony to their lives and actions. However, since change characterizes everything in the cosmos, then the situation at one particular time in life is different from that which is coming to be; each situation is one in process, only to be changed in the succeeding moment, hour, day, or spell of life. But the change that takes place is rhythmic, patterned, predictable, though not necessarily predetermined. In the words of Hellmut Wilhelm: "Change is not something absolute, chaotic, and kaleidoscopic; its manifestation is a relative one, something connected with fixed points and given order."[24] So while change is the changeless basis to all existence its interplay and interconnectedness permits our continued existence, with freedom to conform to the patterns of the universe or to diverge from them.

Change, and the interplay of the forces of life, are described in the *I Ching/Yijing* as *the firm* and *the yielding*. More by transference of idea than any synonymy between the meanings of the words, *the firm* later came to be called *yang*, and *the yielding*, *yin*. But in the early *Chou I/Zhouyi* and the earliest commentaries, *yin* and *yang* do not occur.[25] *The firm* and *the yielding* represent the opposites of activity and receptivity, or movement and stillness, and the tension between both informs all the processes of life. Throughout our daily lives, thoughts advance and subside, arise and disappear. We advance to do this or that and retreat after our efforts. We are active during the day and passive during the night. And we know that the basis of our ability to advance, to act, to think well, to achieve, is dependent on the strength we acquire in the rest and stillness we have in sleep. Receptivity and passivity, stillness and calm, are therefore the dynamic processes of change that prepare us for the more active times of our daily lives. And the tension between the two will always operate to create new experiences or different nuances of old ones. Changes, then, are the tensions infused with dynamism between *the firm* and *the yielding*; they are "the imperceptible tendencies to divergence that, when they have reached a certain point, become visible and bring about transformations".[26] What this suggests is that events in time are perceptible in the future because they are in the process of coming to be. And by assessing the way in which that process is taking place, it is possible to align the balance of the activity and receptivity in the self to harmonize with events in a positive way. This is what proponents of the *I Ching/Yijing* claim the book can do. Each moment in time is a blend of interrelated and interacting fragments. The *I Ching/Yijing*, therefore, is believed to set a moment in time on the wider canvas of a constantly changing cosmic reality.

Later in its historical setting, that which informed all the transformations in the cosmos was posited as *Tao*. The *Appendices*, the *Ten Wings* of the *I Ching/Yijing*, write of *Tao* as the root from which all the transformations spring, "the immutable, eternal law at work in all change . . . the course of things, the principle of the one in the many".[27]

It was sometimes called *t'ai chi/taiji*, "supreme ultimate", *chi/ji* meaning "ridgepole", the essential part of a building that tied it all together. *Tao* as *T'ai-chi/Taiji* is that which generates the tension between opposites that makes changes, transformations, possible, and the power that renews that tension from moment to moment. It is the quiet, spontaneous power that eternally gives energy to the cosmos, to the rhythmic composition of the stars and planets as much as to the energy that a tiny seed needs for germination.

The *Pa-kua/Bagua* or Eight Trigrams

We must turn now to examine the trigrams and hexagrams of the *I Ching/Yijing* in a little more detail and explore how they are used generally and, more specifically, in the context of T'ai Chi Ch'üan/Taijiquan. A text of the *I Ching/Yijing* itself would be valuable to the reader in conjunction with this chapter, for limitations of space allow only an examination of the eight trigrams and not the sixty-four hexagrams they combine to produce.

The *Pa-kua/Bagua*, "Eight Trigrams", are images of processes of change. Each consists of three lines placed one on top of the other, in combinations of firm —— and yielding — — . And there are only eight different possibilities of combination; hence the *Pa-kua/Bagua*. Neither firm nor yielding lines are unchangeable. The firm line is active, moving outwards so that it breaks apart and becomes a yielding line. The yielding line does the opposite by moving inwards so that it eventually becomes a firm line.[28] Of the three lines, in whatever combination of firm and yielding, the top one always represents Heaven, the bottom one Earth, and the middle one, humanity. Being in the middle, humanity has the option of looking upward to Heaven and to spirituality, or to being focused downwards to Earth. The eight trigrams, then, are as shown at the top of the oppositie page.

The arrangement of the trigrams is the earlier, former, pre-Heaven, or primal arrangement, attributed to Fu Hsi/Fu Xi. It is also called the "Yellow River Map" or *ho-t'u/hetu*, and remains an important symbol in Taoist ritual. As can be seen from the arrangement, the trigrams at both ends of each axis are complementary opposites. So *Ch'ien/Qian* is South and summer, while *K'un/Kun* is North and winter. *K'an/Kan* is West and autumn, while *Li* is East and spring. *Ken/Gen* is Mountain, and its opposite *Tui/Dui* is Lake. *Chen/Zhen* is Thunder, an awakening force, while its opposite, *Sun*, is Wind, which drives things away.

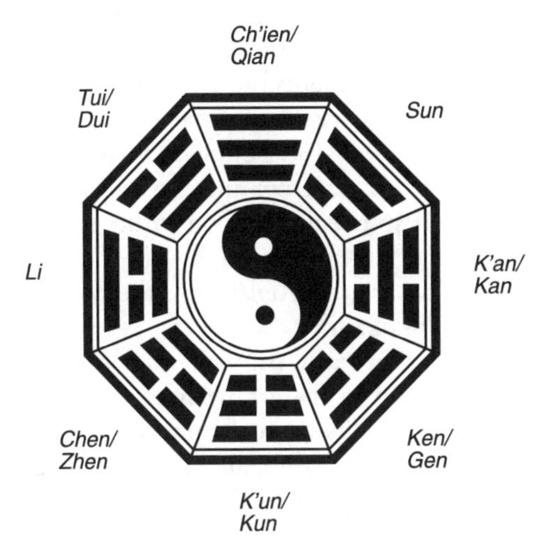

King Wen, however, rearranged the trigrams to represent the motion of change through the cycle of the year. His order is known as the post-Heaven or later arrangement, beginning in the springtime with *Chen/Zhen*:

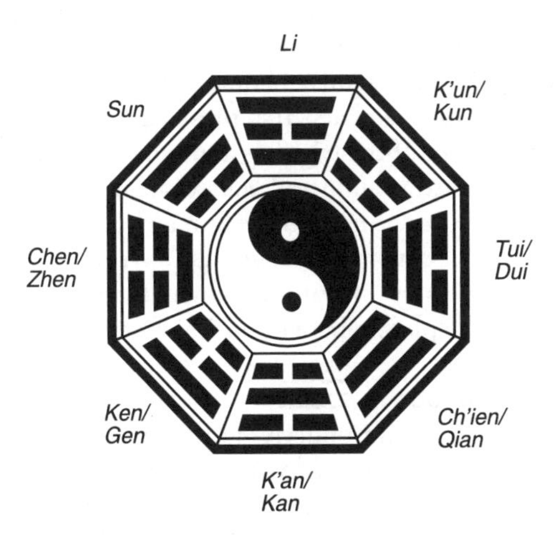

Spring begins the year like the morning begins the day, so *Chen/Zhen*, thunder, wakens the energies of the earth. Then comes *Sun* with its gentle winds, which melt the ice of winter and bring about a time of growth. Then we have summer, *Li*, a time of maturity in the yearly cycle, and of noon in the daily cycle. It is followed by the fruitful time of *K'un/Kun*, the time of harvest, and then the passing into autumn with *Tui/Dui. Tui/Dui* also represents the evening, the time for rest after the day's work, just as the work of the year ends following the harvest. Then, according to the *Shuo-kua/Shuogua*, a battle takes place between the creative force of *Ch'ien/Qian* and the darker forces of cold and winter. It is a time for spiritual reflection within in the face of the darkness without. It is a time followed by the depth of winter itself, *K'an/Kan*. Finally, the trigram *Ken/Gen* is the point of stillness before the whole cycle begins again.

The characteristics of each trigram, each state of change in the universe are represented in the arrangement of the three lines of the trigram. Each trigram has its name, its image (given below in italics) a corresponding family relationship, and a number of general characteristics, the main ones being given in the following:[29]

***Chi'en/Qian* The Creative** ☰

Heaven. The three strong lines of this trigram represent the attribute of strength. Additionally, sublimity, success, beauty, goodness, furthering perseverance and consistency are in its nature. It is a male representation of strength, the father in the family; the king of a nation; action; causality; and in *yin* and *yang* terms is wholly *yang*. It is associated with the dragon and all kinds of horses, the fruits of trees, and Metal in the Five Agents or Elements. It represents South in the early Fu Hsi/Fu Xi arrangement of the trigrams and north-west in the later one, in which it matches late autumn and late evening. It came to be associated with deep red, with the head in the human body, with jade, clarity, the coldness of ice, and with characteristics of roundness and expansiveness, like the fullness of autumn time. It represents productive energy in life. It is the place where opposites meet.

***Tui/Dui* The Joyous** ☱

Lake. The two firm lines underlying the broken line are a sign of stability within, and are associated with joy, happiness and wisdom. In the family the trigram represented a son in the primal arrangement of trigrams, but represents the youngest daughter in the later one, here, its yielding line being last (and so youngest), at the top of the trigram. It is a *yin* trigram. The associative animal is the sheep, the broken line above two firm lines perhaps representing its horns. The image is also suggestive of a yielding outer nature. Thus, it can also represent the concubine.

Water and Metal are its Elements. It is south-east in the primal arrangement of trigrams and West in the later one, making it mid-autumn in the year and the evening of the day. It is associated with enchantresses, in view of the strange things it can hold, and that can be enticed from its depths. It is related to the mouth and tongue of the body, and to pleasure. Since it is a deep and still lake, it reflects images, and so symbolizes deep reflection in life itself.

_Li_ The Clinging ☲

Fire. Here darkness is enveloped in light, the sun, and heat, shown by the two firm or *yang* lines enclosing the yielding or *yin* line. It is thus a light-giving trigram and is associated with external phenomena like the sun, lightning and fire, and internal aspects like the evolution of consciousness, devotion, beauty and purity. It is a *yang* trigram associated in the primal arrangement of trigrams with a son, but in the later one with the middle daughter, since its yielding line is in the middle of the trigram. The pheasant, the toad, crab, snail, turtle and tortoise are associated with this trigram, and Fire is its Element. In the primal arrangement of trigrams it is the East, in the later one the South and so, here, is summer, midday, and intense heat. It is associated with the eye of the body, with weapons, drought, the withered tree, and brightness. It is also associated with self-consciousness, and the corollaries of that in clinging and possessiveness, though it is also indicative of intelligence and understanding. Fire can only rise towards the sky, unlike its opposite of Water, which can only go downwards.

Chen/Zhen The Arousing ☳

Thunder. The strong lowest line with two yielding lines above represents energy and light rising up, reaching through the dark, and so the attributes of this trigram are movement, speed, energy, power and impulse. It is associated with the springtime. Despite its predominantly *yin* lines, it represents the eldest son in the family, indicated by the single firm line being at the bottom and, thus, first in the trigram. It is associated with the dragon in flight, rising up to the sky, or the galloping horse, both represented by the firm line rising upwards. Wood is its Element. It is the north-east in Fu Hsi/Fu Xi's earlier arrangement the North in the later one, and hence associated with mid-winter, midnight, and with thieves who steal at the dark time of the night. It is connected with the ear of the human body and with the colour dark yellow. Generally, it signifies danger, but it is essentially a creative trigram, is young and rapidly developing.

Sun The Gentle ☴

Wind and *Wood*. The firm upper two lines based on a yielding line characterize the trigram as gentle and penetrating like the wind. It is related to what is spiritual, to the intellect and the mind. It is a *yang* trigram and in the family is associated with the eldest daughter, its yielding line being first and at the base of the trigram. It is associated with the cockerel amongst animals, and with the Element of Wood. It is south-west in the primal arrangement of trigrams and south-east in the later one, corresponding to late spring and early summer during the year and morning time in the day. It was connected with merchants, with the colour white and with the thigh and eyes of the body. It is associated with steady progress in tasks or the growth of trees and vegetation. It represents growth and productivity and times of vitality, but also purity and wholeness.

K'an/Kan The Abysmal ☵

Water. The firm line representing strength and light is surrounded by darkness with the yielding lines above and below. The picture is representative of winter, darkness, instability, and danger of being enveloped. It is a predominantly *yin* representation, and is a daughter in the primal arrangement of trigrams but is the middle son of the family in the later arrangement, because the firm line is in the middle position. Water always seeks the lowest point, but it can symbolize spiritual depth as much as the darkness of an abyss. *K'an/Kan* is the darkness of a deep gorge into which water penetrates, or water flowing rapidly through a gorge, thus showing penetrating and piercing characteristics. Water is cold and dark, but it can be heated and can absorb light. The pig is associated with this trigram because it lives in mud and water, and the thief, who hides himself in the watery ditch. The human being who is low in spirits is *K'an/Kan*, as are sickly horses, but also courageous horses. It has curvature, and ability to bend in its nature just like water that fits any shape, so it is the bow and the moon. It is North, mid-winter, midnight, and the time of struggle before the light dawns again.

Ken/Gen Keeping Still ☶

Mountain. Resting and standing fast is the nature of this trigram. The two yielding lines supporting the uppermost firm one suggest passive immovability at the roots. The firm upper line is rooted in the earth of the two lowest yielding lines. In the family it represents the youngest son in the later arrangement of trigrams, being third and top in the trigram, though it is a daughter in the earlier, primal arrangement.

Despite the two *yin* lines, it is a *yang* trigram. It is associated with the dog as the faithful guard, the rat, and some birds. Its Element is Wood. While representing north-west in the early arrangement of trigrams, the later one places it in the north-east, early spring and early morning when night is ending. It was associated with the gatekeepers of the cities, the entrances, with the hand and finger of the human body and with fruits, seeds and knotty trees. While it can represent the stillness of stagnation, it can also represent the stillness of meditative reflection. It is a calm, quiet and restful trigram, but also a firm one.

***K'un/Kun* The Receptive** ☷

Earth. The three yielding or *yin* lines represent pure femininity and, thus, the mother and the queen of a nation. The trigram personifies receptivity, passivity, devotion and a yielding nature, and is a *yin* trigram. The animals associated with the trigram are the mare and the ox. Earth is its Agent or Element. It is North in the primal arrangement of trigrams and south-west in the later one, here representing late summer when fruits ripen, the warm sun of early autumn, and the afternoon in late summer. Its associative colour is black, and the part of the body connected with it is the abdomen. Characteristics are squareness, flatness, docility, harmony, accord and receptivity. In the *Shuo-kua/Shuogua* of the *Appendices* to the *I Ching/Yijing* it is cloth, a kettle, frugality, level, a cow with calf, a large wagon, form, multitude, a shaft, and black soil.[30]

These ancient trigrams are older than the *I Ching/Yijing* itself. Once established in the *I Ching/Yijing* they became subject to wide interpretation and analysis. Importantly, the trigrams represented a fluid and not static picture. They were believed to be changing constantly into each other, and thus depicted the flow of cosmic change. According to the *Shuo-kua/Shuogua*: "Heaven and earth determine the direction. The forces of mountain and lake are united. Thunder and wind arouse each other. Water and fire do not combat each other. Thus are the eight trigrams intermingled."[31]

Heaven and Earth came to be the *yang* and *yin* interactive forces that composed all things in an ever-shifting manner. The interrelation of Heaven and Earth is beautifully expressed by Liu I-ming/Liu Yiming in *The Book of Balance and Harmony*:

> Openness is the form of Heaven, tranquility is the form of Earth. Unceasing self-strengthening is the openness of Heaven, rich virtue supporting beings is the tranquility of Earth. Boundless spaciousness is

the openness of Heaven, boundless breadth is the tranquility of Earth. The Tao of Heaven and Earth is openness and tranquility; when openness and tranquility are within oneself, this means Heaven and Earth are within oneself.[32]

As Cleary points out in relation to Liu I-ming/Liu Yiming's words: "Thus concentration in stillness and active contemplation are regarded as complementary procedures. Certain exercises have traditionally been employed in Taoist practice to clarify, unify, and stabilize the mind so as to achieve the attunement represented as embodiment of Heaven and Earth."[33] This is exactly what T'ai Chi Ch'üan/Taijiquan seeks to accomplish.

The hexagrams

Traditionally and scholastically it has always been believed that the hexagrams were derived from the combination of trigrams and were a later development of them. The eight trigrams combined with each other form sixty-four possible combinations, each a hexagram, a set of six lines placed one on top of the other. The fact that two trigrams make up a hexagram seems to support a trigram > hexagram development. However, hexagrams were probably used before trigrams, the latter becoming important in the late Warring States period for the understanding of the hexagrams themselves.[34] The inscriptions on late Shang oracle bones and Western Chou/Zhou bronzes, with sets of six numerical components very similar to the hexagrams, suggests that they may be prior to the trigrams, and certainly prior to the *yin* and *yang* lines that we now know.[35] It seems, then, that hexagrams were not a natural development of placing two trigrams together. Indeed, it is even posssible that hexagrams and trigrams may have been co-existent from very early times. Xinzhong Yao and Helene McMurtrie certainly think so: "Ancient diviners may have consulted their deities by directly forming a hexagram or a trigram. Both trigrams and hexagrams might well have been tools for divination and other religious rituals, either independently or jointly together."[36]

Importantly, just as the trigrams are believed to interact with each other through processes of transformation, so too the hexagrams are images of states of change. They are considered to represent the fundamental laws and possible states of existence. The firm transforms to the yielding, the yielding to the firm, alternating in rhythmic pattern to form the cycles of life and death, day and night, heat and cold, summer and winter, pleasure and sorrow, movement and stillness. So one hexagram changes to another in constant flux, each hexagram representing the moment in time in the process of change – and discovered at the time of consultation. It is the interrelation of all things that lies at the heart of the philosophy of the *I Ching/Yijing*, interrelation "between all things in the universe from solar systems lying beyond our ken to objects so small that even the microscope has not discovered all of them". In this case, "the same fundamental laws govern worlds, nations, groups of entities, single entities and microscopic parts of entities".[37]

The pendulum of life experiences is never static. At each high point it has to swing back in the other direction, though perhaps with momentary rest before the change in the opposite direction occurs. So success can only be followed by failure, strife by peace, beginning by completion, abundance by scarcity, creativity by passivity and so on: the pendulum always swings back the other way. Understanding such a principle of life encourages optimism in moments of despair and caution in excessive success. The hexagram that emerges following consultation of the *I Ching/Yijing* places the individual psyche in the appropriate context of such ebb and flow, such process of change and transformation, indicating in which direction life is flowing, and how best to deal with it. As we shall see below, the rhythm of opposites is profoundly reflected in the pattern of postures in T'ai Chi Ch'üan/Taijiquan.

Of the two trigrams that combine to form a six-lined hexagram, the lower tends to refer to what is in the process of happening, to what is being created, to the inner self and behind. The upper refers to what is receding or dissolving, what is above, the external environment, and in front, or in the future. The lines of the upper trigram are "going" while the lower ones are "coming". Within a hexagram there are also what are called "nuclear" trigrams. If we read a hexagram from the bottom, the second, third and fourth lines themselves form a trigram, as do lines three four and five. So there are two nuclear trigrams in every hexagram, and these, too, have some bearing on the way in which a hexagram is "read". They provide an "inner" situation to the whole hexagram. The composers of the *I Ching/Yijing* took these nuclear trigrams into consideration when interpreting a hexagram. It is not only a hexagram as a whole, and its nuclear trigrams that present a particular cosmic pattern, but the individual lines of the hexagram. Firm, unbroken lines are "odd" and *yang*. Yielding and broken lines are "even" and *yin*. Such lines are important with reference to their specific places in the hexagram, their relation to other lines, and their order from bottom to top. Unbroken, firm or *yang* lines are indicative of movement, their opposite of broken, yielding or *yin* lines are indicative of rest. It is the changing places of these lines, their ascent and descent, the changing of weak lines to strong ones, and strong ones to weak ones, that mark the ebb and flow of life's situations.[38]

A whole hexagram has to be seen as a fluid, dynamic picture that pulsates through its lines. The first line is the beginning of a process of change, the second, the internal nature of a situation. The third line is that point at which what is internal in the outer trigram is becoming external in the upper one. Thus it is a line representing tension and crisis. The fourth line represents the start of the externalization of the situation, and the fifth, which corresponds to the third line of the "internal", lower, trigram, fully externalizes the situation. The sixth line is the completion or the point at which things turn into their opposite.

When the *I Ching/Yijing* is used, the resulting hexagram may contain what are called "moving" lines. These are lines that are in the process of change from yielding to firm or *vice versa*. The process of change is strong enough to result in a new hexagram obtained by changing the moving lines to their opposites. Such moving lines are indicators of a radically dynamic changing situation, an almost immediate state of change for an individual. A moving, firm or *yang* line is represented by ——o—— , and is an "old *yang*" and a moving *yin* line, an "old *yin*", by ——x—— . Non-moving lines are "young" lines. In analysis, *two* hexagrams are interpreted, the first with its moving lines giving the situation at the moment, and the second, when the old lines have been changed into their opposites, the state into which things are rapidly moving. Moving lines are sufficiently important to override the whole hexagram if there is any contradiction in the interpretation. Lines that are not moving lines are given the numbers seven (*yang*) and eight (*yin*). These are "resting" lines. A *yang* line that is moving to a *yin* one is given the number nine. A *yin* line moving to a *yang* is given the number six.

In summation, *yang* lines are representative of Heaven, of activity and motion, of the male, firmness, strength and light. They are positive indicators. *Yin* lines are indicative of Earth, of passivity, receptivity, and are yielding, weak and dark. They are negative indicators. In the *Ten Wings* of the *I Ching/Yijing*, *yin* and *yang* were accepted as the two interacting forces that inform all phenomenal existence, produced from *Tao* the Ultimate Source of all.

Change and transformation are the reality of the universe according to the philosophy of the *I Ching/Yijing*, and it is in the context of that change and transformation that the human being is placed. The theories informing the *I Ching/Yijing* replaced the usual mythological basis for interpreting life in ancient China. Indeed, China has few myths in comparison to most cultures. And since change and transformation constitute reality, the *I Ching/Yijing* cannot impose fixed laws, it can only present guidelines in relation to the particular flow of events or movement of the universe at a moment in time. It can only encourage self-reflection and responsibility in terms of the present condition in life. Raymond Van Over's words here are especially apt: "If the oracle wishes to direct our action in a specific direction or through a particular channel it will tell us how a Superior Man would conduct himself. In this subtle way our actions are directed toward a positive goal while still allowing us the free will to choose our own ultimate destiny."[39] There is, thus, a self-evolutionary value to working with the *I Ching/Yijing*.

The interrelation and interconnectedness of all things in the universe, both material and subtle, are presupposed by the *I Ching/Yijing*. The changing universe is not a chaotic backdrop on which the human being is placed, but a vast arena on which the interplay of all things forms patterns and rhythms of growth and decay, coming and going, resisting and yielding, expansion and contraction, and so on. Going with the flow of things, rather than in the face of things, is the easier path. The *I Ching/Yijing* is presented as a means by which this is possible, a tool that assists in shaping life.

So the ultimate aim underpinning the *I Ching/Yijing* is to achieve the kind of harmony and balance in life that results in the wisdom of the sage, or the well-being of the *chun-tzu/junzi*, Confucius' gentleman, or superior person,

> one who is perfectly self-controlled and self-sufficient, wholly free from self-seeking and able to stand freely and serenely among forces which toss lesser men to and fro like shuttlecocks, despite their tears and screams. Cheerfully impervious to loss or gain, he acts vigorously when action is needed and willingly performs the much harder task of refraining from action when things are much better left alone.[40]

Becoming such a sage, and the embodiment of wisdom, harmony, naturalness, and particularly virtue, was the ultimate aim of Taoists and is the ultimate aim of the T'ai Chi Master. Like water that finds its way around obstacles, the sage flows with the negative and positive changes that occur in life, in harmony with the ever-transforming universe. For Taoists, this was being in accord with *Tao*; it was identifying oneself with the transformations initiated by *Tao* as the phenomena of all life, at the same time experiencing the oneness of *Tao* in all things. Such a life-condition points to inner stillness while engaged in outward activity, inner harmony while engaged in the ordinary events of the day.

The hexagrams of the *I Ching/Yijing* continually point to the goal of perfection with all kinds of advice, such as developing integrity in one's conduct and helping others to do the same (hexagram 29), or cultivating virtue for the benefit of the world (hexagram 30). Thus, at least the *I Ching/Yijing* contains advice on moral behaviour, on the ways in which the self can evolve. Even if its more active role of response to inquiry is set aside, the more passive role of being an inherently moral guide is of immense value. For there is positive encouragement to do what is good without being harsh on the self, without being unnaturally good. Liu I-ming/Liu Yiming's commentary on the *I Ching/Yijing* brought this factor out well:

> Of old it has been said, always extinguish the stirring mind, do not extinguish the shining mind. When the mind is unstirring it is shining, when the mind does not stop it is astray.
>
> The shining mind is the mind of Tao, the straying mind is the human mind. The mind of Tao is subtle and hard to see; the human mind is unstable and uneasy.
>
> Although there is the mind of Tao in the human mind, and there is the human mind in the mind of Tao, it is just a matter of persistence in the midst of action and stillness: If the shining mind is always maintained, the straying mind does not stir; the unstable is stabilized, and the subtle becomes apparent.[41]

Joseph Needham called the *I Ching/Yijing* a "cosmic filing-system"[42] and a "mischievous handicap"[43] that rather prevented scientific development. *Scientifically* this may well be true. But those who put their faith in the *I Ching/Yijing* are not looking for scientific answers to life's problems. On the contrary, they are trying to explore ways in which they can solve the socio-psychological problems that life is presenting at a moment in time. They are trying, also, to gain greater perception of the particular way in which their present space–time situation harmonizes with the interconnected cosmos.

The *I Ching/Yijing* and T'ai Chi Ch'üan/Taijiquan

The theories embodied in the *I Ching/Yijing* inform the Taoist practice of T'ai Chi Ch'üan/Taijiquan in every sense – energy development, meditation, health, and martial art usage. T'ai Chi is just one of many other traditional Chinese mind and body systems, like *chi-kung/qigong* and *pa-kua chang/bagua zhang*, that put into practice the philosophy, principles and concepts of the *I Ching/Yijing* through actual physical movement.[44] The last section of the *Treatise on T'ai Chi Ch'üan/Taijiquan* contains what are known as the *Thirteen Postures*, and it is these that are essential and fundamental to the practice of any of the martial arts, or to T'ai Chi. The *Thirteen Postures* correspond not only to the eight trigrams, but also to the Five Elements (Activities in the quotation below), and to compass directions. The postures are important enough to cite fully here:

The Thirteen Postures of Warding-Off,
Rolling-Back, Pressing, Pushing, Pulling,
Splitting, Elbowing, and Shouldering
are known as the Eight Diagrams (*Pa Kua*).
Advancing, Withdrawing, Looking-Left,
Gazing-Right, and Fixed-Rooting are known
as the Five Activities (*Wu Hsing*).
Warding-Off, Rolling-Back, Pressing,
and Pushing are then *Chien*, *K'un*, *K'an*, and *Li* –
of the Four Cardinal directions.
Pulling, Splitting, Elbowing,
and Shouldering are then *Sun*, *Chen*, *T'ui*,
and *Ken* – of the Four Diagonal directions.
Advancing, Withdrawing, Looking-Left,
And Gazing right, and Fixed-Rooting are then
Metal, Wood, Water, Fire, and Earth.
Joined together they become
the Thirteen Postures.[45]

While the martial art emphasis is clear from the extract above, the postures are no less applicable to the T'ai Chi *form*, as we shall see.

The eight trigrams of the *I Ching/Yijing* directly correspond to the eight energies or "gates" in the T'ai Chi *form*. Each is a special posture or technique of movement, and incorporates at least two of the Thirteen Postures. The eight postures corresponding to the eight trigrams are listed below. Each of the eight postures presents a change of energy direction. This corresponds to the state of change in the universe as represented by the eight trigrams of the *I Ching/Yijing*, as represented overleaf.

Ward Off is related to *Chi'en/Qian*, Heaven.
Roll Back is related to *K'un/Kun*, Earth.
Press/Squeeze is related to *K'an/Kan*, Water.

Push is related to *Li*, Fire.
Rend/Split is related to *Chen/Zhen*, Thunder.
Bump is related to *Ken/Gen*, Mountain.
Pluck/Grasp is related to *Sun*, Wind.
Elbow is related to *Tui/Dui*, Lake.

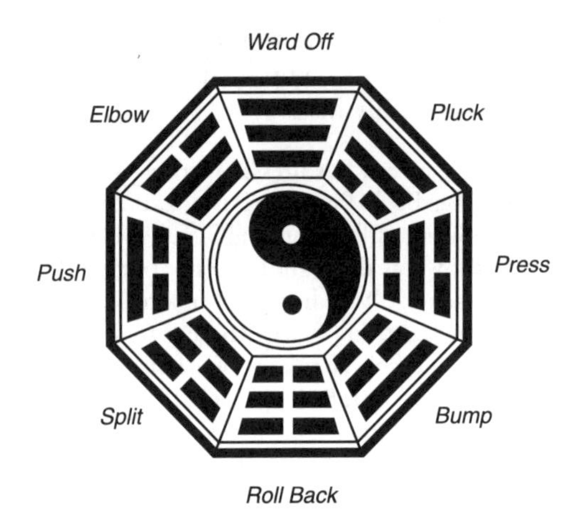

Since every movement performed expresses at least two of the eight energy techniques, this will correspond to the balance of *yin* and *yang* and the working of opposite energies in the movements of the *form*. We need now to examine the eight techniques or postures in detail.

Ward Off: Chi'en/Qian

Ward Off occurs when the weight is moved forward onto the front foot and the leading *yang* arm is bent across the chest, as if holding a ball to the chest. The rear hand, which is classed as *yin*, is held either by the side of the body with the palm facing downward, pressing energy or, in some other styles of T'ai Chi, just behind the front forearm, with the palm facing toward the front forearm in the press position. In the photograph, the first option is shown with the palm facing the floor. The energy movement of the *Ward Off* technique is outwardly expanding in either a forward or upward direction. It has the feeling of roundness with the front arm and chest, and appears as if bouncing any incoming energy away just like a ball. The *Ward Off* posture is seen in the T'ai Chi movements of *Grasp the Sparrow's Tail* and *Wave Hands in Clouds*; the technique corresponds to the trigram of The Creative, Heaven.

Ward Off: Chi'en/Qian

The attribute of *Ward Off* is strength, thus it is classed as *yang*. In the Five Elements it is the Metal Element, and its direction in the earlier arrangement of Fu Hsi/Fu Xi is South, and in the later arrangement, north-west. It is associated with the head in the human body.

Roll Back: K'un/Kun

The *Roll Back* technique is a yielding or giving-way method. The weight is on the rear leg and the rear *yin* palm is facing upward as if holding or lifting something. The leading *yang* palm is facing downward as if pressing on something, as seen in the photograph on the next page.

The *Roll Back* technique can also be broken down further into either a small *Roll Back* or a large *Roll Back*. The overall feeling of expression of energy in the *Roll Back* technique is of yielding, pulling or uprooting the attacker off balance. In the *form* the *Roll Back* technique is seen in the posture of *Grasp the Sparrow's Tail*. The *Roll Back* corresponds to the trigram of The Receptive, Earth. Its attribute is to be yielding and so it is *yin*. In the Five Elements it is the Earth Element, and its direction is North in the earlier arrangement and south-west in the later arrangement of trigrams. It is associated with the abdomen in the human body.

Roll Back: K'un/Kun

Press/Squeeze: K'an/Kan

The *Press* technique is performed with the two hands facing each other, as if squeezing air out of a ball or balloon. It can be performed in a horizontal, side to side or forward and backward direction and it can also be performed in a vertical upward and downward direction as seen in the two corresponding photographs on the opposite page.

The front hand is *yang* and the rear hand is *yin*. The feeling of energy expressed in the *Press* technique is of holding or containing. Again, the *Press* technique is seen in the posture of *Grasp the Sparrow's Tail* of the T'ai Chi *form*. The *Press* technique corresponds to the trigram of The Abysmal, Water. Its attribute is instability and is *yin*. In the Five Elements, it is the Water Element and its direction is West in the earlier arrangement of trigrams and North in the later one. It is associated with the kidneys in the human body.

Push: Li

The *Push* technique is performed in either a forward, downward or upward direction. It is done with a single hand or with both. The energy of the *Push* technique is outward, away from the body, and in its T'ai Chi martial art usage it may be used either to control the attacker's limbs, or to push directly against his or her body in a downward or forward direction. In the T'ai Chi *form* the action is done with the fingers pointing forward. Then, right at the end of the movement, the wrist drops downward, forward or upward and the palm lifts to an upright position, issuing the vital energy out through its centre.

Squeeze: K'an/Kan

Press: K'an/Kan

The action of the *Push* technique is shown in the postures of *Brush Knee Side Step*, *Grasp the Sparrow's Tail* and *Repulse the Monkey*. The *Push* technique corresponds to the trigram of The Clinging, Fire. Its attribute is consciousness and it is *yang*. In the Five Elements it is the Fire Element. Its direction in the earlier arrangement is East and in the later it is South. It is associated with the eyes and the heart in the human body.

Rend/Split: Chen/Zhen

As a martial art movement, the *Rend* technique has the feeling of splitting a piece of wood into two parts. The energy direction is forward and to the side; the shoulder, upper and lower arm are used to uproot the attacker. The technique is performed with the leading leg placed either to the inside or outside of the attacker's legs. The leading arm performs the *Rend* technique moving forward and to the outside of the leading leg. This gives the feeling of two energies moving in opposite directions. The leading leg slightly presses inward against the attacker's leg, while the leading arm's energy is moving outward to the side, pressing against the attacker's body, bouncing him or her over the leg – hence the feeling of splitting wood in two. In the T'ai Chi *form* the technique occurs in the posture of *Parting the Horse's Mane*. The *Rend* technique corresponds to the trigram of The Arousing, Thunder. Its attributes are movement, and it is classed as *yin*. In the Five Elements it is the Wood Element. Its direction is north-east in the earlier arrangement of trigrams and is North in the later one. It is associated with the ear and left abdomen in the human body.

Bump: Ken/Gen

The *Bump* technique means to use the shoulder, back, hip, thigh or knee to knock the attacker off balance. The direction of the energy used can be forward, downward, sideways and upward. The martial art aspect of the *Bump* technique is only used in close-range situations, and if it is used skilfully it destroys the attacker's root by knocking him or her off balance. It is also used to take the opportunity to execute further action, like a kick or strike. The *Bump* technique is a very powerful method, causing damage to the attacker by knocking him or her to the floor. The energy released is a short explosive energy that is sudden and powerful. It is, then, a martial art technique. It corresponds to the trigram of Keeping Still, Mountain, for its attribute is stillness. It is *yang*, and in the Five Elements it is Wood. Its direction is north-west in the earlier arrangement of trigrams and north-east in the later one. It is associated with the hands and neck in the human body.

Pluck/Grasp: Sun

The *Pluck* technique means to grasp the attacker's limbs or joints in order to immobilize him or her for further attack. The action of *Pluck* or *Grasp* is not just done with the hands and fingers, but it can also be performed with the arms. The energy of the *Pluck* movement is downward or sideways and may be used to lead the attacker off balance. Once the attacker's limb is grasped, immediate control, not only of the attacker's balance, but also of the flow of vital energy into the limb itself, occurs. In the *form* postures the *Pluck* action is seen in *Wave Hands in*

Clouds, *Play the Lute*, *Pick the Needle Up* and *Single Whip*. The *Pluck* technique corresponds to the trigram of The Gentle, Wind. Its attribute is intellect, and it is classed as *yang*. In the Five Elements it is Wood. Its direction is the south-west in the earlier arrangement of trigrams and south-east in the later arrangement. It is associated with the thighs and lower back in the human body.

Elbow: Tui/Dui

The *Elbow* technique is used both in attack and defence. In its offensive use the *Elbow* is used to strike the attacker, or it is used to press against the attacker as a means to offset balance. In its defensive action, it is used to neutralize an attempt to lock any of the joints on the arms, by using a circular, yielding action. This circular, yielding movement makes it possible to coil around the attacker's own limb as a means to immobilize him or her, or prevent further attack. The *Elbow* technique is a very powerful weapon and, like the *Bump* technique, it is only used in close range situations, yet we still find it in the T'ai Chi *form* in the postures of *Wave Hands in Clouds* and *Single Whip*. The *Elbow* technique corresponds to the trigram of The Joyous, Lake. Its attribute is wisdom. It is *yang*, and in the Five Elements it is associated with either Water or Metal. Its direction is south-east in the earlier arrangement of trigrams and West in the later one. It is associated with the mouth and the right side of the abdomen in the human body.

Although the Eight Gate techniques are associated with the eight trigrams, they do not follow each other in the same order every time, otherwise the energy would become stagnant, rigid and obvious. Similar to the Eight Gate postures are the eight palm positions (*pa-shou/bashou*). These are distinct positioning of the arms and hands in the T'ai Chi movements. Whereas the Eight Gate techniques correspond to a particular direction of *energy* that the individual is moving towards, the eight palm positions correspond to the direction that the centre of the palms are facing.

Heaven: Chi'en/Qian   The Creative
The Heaven and *yang* palm position is performed with the centre of the palm facing upward.

Earth: K'un   The Receptive
The Earth and *yin* position has the centre of the palm facing downward.

Fire: Li   The Clinging
In the Fire and *yang* position the centre of the palm faces forward.

Water: K'an/Kan   The Abysmal
The Water and *yin* position is performed with the centre of the palm facing inward, but with the hand in a horizontal position, fingers pointing forward.

Mountain: Ken/Gen   Stillness
In the Mountain and *yang* position the palm faces inward, but with the hand in a vertical position, fingers pointing upward.

Thunder: Chen/Zhen   The Arousing
The Thunder and *yin* palm position is performed with the palm facing inward towards the body, but in a horizontal position.

Wind: Sun   The Gentle
The Wind and *yin* palm faces inward with the fingers either pointing downward or upward, but in a vertical position.

Lake: Tui/Dui   The Joyous
The Lake and *yang* palm faces diagonally downward or upward.

Each of the eight hand positions are found in the T'ai Chi *form*, each palm direction changing into another, each generating the energy for the next in a smooth, interchanging way.

T'ai Chi Ch'üan/Taijiquan postures and the hexagrams of the *I Ching/Yi Jing*

Not only does T'ai Chi Ch'üan/Taijiquan utilize the eight trigrams but it also includes the sixty-four hexagrams as well. For example the *Pluck/Grasp* technique is performed with the rear hand, corresponding to the *I Ching/Yijing* trigram of *Sun*, The Gentle. With the front hand the *Ward Off* technique follows, which corresponds to the *I Ching/Yijing* trigram of *Chi'en/Qian*, The Creative. When we place the two trigrams together we have the hexagram Temptation. Another example is to use the *Push/Press* technique with the rear hand, which corresponds to the trigram of *Li*, Fire. Then, the front hand or arm performs the action of the *Rend/Split* technique that corresponds to

Chen/Zhen, Thunder; this will give us another hexagram from the *I Ching/Yi Jing* which is hexagram Zenith. These examples illustrate the extent to which the movements of T'ai Chi Ch'üan/Taijiquan are connected to the *I Ching/Yijing*. Each set of postures or sequences that make up the whole T'ai Chi *form*, then, also corresponds to a particular hexagram from the *I Ching/Yijing*. Below are some examples of the T'ai Chi postures with their corresponding hexagrams.

The opening posture of the T'ai Chi *form* is represented by hexagram 35 *Chin/Jin*, which represents progress. The hexagram is composed of the trigram *Li*, Fire, above the lower trigram of *K'un/Kun*, Earth. This symbolizes the sun rising above the earth at the start of each day. The student stands upright as he or she begins the *form*. The legs are parallel to one another. Then the student rises from the thighs in a parallel position, slowly lifting the hands together to the chest and then slowly lowering them down again. The second posture is known as *Part the Horse's Mane* and is represented by hexagram 59 *Huan*, which means Dispersal. It is composed in the upper trigram by *Sun*, Wind, and in the lower trigram by *K'an/Kan* Water.

The upper trigram *Sun* symbolizes a hand moving towards the head to perform a striking action; the lower trigram *K'an/Kan* symbolizes movement from the legs. The student steps forward with the leading leg, and at the same time sweeps forward with the leading arm. The moving *yang* arm's palm is facing upward; the non-moving *yin* palm faces downward alongside the hip.

The third posture is known as *White Crane Spreads Wings*. It is based on hexagram 22 *Pi/Bi*, which means Grace. The upper trigram is *Ken/Gen* Mountain and indicates a hand or wing. The lower trigram is *Li*, Fire, which the *I Ching/Yijing* indicates as a white bird or horse. Hence the hexagram gives the picture of a white bird gracefully spreading a wing. The weight is transferred onto the rear leg; the front heel is raised with just the ball of the foot touching the ground. The right arm is raised to eye level with the arm bent and the palm facing inwards towards the head. The left arm lowers to rest alongside the hip with the palm facing downwards.

The fourth posture, which is known as *Brush Knee Side Step*, is based on hexagram 18 *K'u/Ku*, which means Repair. The upper trigram is

Ken/Gen Mountain and the lower trigram is *Sun* Wind. The image used for this hexagram of the *I Ching/Yijing* is The Wind Blows Low on the Mountain, another way of expressing *Brush Knee Side Step*. The student steps forwards with the leading leg, the leading *yang* arm sweeps low over and around the front knee, palm facing downward. The rear *yin* arm pushes forward at chest height, palm facing forward.

17

The fifth posture is known as *Play the Lute*, using hexagram 17 *Sui* "Adapting". The upper trigram is *Tui/Dui* Lake, and the lower trigram is *Chen/Zhen* Thunder. The trigram Lake suggests a joyous activity, whereas the actual movement means to hold or play a traditional Chinese instrument known as a *pi-pa/biba*, a wooden lute or guitar. The lower trigram, Thunder, suggests a firm stance. The student places his or her weight on the rear leg. The rear *yin* hand is in front of the navel with the palm side on, fingers pointing forward. The lead *yang* hand is ahead of the rear hand, but in line with it. The palm is side on, fingers pointing forward. The lead leg is slowly raised and then lowered onto the floor with the heel touching the ground and the toes raised from the floor.

Thus, all the movements of the T'ai Chi/Taiji *form* are correlated with the hexagrams of the *I Ching/Yijing*. The intention underpinning such correlation is no different to the fundamental principles of the *I Ching/Yijing*. That is to say, there is a conscious effort to reflect the rhythms and harmony of the cosmos in the principles of both the *I Ching/Yijing* and the T'ai Chi *form*. Serious practitioners of T'ai Chi understand such deeper meanings inherent in their practice and search by means of it for a life that is in harmony with cosmic forces. Raymond Van Over put this sensitively when he wrote:

> The writers of the *I Ching* recognized this archetypal and ardent striving for universal identification. They looked not at transient values, or superficial answers such as commercial and social success, but rather at the rhythm of the flower as it thrusts from the ground, blossoms, spreads its seed, wilts, and returns from whence it came. Such, to the writers of the *I Ching*, held a profound meaning. Where there was only mystery for many and fear of the transience of life for others, there resided an eternal truth for a few. This movement of life, its necessary ultimate destruction and eternal recurrence, its polarity of principles and energies, dictated a

way of life that could, if based upon insight and wisdom, pattern itself after the cosmos.[46]

Such words epitomize rather well the inner meaning of the *I Ching/Yijing* for those who accept its validity. To regard it scientifically is to miss the *spiritual* connectedness with the cosmos that its proponents wish to achieve. At the end of the day, there will be those who will view the *I Ching/Yijing* as no more than the fanciful ramblings of ancient soothsayers; others will find it a useful guide. And in Hellmut Wilhelm's words: "Even if we shrink from approaching the book with the willing faith of an oracle seeker, we can still meditate on this image of the cosmos for its own sake and seek to understand it."[47] One fact remains, the *I Ching/Yijing* seems to have stood the test of three millennia of time, and that in itself is remarkable. In the context of Taoism, it is an accepted text that Taoists took ownership of from their distant beginnings to present times and as part of its present expression it underpins the philosophy and practice of T'ai Chi Ch'üan/Taijiquan.

5 Phases

As was seen with the analysis of the trigrams and hexagrams of the *I Ching/Yijing*, and the nature of *yin* and *yang*, a cyclical motion of change underpins all life. And that cyclical motion of change is the only permanent reality: change is the changeless reality of the universe. But in each repetition of a cycle the space for change is infinite; there is renewal without identical copying, alternation with difference. Just as no springtime can be the same as any other period of springtime in the past, so change characterizes the changeless cycles of the seasons, night and day, darkness and light, and the many dualities that make up existence. Such a view of the universe makes it self-creative and self-sustaining, with all phenomena caught up in the rhythm of cyclical motion. Thus, while plurality is self-evident in the universe, the totality of that plurality is interconnected and interrelated by the forces that inform it. These forces are the Five Elements or Agents – Wood, Fire, Earth, Metal and Water. Robinet commented on their importance in Chinese philosophy:

> All creatures are categorized, listed under one of these rubrics. All kinds of resonances and influences can be discovered in the system founded on this principle of classification, some of them opposing, some of them attracting. A basic guiding principle is that things which resemble each other go together. As a result, certain actions and interactions can be explained or predicted, both in space and in time, horizontally (from one end of the world to the other) as well as vertically (from earth to heaven).[1]

The Five Elements, then, underpin all nature and all life.

The Five Elements are known collectively as the *wu-hsing/wuxing*.

Wu means "five", but the word *hsing/xing* is more problematic. Traditionally it has been translated as "Elements" much in line with the Greek and Indian conception of the elements of earth, air, fire and water as the constituents of manifest existence. But Chinese *hsing/xing* has a much more dynamic meaning. This can be seen instantly in its root meanings – to prosper, to begin, to increase, to rise, to raise, to walk, to do, to act, to travel.[2] Thus, *movement* is characteristic of each of the Elements. They are *activators*, each with its particular kind of movement. It is for this reason that the translation "Agents" more readily describes their cosmological function. Tsou Yen/Zou Yan called them *wu-te/wude* "Five Powers", because he related them to the rise and demise of dynasties. They were also called Five Processes, indicative of their properties – Fire rising and burning, Water saturating and sinking, for example.[3] In pre-Han times they were called Five Materials (*wu-ts'ai/wucai*),[4] and from Han times onwards, they were referred to as Five Phases, an appropriate term given the cyclical dominance of each of them in turn in all dimensions of life, as we shall see below. Such descriptors illustrate two points. The first is that the origins and growth of the concept of the Five Elements were not neatly linear and, second, that the Elements could be applied in a variety of ways. Indeed, it is this last point that we must take up in more detail below, for the theory of the Five Elements is very much alive in a number of fields in the present day and age, and is very important in the practice of T'ai Chi. In all, the term *Agents* is perhaps the most all encompassing, and does the least to confine the overall use of all Five, but in the T'ai Chi tradition, they are known as Elements, and for the purposes of this present chapter, this is the term that will be used. The reader should note, however, that the terms Agents and Phases are widely used, the latter term by more modern, academic sources, though it is somewhat time-orientated. In martial arts, especially in T'ai Chi Ch'üan/Taijiquan, however, the term *Elements* is the norm.

The Five Elements, then, are *active* motivators. They are functional, bringing into being and ending the phases and changes evident in the world. Through their mutual functioning all things come into being and pass away. Air is excluded for it is the all-pervasive oneness of *ch'i/qi*, the vital breath or energy from which *yin* and *yang* and the Five Elements themselves emerge. Instead, Wood is included because of its more obvious functional and indispensable role in existence, for it represents growth and the ability to flourish. So the Five Elements are both abstract principles and dynamic forces. The former prevents their being reduced to basic, static substances, and the latter ensures their active roles in informing the interconnection of all things. All phenomena in life will correspond to one of these Elements.

Historical development of the Five Elements

Like so many aspects of Taoism and Chinese thought, the antecedents of the Five Elements must surely be found in the ancient observations of nature. The four seasons, especially, had their respective characters and rhythmic cycles, which four of the Elements, at least, could be seen to reflect, and Earth came to be the central Element that facilitated the activity of the other four. It is likely that the theory of Five Elements was imposed on older systems, gradually being applied to five deities and the four cardinal points around a fifth centre.[5] It was probably among the ranks of the *fang-shih/fangshi* that the cosmological theories relating to the Five Elements gathered ground.

Our earliest sources of information regarding the Five Elements are two texts, the *Lü-shih Ch'un-ch'iu/Lüshi Chunqiu*, *Annals of Spring and Autumn from the State of Lü*, which contains what is called the *Monthly Commands* (extant also in the *Book of Rites*), and the *Hung Fan/Hongfan* or *Grand Norm* found in the *Book of Documents*, the *Shu Ching/Shujing*. The *Lü-shih Ch'un-ch'iu/Lüshi Chunqiu* is an eclectic work composed in the late third century BCE by numerous scholars, and reflects the views of late Chou/Zhou philosophers. It is in this document that the phases of the Five Elements are correlated with dynasties and colours. Thus, the legendary Yellow Emperor ruled by the power of Earth with yellow as his colour. Earthworms and mole-crickets appeared before he rose to power to indicate the ruling Element. Grass and trees appeared when Yü/Yu came to power, so Wood became his ruling Element and green his associative colour. Similarly, T'ang/Tang, the founder of the Shang dynasty, was associated with Metal and the colour white since knife-blades appeared in the water. The appearance of a fiery flame and a red bird holding a red book in its mouth made King Wen rule by the Power of Fire, with red as his colour. The *Annals of Spring and Autumn* indicated that Water would be the Power associated with the next ruler, along with the colour black, before the cycle revolved again to Earth. The early correspondents to the Five Powers were, therefore, the respective dynasties and their correlative colours:

Earth	*Wood*	*Metal*	*Fire*	*Water*
Yellow Emperor	Hsia/Xia	Shang	Chou/Zhou	–
Yellow	Green	White	Red	Black

The *Monthly Commands* connected the Five Elements more finely with the months of the year, with appropriate colours to be worn, and even with the musical notes to be played. Climatic disasters would ensue if conformity to the patterns of the dominant Element were disregarded. Of the Five Elements, the *Hung Fan/Hongfan*, the *Grand Norm* or *Great Plan* states:

> The first is named water, the second fire, the third wood, the fourth metal, the fifth earth. The nature of water is to moisten and descend; of fire to burn and ascend; of wood, to be crooked and straight; of metal, to yield and to be modified; of earth, to provide for sowing and reaping. That which moistens and descends produces salt; that which burns and ascends becomes bitter; that which is crooked and straight becomes sour; that which yields and is modified becomes acrid; sowing and reaping produce sweetness.[6]

The cosmological cycles of the Five Elements were extended to directions, planets, deities, animals, emperors, mountains, musical tones and all kinds of phenomena, as we shall see below.

While the *Yin-Yang* school and the Five Elements school seem to have existed separately at first, it was Tsou Yen/Zou Yan who brought about a coalescing of the two, and by Han times the *Yin–Yang* school and the Five Elements school were interchangeable names. It was an important correlation of two strands of thought that had an enormous impact. The interrelation of Heaven, Earth and human affairs became such that the seasons and the general welfare of humankind could be affected by the proper or improper actions of the ruler – he who embodied Chinese humanity. The coalescing of the two powerful theories of *yin* and *yang* and the Five Elements served to illustrate a direct correlation between the macrocosm of Heaven and the microcosm of the human.

Tsou Yen/Zou Yan called the Five Elements *wu-te/wude*, Five Powers. Perhaps he drew on earlier theories of *yin* and *yang* and early ideas of the Five Elements, *wu hsing/wuxing*, as found in the *Grand Norm*.[7] However, the amalgamation of *yin* and *yang* and the Five Powers formed a formidable theory and philosophy of history centred around the influential school founded by Tsou Yen/Zou Yan in the state of Ch'i/Qi. As a result of Tsou Yen/Zou Yan's efforts, the idea that ruling powers followed the natural fixed sequences of the Five Powers was sufficient for the first Chinese Emperor Ch'in Shih Huang-ti/Qinshi Huangdi in 221 BCE to claim his right to rule in alliance with the ascendancy of the Power Water. Accordingly, he accepted black as his imperial colour. The succeeding Han dynasty then reverted to Earth and the colour yellow.

The function of the ruler came to be shifted towards aligning himself with the natural sequences of the Five Powers during the cycle of the year – a very different perspective from that of the Confucians. Rubin writes:

> The proponents of Tsou Yen's theory understood the role of the politician in a manner entirely different from Confucians: if for the latter the central purpose had consisted in helping and educating the people, for cosmologists the crucial part of political art was the ruler's ability to understand the timing of dynastic change and to align himself with the power of the future by introducing measures that bring the state ceremonies and calendar into accord with this power. Such a task demands that a politician recognize the portents presaging the epochal change.[8]

It was the proponents of Tsou Yen/Zou Yan's school that provided the expertise in interpreting the ways in which the ruler could align himself with natural forces. Given such knowledge it would be possible for a ruler to act in such a way that no misfortunes could occur in the natural, corporate life, or in his own personal life. It was in this context that the *Monthly Commands* provided explicit guidance. Here, the Five Powers are correlated with the seasons, Wood with spring; Fire with summer; Metal with autumn; Water with winter. And the actions of an emperor – from governing down to the colour of his clothes and what he may or may not eat – depended on the prevailing Power. The *Monthly Commands* tells us, for example, that if the ruler follows the regulations set out for summer at the wrong time rain will fall out of season, the leaves will fall from trees and plants too early, and the state will be uneasy and fearful. The balances of *yin* and *yang* throughout the year, combined with the Powers, regulated the life at court, the times when the ruler should reward or punish, the area of the palace in which to live, the colours to wear, the ritual to observe. While such practices declined subsequent to the Han dynasty, it is notable that even the last Emperor of China ousted by the Republic of China in 1911 was called "Emperor of [the Mandate] of Heaven and in accordance with the Movements [Five Agents]".

The Five Elements as cosmological functions

The Five Element theory depicts the rotation of the Elements in both a generating and a conquering cycle. In the generating or mutually-producing cycle, Wood generates Fire; Fire generates Earth; Earth generates Metal; Metal generates Water; Water generates Wood. Here, the logical sequence is taken from ordinary observation of nature. Wood fuels a fire. Fire creates ashes and so forms earth. Earth provides the environment for metal that forms in its veins. Metal encourages underground waters or provides a surface for dew as a result of condensation. Waters encourage the growth of plants and trees – the wood that feeds fire. And so the cycle begins again. Here, the generating cycle is linked with the seasons, too. The wood of spring generates the fire of summer. Fire generates the earth itself. The earth generates the metal of autumn, and from autumn we pass to the water of winter.

In the conquering or mutually-overcoming cycle, where the Elements overcome each other, Wood overcomes Earth; Earth overcomes Water; Water overcomes Fire; Fire overcomes Metal; Metal overcomes Wood. Again, the sequence is taken from natural observation. Wood overcomes earth as the roots of trees and vegetation take over, or as the plough overcomes it. Earth overcomes water by obstructing its path, as in dams, or by filling rivers with mud and silt. Water overcomes fire by destroying it completely, and fire is the element that can melt metal. Metal then overcomes wood by chopping it. The logic of the order here in the context of ancient Chinese culture is noted by Graham: "Among Chinese proto-scientific concepts the conquest cycle stands out as independent of all correlations, and probably derives directly from observation of the five basic resources at the workman's disposal. Struggling with water, fire, metal, wood or soil, there is little room for disagreement as to which of the others is most required to dam, quench, melt, cut or dig the resisting material.[9]

The two different cycles are detailed in the diagram overleaf.

The *Huai-nan-tzu/Huainanzi* combines the generating and overcoming cycles to show that each of the Elements passes through a rising and declining cycle – the *yin* and *yang* of each Element. When at its zenith, each Element can generate the next one, but at the same time can overcome the Element that is at its weakest, "death" in the chart below. Throughout the cycles each Element follows the one that it cannot overcome, as detailed in the list following the diagram.

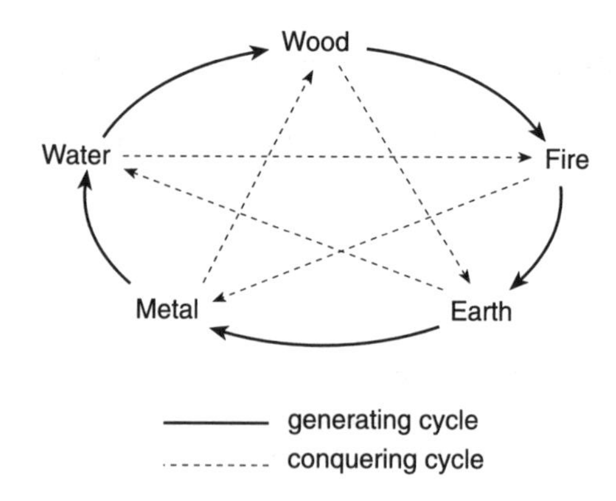

Birth	Wood	Fire	Earth	Metal	Water
Zenith	Water	Wood	Fire	Earth	Metal
Ageing	Metal	Water	Wood	Fire	Earth
Immobilization	Earth	Metal	Water	Wood	Fire
Death	Fire	Earth	Metal	Water	Wood

Importantly, what this table shows is that there is continued interaction between the Elements. Since the Five Elements were the constituents of all phenomena, they were believed to be present in the three realms of Heaven, Earth and humanity. Their mutual interaction and balances and imbalances at any one time had a profound effect on human existence. Given the rise and decline of each individual Element, it followed that the early cosmologists saw human and natural events as being dictated very much by the particular phases of the Five Elements. Such was the case not only on the larger canvas of historical dynasties, but also on the cyclical events of the days, months, seasons and years, even the human body. While one Element might be predominant at a particular time of the day, month, season or year, the relative strengths and weaknesses of the others also had their effects.

In later alchemical texts the Element that generates the following one is called the mother, and that which it generates is called the son. In the overcoming cycle, the Element that overcomes is called the father, and that which is overcome, the wife. Additionally, each Element has two sons. The interaction between sons themselves, between mother and son, father and wife are all symbols of the interaction of the forces that make the seasons, as well as such things as the relation between the different organs and parts of the body. Important, too, is the connecting of the Elements with the trigrams of the *I Ching/Yijing*. Thus we have:

Ch'ien/Qian	Metal	**Sun**	Wood
Tui/Dui	Metal	**K'an/Kan**	Water
Li	Fire	**Ken/Gen**	Earth
Chen/Zhen	Wood	**K'un/Kun**	Earth

The operation of *yin* and *yang* determines the seasons and the dominating Element for that season. For some time the trigrams and hexagrams of the *I Ching/Yijing* stood independently as a cosmological scheme. The *Monthly Commands*, indeed, reflects such a separation. However, by early Han times the process of applying the theories of *yin* and *yang* and the Five Elements in wider contexts was well in place. In the amalgamation of *yin* and *yang* with the Five Elements, the latter became the active Elements by which *yin* and *yang* could operate, and each Element had its *yin* and *yang* cycle. Each of the Elements was assigned a *yin* or *yang* predominant force. Thus, Wood was lesser *yang*; Fire was great *yang*; Metal was lesser *yin*; Water was great *yin*. Earth, the central Element was the harmonizing point of them all. The fairly easy amalgamation of the different cosmological views was possible because of the Chinese view of an interdependent, interacting and interrelated universe that was ultimately a unity of its many parts.

The nature of the Elements

Wood is the Element associated with springtime when green leaves shoot out and vegetation revives from winter. It balances with its opposite of Metal, the Element of the autumn, when trees begin to lose their leaves, their branches becoming brittle, rigid and metallic. Fire is clearly the Element of summer, its warmth and heat contrasted by the coldness and darkness of its opposite Element of Water, the Element of winter. These were easy correlates of the full waxing and waning of *yin* and *yang*. Water was an important symbol in Taoist philosophy because of its naturalness, its ability to achieve its goal by gently wearing away its rocky banks, or adapting itself to fit any vessel. According to one text:

> Hence the solution for the Sage who would transform the world lies in water. Therefore when water is uncontaminated, men's hearts are upright. When water is pure, the people's hearts are at ease. Men's hearts being upright, their desires do not become dissolute. The people's hearts being

> upright, their conduct is without evil. Hence the Sage when he rules the world, does not teach men one by one, or house by house, but takes water as his key.[10]

The Element Earth was special in that it was central and pivotal to the other Elements. Wood grows from earth, fire rises up from it, metals are found in it, and water is absorbed by it. Robinet commented:

> Earth is the center, providing cohesion to the whole. In the circle that makes up the round of the Five Agents, Earth controls transitions from one Agent to another, and it is located at the frontier that both joins and separates them: that is, Earth is where we cross from the areas of the Yang Agents (Wood and Fire) to those of the Yin Agents (Metal and Water), at the boundary of each of the sectors, the crossing points from one to another.[11]

In its central position, Earth is spatially at the centre of the four compass points and in terms of time is dominant at a point between summer and autumn.

The theory of correspondences

It was during the Han dynasty that the applications of the Five Elements begun by Tsou Yen/Zou Yan were extended not only to dynasties and historical cycles but to all manner of phenomena – the seasons, cardinal points, planets, bodily organs, calendrical signs, musical notes, colours, tastes, smells, numbers, and many other aspects. However, such correspondences necessitated the reduction of major phenomena also to five basic aspects. Sarah Allan suggests that the ancient Chinese division of the world into five geographical parts was the inspiration for the later significance of the number five.[12] Indeed, she points out that this geographical division amounted to four quarters and a central part, and that the number five was important in oracle bone inscriptions in Shang times. There were five major mountains and the deity Shang-ti/Shangdi had five ministers, perhaps thought to preside over the five geographical regions.[13] By Tsou Yen/Zou Yan's time the number five had become a sacred number and five Confucian virtues were the underpinning morality of the state. Categorizing all things in groups of fives was an attempt to unify and systematize the known universe. Bodde wrote: "This splitting up of the world into sets of fives is a typical manifestation of the rationalistic Chinese mind, which tries to find order and plan in all things, and which has therefore taken a particular delight in inventing numerical categories of all kinds, not only in fives, but in many other numbers."[14]

For convenience, the correlates of the Five Elements are listed in the table below:

	Wood	*Fire*	*Earth*	*Metal*	*Water*
Seasons	spring	summer	late summer	autumn	winter
Directions	East	South	centre	West	North
Time	morning	noon	–	evening	night
Month	1–2	4–5	3, 6, 9, 12	7–8	10–11
Weather	wind	heat	humidity	dryness	cold
Animal symbols	Blue Dragon	Red Bird	Yellow Dragon	White Tiger	Black Tortoise
Deities	Fu Hsi/ Fu Xi Tai-hao/ Daihao	Shen-nung/ Shennong Yen-ti/ Yan Di	Huang-ti/ Huangdi	Shao Hao	Chüan-hsü/ Juan Xu
Divine ministers	Kou-mang/ Gou Mang	Chu-yung/ Zhu Yong	Hou Tu/ Houdu	Ju-shou/ Ru Shou	Hsüan-ming Xuan Ming
Planets	Jupiter	Mars	Saturn	Venus	Mercury
Colours	blue-green	red	yellow	white	black
Stems	*chia/jia* & *i/yi*	*ping/bing* & *ting/ding*	*wu, mu* & *chi/ji*	*keng/geng* & *hsin/xin*	*jen/ren* & *kuei/gui*
Pitch-pipes	*chiao/jiao*	*chih/zhi*	*kung/gong*	*shang*	*yü/yu*
Sacrifices	inner door	hearth	inner court	outer court	well
Numbers	eight	seven	five	nine	six
Creatures	scaly	feathered	naked	furred, hairy	shelled
Domestic animals	sheep	fowl	ox	dog	pig
Wild animals	tiger	stag	bird	bear	monkey
Grains	wheat	millet	rye	rice	peas
Body organs	liver	heart	spleen	lung	kidneys[15]
Connected organs	gall bladder	small intestine	stomach	large intestines	bladder
Sense organs	eye	tongue	mouth	nose	ear
Body parts	muscles, nails	pulse, complexion	flesh, lips	skin, body hair	bones, hair
Fluid	tears	sweat	lymph	mucus	saliva
Growth	germination	growth	trans-formation	reaping	storing
Emotions	anger	joy	worry	grief	fear
Energy	blood	psychic	physical	vital	volitional
Body sounds	crying	laughing	singing	sobbing	groaning
Tastes	sour	bitter	sweet	acrid	salty
Smells	"goatish"	burnt	fragrant	rank	rancid
Virtues	love	wisdom	faith	righteous-ness	propriety

	Wood	*Fire*	*Earth*	*Metal*	*Water*
Ministers	for Agriculture	for War	for Works	for the Interior	for Justice
Society	the people	the state	the prince	the vassal	products
Greatnesses	beginning	change	ultimate	simplicity	origin

The above table illustrates well how the reflections on the balance between nature and human life, and beliefs in the interrelatedness of the entire cosmos, informed the Chinese psyche. The phenomenal world is portrayed as pulsating interchanges of different energies promoting and repelling each other in a multiplicity of combinations that result in what we view as life, both material and immaterial, and also spiritual. The Five Elements theory explained the way the whole world was perceived, from the macrocosmic deities to the bodily functions of the individual. The correlations posited between the transformations in nature and those of the human body illustrated the existing harmony between macrocosm and microcosm.

The Five Elements cosmology is also an attempt to create an explanation for life in terms of perpetual rhythm and pattern. Linked with the theory of *yin* and *yang*, the springtime brought about by the Element Wood, is a time of generating, of birth, and the rising of the light of *yang* from the *yin* cold and darkness of the winter time. Cosmologically, it is the beginning of creation. Microcosmically, it is the dawn of the day, and the birthing process in living beings. As the warmth of Fire succeeds, *yang* strengthens to its fullest to permit the growth and development of all things. It is a time of great production and growth. Then, once again, *yin* begins to rise in *yang* and the fulfilment of processes is brought about through the Element of Metal. As in the autumn, the time of fruitfulness, of bringing to an end the toiling on the land, nature comes to completion. Then comes the time of decay and death, the dark, the cold, brought about by Water. *Yin* is at its maximum, though the light of *yang* is now ready to begin once again its expansion to bring about rebirth. The medium for these changes is the Element of Earth, which interacts with the other Elements assisting the transformations from one stage to the next.

The Five Elements have also determined the Chinese calendar. Tradition has it that periodic cycles of sixty years were set up by the chief minister of Huang-ti/Huangdi, the Yellow Emperor. Each of the Elements has two "sons" or stems, a *yin* one and a *yang* one. These are noted in the table above, and are called the "Heavenly Stems". Each of the stems has a colour; green, for example, is the *yang* aspect of Wood and blue is its *yin* aspect. Rotating also with the ten Heavenly Stems are twelve "Earthly Branches" each symbolized by an animal – monkey, rooster, dog, pig, rat, ox, tiger, rabbit, dragon, snake, horse and goat. Given the two rotations, a particular colour from the Heavenly Stems and an animal from the Earthly Stems can only coincide once every sixty years. In referring to a year, both the Stem and the Branch is given – the year of the green goat, the year of the purple dog, for example. Sixtieth birthdays are causes for considerable celebration, since a sixty-year-old person would have completed the important cycle. While the Elements are aligned with the seasons, each one will also be predominant in a particular year. Since they are also assigned to the months of the year, the days, and the hours in the day, horoscopes – so popular in Chinese tradition – were calculated by the Elements.

Wider influences

Along with *yin* and *yang* the Five Elements theory underpinned later theories in alchemy, medicine, science, astronomy, geomancy, and art, for example. In medicine, the *Huang-ti nei-ching/Huangdi Neijing*, the *Yellow Emperor's Classic of Internal Medicine*, describes how the essential energy of the body, *ch'i/qi*, needed to be nourished by appropriate actions and living according to each of the four phases and seasons of the year. Thus, in spring, when Wood dominates:

> Together Heaven and earth give life,
> The myriad creatures thereby blossom.
> Sleep at night and rise early,
> Stroll at ease around the yard,
> Loose the hair, relax the body,
> Allow intent to come to life.
> Let it live, don't kill it:
> Give to it, don't steal from it:
> Reward it, don't punish it.[16]

Living in such a way in springtime is the means by which the body is able to stay healthy, and avoid summer colds. Such appropriate existence ensures efficient functioning of the liver. For summer, the *Huang-ti Nei-ching/Haungdi Neijing* reads:

> The *ch'i* of Heaven and earth mingle,
> The myriad creatures flower and ripen.

Sleep at night and rise early,
Don't be too greedy for the sunshine,
Don't let intent get out of hand,
Let flowering fulfil its growth,
Allow the *ch'i* to seep out from you,
As though the not-to-be wasted were outside.[17]

Here the response to the Fire Element of summer is a time of outgoing energy. The heart is protected by right living during these months, the results of neglect of it being the experience of fevers in the autumn. For autumn, under the influence of Metal, the *Huang-ti Nei-ching/Huangdi Neijing* reads:

The *ch'i* of Heaven is then gusty,
The *ch'i* of Earth is then bright.
Sleep early, rise early,
Be up with the cock.
Keep intents firm and stable,
To ease the penalties of autumn.
Gather in the harvest of daemonic ch'i,
Keep the *ch'i* of autumn calm.
Don't let intent stray outside,
Keep the *ch'i* in the lungs clear.[18]

Autumn is the time of the harvest, the time of gathering in, and this is applied to the energy and essential life-force of the body, too. Unless this is done, the lungs will be harmed and diarrhoea will be suffered in the wintertime. For the Water of winter, the *Huang-ti Nei-ching/Huangdi Neijing* says:

Water freezes, ground cracks,
Don't put strain on the Yang.
Sleep early, rise late,
Be sure to wait for the sunshine.
Keep an intent as though lurking, hiding,
As though it were a private thought,
As though you had succeeded already.
Avoid the cold, stay near the warm,
Don't allow the seeping through the skin
Which lets the *ch'i* be quickly stolen away.[19]

This is the advice of the *Huang-ti Nei-ching/Huangdi Neijing* on how to spend the cold of winter. If the advice is ignored then the kidneys will be harmed, and impotence will result in the springtime, when energy cannot be given out since it has not been properly stored up in the winter.

What is interesting about the *Huang-ti Nei-ching/Huangdi Neijing* is the emphasis it places on a holistic view of life: outward activities thus affect the internal functioning of the body. The body is viewed as a whole, its parts interactive and delicately balanced between *yin* and *yang* energies. The internal organs of the body are hollow (*fu*) or solid (*tsang/zang*). The *yin* organs are the internal ones, like the liver, lungs, spleen, kidneys and heart. The *yang* organs are those concerned with externally manifested functions; they are organs such as the stomach, large and small intestines, bladder and gallbladder. Each of the Five Elements has its *yin* and *yang* organs:

	Yin	*Yang*
Wood	liver	gall bladder
Fire	heart; heart constrictor (pericardium)	small intestine; heat supply
Earth	spleen; pancreas	stomach
Metal	lungs	large intestine
Water	kidneys	bladder

The Five Elements are still used in modern Chinese medicine. In a standard textbook for modern-day practice of acupuncture and moxibustion, their function is clearly explained: "In traditional Chinese medicine the theory of the five elements is applied to generalise and explain the nature of the zang-fu organs, the inter-relationships between them, and the relation between human beings and the natural world. It thus serves to guide clinical diagnosis and treatment."[20] While recognizing the limitations of the theory and the need for greater development of it, the Five Element theory is still retained as a useful tool: "When the theory of the five elements is applied in traditional Chinese medicine, the classification of phenomena according to the five elements and their interpromoting, interacting, overacting and counteracting relationships are used to explain both physiological and pathological phenomena, and to guide clinical diagnosis and treatment."[21] Then, too, the "mother–son" relationship, noted earlier, between the generating or promoting Element, and that Element which it promotes is still retained in clinical text books. In such medical practice the Five Element theory and *yin* and *yang* are complementary to the extent that the use of one must include the other.

In alchemical breathing exercises, the Five Elements were linked to five breaths necessary to nourish the five vital organs of the body associated with each Element. Such exercises were designed to suit each season of the year with its dominant Element. In alchemy, too, five basic ingredients represented the Five Elements, Earth usually being the central power representing the intermediate place between all opposites. In geomancy, where the positioning of a temple, grave or important building needed to match the natural forces of the site, the Five Element directions were also employed. From Han times on, the theory also penetrated the world of art in terms of the colours and animals representing the Elements. Cities were built directionally according to the principles of the Five Elements, and the family altar, likewise, was carefully constructed in line with the theory. In short, the concept and application of the theory of Five Elements, Agents, Powers or Phases, has been widespread in Chinese, and certainly Taoist, culture.

With the trigrams and hexagrams of the *I Ching/Yijing*, *yin* and *yang*, and the Five Elements, we have a cosmological picture of the universe based on the interrelation of all things in the universe. Schirokauer points out that it was a very satisfying view of the world: "Not only did it explain everything, it enabled men to feel at home in the world, part of a temporal as well as spatial continuum. It provided both an impetus to the development of science and the basis for a sophisticated theoretical framework for explaining the world."[22] The three theories were not originally Taoist or Confucian, but were generically Chinese. However, they provided such a systematic view of the universe that both Confucianism and Taoism accepted them as their fundamental cosmology. They are theories that came to be embedded deeply in the subconscious of Taoist culture. We must now turn to examine their particular relevance in T'ai Chi Ch'üan/Taijiquan.

The Five Elements and T'ai Chi Ch'üan/Taijiquan

The Five Elements and the changes of the *I Ching/Yijing* guide the student of *Tao* in the practice of T'ai Chi Ch'üan/Taijiquan whether in the movements of the *form*, or in martial art praxis. In the *form*, the Five Elements relate to the development of health maintenance, and to development of the vital energy in meditation. It is usually in the T'ai Chi *form* that individuals have their first contact with Taoist health, meditation and martial arts. Knowledge of the Five Elements assists in the understanding of their practice of T'ai Chi.

The Five Elements, as we have seen above, are Metal, Water, Fire, Wood and Earth. In the *form*, the legs are considered to be the Earth

Element, because they are connected to, and rooted deeply into, the ground. The torso is the Wood Element, as it is like the trunk of a tree, upright and supple. The arms are the Water Element, as they can flow softly in any direction without being hard or stiff. The mind is considered to be the Metal Element; this means that concentration is sharp and strong. Last, breath is considered to be the Fire Element. Breath guides and develops the vital energy that is warm or hot, and that circulates throughout the body in every movement that is performed.

Five Elements for health

The physical movements of the torso have a beneficial effect on the functions of the internal organs of the body. When we associate the Five Elements with traditional Chinese medicine, then the lungs are linked to the Metal Element, the kidneys to Water, the liver is associated with Wood, the heart with Fire and the spleen with Earth. By practising T'ai Chi on a regular basis the individual strengthens, and brings into balance, the functions of the five *yin* internal organs, because the movements have an internal massaging effect.

The lungs: Metal

Where the actions allow the individual to raise either one or both arms above his or her head, a beneficial effect on the working of the lungs occurs. In traditional Chinese medicine the lungs are in control of the vital energy and respiration, and are the uppermost organ. So when the air comes into the lungs it then extracts the clean *ch'i/qi*, vital energy, and passes it onwards to the other internal organs. Also, the arms above the head have the effect of draining the lymphatic system, which helps the body to flush out the build-up of toxins. The lungs control the descending of the vital energy into the other internal organs.

The heart: Fire

When the arms are stretched and raised up to shoulder height, the working of the heart is benefited. In traditional Chinese medicine and in Western medicine the heart is the controller of the blood. Through the slow and gentle movements of T'ai Chi, in conjunction with deep diaphragmatic breathing, the blood and tissues are alkalized. The heart can then pump more fresh blood round the whole body, removing any stagnant blockages and toxins.

The spleen: Earth

When the torso twists to the left in the *form*, the spleen is massaged. The spleen in traditional Chinese medicine governs transformation and transportation: it also controls the blood. The spleen transforms the vital energy, *ch'i/qi*, that we receive from eating and drinking and transports it to the other internal organs. The spleen also controls the raising of the vital energy.

The liver: Wood

Twisting the torso to the right side in the movements of the *form* gently massages the liver and promotes its functioning. According to traditional Chinese medicine the liver stores the blood. It also ensures the smooth flow of the vital energy. The liver regulates the volume of blood in the whole body in conjunction with physical activity. In females it regulates menstruation. When the body is at rest the blood flows back to the liver. When the body is active the blood flows into the muscles.

The kidneys: Water

Bending slightly forward from the waist, or sinking downward by bending the knees, aids the functioning of the kidneys. In traditional Chinese medicine the kidneys store the body's essence and govern birth, growth, reproduction and development. They produce marrow, fill up the brain and strengthen the bones. They govern water and control the reception of the vital energy, *ch'i/qi*. The essence of the kidneys is a very precious substance that we inherit from our parents. If the kidney essence is strong then the bones of the body will be strong as well. According to the Five Elements theory the kidneys are associated with Water. Thus, they govern the transformation and transportation of the body fluids. The kidneys have the function of providing vital energy for the bladder to store and transfer urine. The kidneys act as a gate that can open and close allowing urination to be normal in quantity and colour. Like the lungs, they control the reception of clean vital energy into the body. The lungs cause the vital energy to descend downwards into the kidneys and the kidneys respond by "holding" the vital energy down. If the kidneys cannot hold the vital energy down, then the energy will surge upwards into the chest causing congestion that may lead to chronic asthma.

The movements of the body in conjunction with the practice of the T'ai Chi *form* aid the functioning of the five *yin* organs of the body. It is said that the physical *yang* movements of the body will have the opposite effect on the *yin* organs inside the body. Thus, the outside and inside are deeply interrelated. The physical, emotional and mental aspects of the body are interconnected, and will respond both in a *yin* or *yang* action. For example, if the physical movements on the outside of the body are soft, gentle and *yin*, then there will be a *yang* positive effect on the internal organs. Then, the emotions will become more in balance and the mind will become clear. But if the physical actions are hard and damaging, *yang*, there will be a *yin* negative reaction on the internal organs; the emotions will be out of balance and the mind will be scattered.

Balancing the emotions through T'ai Chi Ch'üan/Taijiquan

The Five Elements, therefore, are also associated with the balance of the individual's emotional state. Each of the particular elements is connected to an organ, which then corresponds to the negative or positive expression of an emotion.

- The lung's *yin* negative emotion is sadness, grief. The *yang* positive emotion is courage.
- The heart's *yin* negative emotion is cruelty, hatred. The *yang* positive emotion is love, honour, respect.
- The *yin* negative emotion of the spleen is worry. The *yang* positive emotion is fairness.
- The *yin* negative emotion of the liver is anger. The *yang* positive emotion is kindness.
- The *yin* negative emotion of the kidneys is fear, stress. The *yang* positive emotion is gentleness.

Through regular practice of T'ai Chi the balance of the emotions is maintained. If the emotions are kept in balance the vital energy of the body is developed and strengthened. In the practice of Taoist meditation it is important that the emotional aspect is kept in check. Learning to do a Taoist inner-dissolving exercise, where the individual mentally looks deep inside his or her self, helps this. To do this, the individual concentrates his or her mind on a particular organ of the five *yin* organs and begins to dissolve mentally any negative emotions or blockages that he or she may come across. These blockages take several training sessions over a long period of time to remove, depending on the actual emotional state of balance of the individual. Such concentration is practised either in a stationary position, like sitting or lying down, or it can be done while walking or performing the slow movements of T'ai Chi. There are many different training methods used to help the individual visualize the removal of emotional blockages. One, is to think of the blockages as blocks of ice that the individual begins to melt, decreasing their size gradually until they actually disappear into a watery substance that is flushed away by the surging of the unblocked negative energy. If the blockage of negative energy has manifested itself over a long period of time then, as the individual slowly begins to dissolve it, he or she might begin to feel the negative energy release itself slowly or very quickly. It will cause a certain reaction as it is released from the body. The individual might begin to weep or cry, which is a *yin* emotion of the lungs being released. Or, there might be a show of anger by yelling and shouting, which is a *yin* negative emotion being released from the liver.

Once the individual has gone around all of the five *yin* organs, dissolving any blockages that are found, each organ is thanked for the work that it performs every minute of the day and night. Thus, love and compassion are expressed for the transforming of the negative emotion of each organ into useful ones. It is essentially through such practice that the individual develops a greater sensitivity and connection of his or her mind to the workings of the internal organs. In this way good health and a balanced emotional state are maintained. But, most importantly, the practitioner will be able to develop and harness the vital energy of the five *yin* organs and begin to fuse the energies together for the deeper aspects of Taoist meditation. Such a level of energy development is called the "fusion of the Five Elements", and obviously takes a great deal of time and dedicated practice to achieve. It will combine both seated meditation as well as moving meditation to harness each organ's vital energy and store it in what is called the lowest elixir place that is located just below the navel. In Taoist meditation this is known as *tan-t'ien/dantian*, or the "lower cauldron". As *Lao Tzu/Laozi* said in the book of *Wen-tzu/Wenzi*:

> Heaven loves its vitality, earth loves its constants, humanity loves its feelings.
>
> The vitality of heaven is the sun and moon, stars and planets, thunder and lightning, wind and rain.

> The constants of earth are water, fire, metal, wood and soil.
>
> The feelings of humanity are thought, intelligence and emotions.[23]

The fusion of the Five Elements is a form of Taoist internal alchemy. It is an advanced and high-level practice, where the individual fuses together the vital energy of each of the five *yin* organs and glands to produce a pure energy. Such pure energy takes the form of a crystallized energy ball, like a crystal or pearl. It takes a long time to create it inside the lower cauldron or *tan-t'ien/dantian*, and not everyone develops an energy ball like this. However, what might develop is a great amount of heat within the lower cauldron, or an awareness of strong concentration for long periods of time occurs. Through the regular practice of the T'ai Chi *form* the mind is developed and disciplined sufficiently to concentrate and guide the vital energy from the five *yin* organs into the lower cauldron. The forming of the energy ball is the first step of the Five Element fusion exercise that transforms the individual's consciousness to a new and high level of awareness.

Martial arts

The two-person exercise known as *Pushing Hands*, which has been mentioned in a number of contexts already, is applicable to both the *form*, and T'ai Chi as a martial art. Here, two individuals try to uproot each other's balance while remaining in contact with each other. They try to push each other off balance by using the other person's strength against him or her. Maintaining balance and equilibrium is the key to the exercise. Chang San-feng/Zhang Sanfeng mentions in his *T'ai Chi Ch'üan Ching/Taijiquan Jing.*

> Step forward, step back,
> look left, look right,
> and central equilibrium
> are the five elements.[24]

Pushing Hands involves not only the Five Elements but also *yin* and *yang*, with a balancing or controlling *yin* aspect and a destructive or counter-controlling *yang* aspect. The diagram below relates the Five Elements to the stepping actions that can be used in the *Pushing Hands* exercise as a martial art and in the practice of the T'ai Chi *form*, illustrating the directions in which the individual moves. The diagram is reputed to have been created and used by Chang San-feng/Zhang

Sanfeng to describe the theory of the Five Elements in the practice of T'ai Chi. *Pushing Hands* is a popular form of exercise found in all the many different schools or styles of T'ai Chi. It is an exercise that develops sensitivity, balance, co-ordination and concentration. There is a saying that to be able to control another person, you must first be able to control yourself. In the practice of T'ai Chi we study and practise the *form* to discipline ourselves, and we practise the *Pushing Hands* exercise as a means to learn how to control another person's balance and energy.

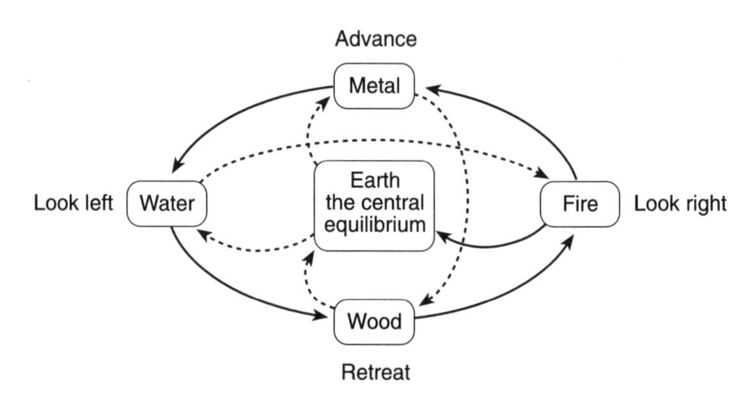

As shown in the diagram the Earth Element is the controlling Element that links the other four Elements together. In the *Pushing Hands* exercise, a *yin* controlling method occurs when the opponent moves ahead by stepping to either side. If a forward step is taken just as the opponent is in the middle of transferring weight onto his or her other leg, while stepping sideways, then he or she is easily unbalanced since there is no root, or firm connection to the ground. Here, the body is light and soft as water and is momentarily in a state of vulnerability. This would be known as Metal overcoming Water. On the other hand, slowness in trying to unbalance an opponent, allowing him or her to regain balance while you, yourself, are still stepping forward, places one's own balance in jeopardy. This is known as Fire overcoming Metal. All of this happens within a split second. In the event that an opponent pushes without simultaneously stepping forward, then one of his or her limbs is gripped while he or she steps backward, thus pushing the opponent off balance. Here Wood is overcoming Earth. But, if you step backward prematurely, so that your partner can both see and feel what you have done, he or she is then able to step forward and push you off balance.

This would then be Metal overcoming Wood. Critical in such martial art praxis is the understanding of the energy generated or dissipated by the opponent. In the *Notes to the Original "Treatise"*, supplying comments on the *Treatise on T'ai Chi Ch'üan/Taijiquan* of Wang Tsung Yüeh/Wang Zongyue, we find the words:

> Striking the opponent when his attack is imminent but has not yet issued forth is called "striking the contained energy". Awaiting the opponent's touch in stillness and striking after his attack is already under way is called "striking the incoming energy." Striking the opponent after he has landed on emptiness and seeks to change his energy is called "striking the retreating energy." Looking at it in this way and paying close attention to study, one naturally attains spontaneity and perfect clarity.[25]

The principle of the Five Element theory in the Tai Chi Ch'üan/Taijiquan *form* corresponds to the cultivation of the vital energy from the five directions. The direction of North benefits the kidneys, which is attributed to the Water Element. The South direction benefits the heart and is attributed to the Fire Element. The West direction benefits the lungs and is attributed to the Metal Element. The East direction benefits the liver and is attributed to the Wood Element. Standing in one place corresponds and benefits the spleen and is attributed to the Earth Element. So, by performing the *form*, the individual harnesses and cultivates the vital energy that surrounds his or her self from all directions for the benefit of health maintenance, and for meditation purposes. In order to become closer to *Tao*, Taoists realized that, through the theory and understanding of the Five Elements, they could look deeper into themselves and become consciously aware of the balance between Heaven, Earth and humanity.

6 Energy

Like so many other cultures and religions, the dream of immortality, of the continued existence of the self beyond the grave, was no less featured in the Chinese search to make sense of the life that preceded death. For many Chinese, and certainly for Taoists, immortality became the goal of life. And this was not really a strictly *religious* goal, for it had nothing to do with communication with a divine being in an afterlife, or the metaphysical fusion with a divine force. It was more a sense of a long bodily life, *ch'ang-sheng/changsheng*, which stretched so far into the future that it became eternal. Thus, there is a continuum of existence without the break from life to death, albeit that death appeared to happen. The goal came to be the replacement of the physical, mortal, perishable body with an equally physical, but immortal and imperishable body that developed gradually within the body framework. It was alchemy that provided the means for such transformation. Similar ideas inform the theory that underpins the practice of T'ai Chi Ch'üan/Taijiquan, which has adapted many concepts of inner alchemy into its theoretical framework.

As the forerunner of metallurgy and chemistry, ancient alchemy was the process by which base metals were transmuted into gold. In a physical sense, too, it was the transmutation of the mortal body into an immortal one. Since gold was an immutable substance, turning the bones to gold and the flesh to jade were believed to be ways in which the physical body could also become immutable. Taoists adopted both these pathways. The Chinese use the word *tan/dan*, which means "cinnabar" "elixir" or "pill", to refer to alchemy in its widest sense. Cinnabar is a red mineral from which we get mercury, which, like gold, was believed to be a *Tao*-like substance, that is to say, a basic substance in the universe. To use Schipper's words, "these minerals and metals are the products of the interaction of cosmic energies and time and thus constitute the quintessence of our planet".[1] Sometimes, the two words "gold-cinnabar", *chin-tan/jindan*, are combined as the term for alchemy. Chinese distinguishes between alchemical practices that are conducted in the laboratory, and are concerned with the transmutation of metals and minerals as "outer", "external" alchemy with the word *wai*, and the "inner", "internal" transformations of the body as *nei*.[2] In the pages that follow, then, we shall be referring to outer alchemy or *wai-tan/waidan* and inner alchemy or *nei-tan/neidan*.

While turning base metals into gold was certainly a goal in itself, both outer and inner alchemists sought to promote good health, youthful vitality, longevity and eternal life. It was simply the interpretation of the means that differed. Both sought purification and perfection, one of metals and the other of the body, though many great alchemists of the outer alchemy schools were also dedicated to the perfection and immortality of the body through the ingestion of substances perfected in the laboratory. In this sense, both outer and inner alchemists conducted *physiological* alchemy, as it is sometimes referred to. But pure inner alchemy did not need the external aids of ingested substances mixed in the furnaces of the laboratory to gain immortality. Here, the path was thoroughly internalized by concentration on the inner body itself in order to transform it into *Tao*. It is such inner alchemy that is relevant to T'ai Chi Ch'üan/Taijiquan.

A duality and complementarity of the material and the physical pervades both inner and outer alchemy – not least because the Chinese never separated the physical body from the spiritual self or the mind, as we shall see. In the three aspects of the universe – Heaven, Earth and humanity – only humanity is perishable. This may have led to the belief that since all emanates from *Tao* there must be some aspect of the human self that also has the same immutability and permanence of *Tao*: it merely has to be recreated. Secrets of the creation of an immortal self were, however, carefully guarded, and the language of the texts was deliberately partial, symbolic, misleading and only for initiates. Traditions were oral before being committed to esoteric language that today makes it difficult to decipher without the aid of good commentaries.

There was also an overlap between outer and inner alchemy in practice, language and, as noted above, aim, especially in their earliest phases. Outer alchemists might concentrate also on inner meditative practices and inner alchemists on an alchemical "Golden Pill" to finalize their process of immortalization. Some alchemists were both outer and inner at the same time, and many alchemical texts reflect the same *wai-tan/waidan–neitan/neidan* character. However, the great flowering of outer alchemy in the T'ang/Tang dynasty was to mark also its demise and, thereafter, particularly in Sung/Song times, the complementary nature of the two gave way to the precedence of inner alchemy. However, the legacy of outer alchemy to its inner counterpart was a commonality of language, so that inner alchemists used the language of the laboratory to depict the inner transformations of the body into an immortal self.

The origins of alchemical ideas

The origins of alchemy reach far back into the distant shamanic practices that obtained well before Taoism. It is to the ancient practices of the shamans – the workers of magic who could enhance life through spells to ward off illness, disease and malevolent spirits – that alchemy owes its beginnings. In addition, there are the tales of great sages who could ride the clouds on the backs of dragons, defy the ageing process and death, and enjoy immortality. Here we have the ideas of magical extension of life beyond its normal years. By the fourth century BCE there seems to have been what Daniel Overmyer terms an "active quest for immortality" in a variety of ways.[3] But on a more philosophical level, innate in the Chinese psyche was also – as we have seen in earlier chapters – a sense not only of the interrelation of microcosmic Earth with macrocosmic Heaven, but also belief in what Needham described as an "organist conception in which every phenomenon was connected with every other according to a hierarchical order".[4] Such a view led to the replication of the macrocosm of the universe within the microcosm of the human body, even with the same hierarchical distinctions. Such a concept is at the root of inner alchemy. And in the same way that Heaven and Earth are characterized by the rhythmic changes of *Tao* so, also, is the energy and breath of all life. Sivin illustrated the point admirably:

> In China the earliest and in the long run the most influential scientific explanations were in terms of time. They made sense of the momentary event by fitting it into the cyclical rhythms of natural process. The life cycle of every individual organism – its birth, growth, maturity, decay, and death – went on eternally and in regular order: the cycle of day and

> night, which regulated the changes of light and darkness, and the cycle of the year, which regulated heat and cold, activity and quiescence, growth and stasis. It was the nested and intermeshed cycles of the celestial bodies that governed the seasonal rhythms and, through them, the vast symphony of individual life courses.[5]

Alchemy was sensitive to such pulsating and rhythmic forces and energies in the macrocosm, and saw them as no different in the laboratory furnace or the human body. Thus, all alchemy was conducted in conjunction with the phases of the cosmos – the moon, the sun, the stars, the time of year, month, week, day. Harmonizing the microcosm of the body – whether with a Golden Pill or through inner meditation and visualization – with the macrocosm and dynamism of *Tao* was the philosophical idea that informed alchemy in the past and present, including the practice of T'ai Chi today.

The first Chinese alchemists were traditionally the legendary emperors Huang-ti/Huangdi and Yü/Yu. Emperor Huang-ti/Huangdi was taught about *Tao* and such topics as medicinal substances and meditation by a number of immortals. Legend has it that, after ruling for more than a hundred years, he rose to Heaven on the back of a dragon, along with some of his court. The legendary Emperor Yü/Yu was credited with the smelting of metals and the differentiating of them into *yin* and *yang* categories.

But it was particularly with the widely skilled *fang-shih/fangshi* that alchemical practices were obvious. Their skills in magical healing and attempts to prolong life through herbs and minerals were to have a significant impact on Taoism. Those interested in longevity and immortality were the forerunners of the great alchemists. They occupy a long span of historical time from the early centuries BCE to well into the early centuries of the first millennium. They created potions for immortality from plant, mineral and animal sources. They advocated breathing techniques, gymnastic exercises, dietetics, and sexual practices for the promotion of longevity, and kept alive the notion of the spirit world that invaded the human realm. Indeed, Robinet considered that inner alchemy derived "in direct lineage" from the *fang-shih/fangshi*.[6] One well-known *fang-shih/fangshi* of the second century BCE was Li Shao-chün/Li Shaojun, who won the favour of Emperor Wu for his experiments in making gold, and for his medical practices. He later was reputed to have become an immortal[7] and is recognized today as the first Chinese alchemist.

The Golden Elixir

The foundation of much alchemical practice was the belief in the possibility of creating a drug, a pill or an elixir that would prolong life indefinitely, reverse the ageing process to permit youthful energy and bring about an immortal existence. As one author puts it: "Procreation may be nature's necessity, but immortality would be mankind's masterpiece."[8] The modern term for such praxis is *macrobiotics*, albeit one that has more natural connotations in today's world. Substances used to make the ultimate of pills, *the* Elixir, varied from herbs and plants to minerals and animals. Some believed in a specific plant of immortality to be obtained from the elusive islands in the ocean in the East. But while emperors sent expeditions to procure it, the islands and the plant were never found. While such an aim might seem to be a worldly one, Sivin points out that it was an aim that still had "self-cultivation, a means toward transcendence" as its informing goal.[9] The Elixir is identified with the butterfly's transformation from its chrysalis; the transformation of the yolk of an egg into a baby chick; a fish resting in still water; the moon rising in the evening across a still lake; the morning mists on green hills. It is the naturalness that is the expression of *Tao* in the universe. For outer alchemy, the Elixir is an ingested, purified substance. For inner alchemy it is the stilling of the mind to emptiness, to singleness and unity of mind – a gathering of inner energy that begins the process of the formation of an inner Elixir. Here, the Elixir is seen as an internal essence that is innate in humankind, a pure, spiritual energy that has been refined to perfection, "the unfragmented original essence" as Liu I-ming/Liu Yiming called it.[10] However, ordinarily, it remains unrefined and lost to the desires and enticements of worldly living – a state of living, as we shall see, that T'ai Chi seeks to reverse.

The Taoist anatomy of the body

The traditional Taoist view of the inside of the body is one of a microcosm that reflects in its entirety the macrocosm of the universe. Imagine a journey through your own body that is like a journey through the earth, the stars, the planets and the whole universe. Inside the body are the mountains, lakes, oceans and plains of the earth, the spirits and deities that inhabit the heavens, and the primordial essences that are the stuff of the universe before it ever came into being. The outcome of such a belief is that the body is an expression of *Tao*. The physical being is not that which has to be denied in the search for a subtle self that transcends it as a soul. The physical being itself has the answers to the problems of life. It, itself, is capable of reversing the attitudes of mind that connect it with the materialism of the world, back to the primordial *Tao-ness* that it really is.

We all know that emotions affect our energies in life. The mind is difficult to still, the heartbeat is affected by fear, emotional upset, sex, anxiety, excessive happiness or sorrow. Leakage of energy in the body leads to tiredness, sometimes exhaustion and illness and contributes to ageing. One of the aims of internal alchemy is to prevent such leakage of energy. And, like the rhythm of *yin* and *yang* in the cosmos, the body develops its *yang*-evolving energies during the first part of its life, before the declining, ageing *yin* takes over and gradually increases until the point of death, when *yang* is used up. *Yang*, too is representative of the subtle and spiritual aspects of the self, *yin* of the grosser, physical self, just as Heaven was formed from cosmic *yang* energy and Earth from cosmic *yin*.

The body also has energy channels that convey energy throughout the body, as well as important "openings". These are crucial to the understanding of T'ai Chi. When blocked, illness occurs through imbalance. Such a theory lies at the heart of the practice of acupuncture. There are special circulations of energy that we shall look at later in more detail, but here we need merely to note that the flow of energy without blockage is essential for the development of the body: in Taoism, it was essential for immortality. The flow of energy, *ch'i/qi*, in the body is believed to match the flow of cosmic energy when operating without impediment. Some is *yin*, passive and descending, and some is *yang*, active and rising. The cosmic energy of the universe is, then, mirrored in the whole body. And, in the same way that the universe is a unity of both physical and subtle matter, so the physicality of the body alongside its subtle energies and aspects are seen as a unity. There is no dualism of spirit and matter in the Taoist, Chinese, or T'ai Chi concept of the self. Immortality, then, would be as much of the body as of the spiritual essence.

Three cinnabar fields are also found in the body, roughly, the lowest in the abdomen, the middle in the thorax, and the uppermost in the head. They are the *tan-t'ien/dantian*, also called the "elixir fields". The lowest is placed between the kidneys, a space, Robinet stated, that "symbolizes the mid-point between Yin and Yang, the equivalent of the Supreme Pinnacle, the Center, and the highest point of the world that encloses

Yin and Yang. It is both the primordial couple and the place of their union, and at the same time the child born of them".[11] It is here, then, that the process of immortality begins with what is called a Spirit Embryo, and is the place where energy is generated. It is, therefore, the most important of the three fields. The middle field, often referred to as the "Yellow Court", the "Crimson Palace" or "Golden Palace", is in the area of the "Golden Gate Towers" below the heart and spleen. The uppermost field is about three inches within the head from the point between the eyebrows, and is sometimes referred to as the "Mud Pill Court", or the "Palace of Ni-huan".[12] Names, terms, and locations are, however, not at all consistent. Each of the regions is an area of heat, suggested by the word *tan/dan* – they are the furnaces of the body that will replace those of outer alchemy.

Also in the body are three important "gates" or "passes" through which energy passes. Such gates are to be found along the spine, and control entry into the cinnabar fields. The lowest is situated at the coccyx, or between the kidneys. The second is in a vertebra of the chest, between the shoulder blades. The top one, also called the "House of Wind", is at the occiput, where the spine joins the skull. Then there are nine orifices, which are the three fields, the three "gates" and three other points in the head. These nine are crucial to the circuit of energy, *ch'i/qi*, through the appropriate meridians. There are also "bridges" that serve the purpose of linking the major meridians.[13]

In Taoism generally, the body was believed to be host to the deities of the universe, and to *Tao*. The entanglements with the world obscured this reality, and the inner body was neither known nor nourished. The deities of the inner self that nourished the inner energies and nature were what kept it alive, kept it functioning. When they departed, there could be no life at all. In a wonderfully expressive statement of the goal here, Robinet wrote of the adept:

> By contemplating himself and by locating himself in a correctly aligned geometric schema that represents the cosmos as a sort of mandala, he finally identifies himself correctly and ritually in relationship to the axis of the world. Further, by rediscovering the Prime Mover, he rediscovers the order of the world and his own relationship to it. The two movements go together. He must impose order on the world to reconcile it to himself and to reconcile himself with himself.[14]

These words would also be applicable to the theory informing T'ai Chi Ch'üan/Taijiquan. Such an alignment is brought about by contemplation of the inner nature of the self that is ultimately *Tao*. But the *Tao* that is experienced in its totality within is concomitant with the development of a new body that is *Tao*, a new spiritual body of cosmic unity, a spiritual self that merges with the cosmos. We must turn now to examine how that comes about.

The Three Treasures

Critical to the understanding of the body, to the understanding of T'ai Chi, to the experience of *Tao*, and to the attaining of immortality through the development of a new spiritual self, a spiritual Embryo that develops into an immortal body, are the Three Treasures – *ching/jing*, *ch'i/qi* and *shen.* They are sometimes called Three Flowers, Herbs or Jewels. It is these Treasures that make life possible. Cosmically, they are the functioning of the energies of *Tao* in the universe, just as they are responsible for the life-giving essences of the body. While the first two of these may have been rather undifferentiated in earliest times, they all came to have different, yet interrelated, functions in the cosmos as much as in the human body. They are energies within the body, but energies that were once pure *Tao*. Restoring the original purity of each, and their primordial nature and unity, is the aim of inner alchemy and of T'ai Chi Ch'üan/Taijiquan. Each obtains both inwardly, in each individual life, and cosmically, in the universe itself. *Ching/jing* is the vital essence, vitality, sometimes equated with semen, though it has wider meanings; *ch'i/qi* is vital breath and energy; *shen* is spirit. The importance of the Three is illustrated in the following extract from the *Secret Instructions of the Holy Lord on the Scripture of Great Peace*:

> To pursue long life you must guard energy and harmonize spirit and essence. Never let them leave your body, but continue to think of them as joined in one. With prolonged practice your perception will become finer and subtler. Quite naturally you will be able to see within your body. The physical body will become gradually lighter, the essence more brilliant, and the light more concentrated. In your mind you will feel greatly restful, delighted and full of joy. You will go along with the energy of Great Peace. By then cultivating yourself, you can turn around and go along with all without. Within there will be perfect longevity; without there will be perfect accordance with the order of the universe. Without the exertion of any muscle you naturally attain Great Peace.[15]

Such is a description of the effects of harmonizing these three essential components of existence. The greater the degree of harmony, the greater the strength and longer the life of the individual. Leakage of any essence or energy from the body is, as was noted above, inimical to health and long life, and leakage occurs through engagement in the world in such a way that stress, anxiety, emotion, sorrow, excessive eating, drinking, desires, aversions – all contribute to loss of the Three Treasures. Conversely, maintaining the Three Treasures and refining them into one energized unity, results in immortality, for the primordial essence of all life that is *Tao* becomes the very essence of the self.

Ching/jing

Ching/jing is *yin* vital essence, that which generates all life. It provides us with our state, or lack of, well-being, depending on its levels and quality. At its coarsest level, it is bodily male and female sexual fluids, which generate new life, and reside in the lowest cinnabar field. But it can, in addition, refer to wider secretions of the body,[16] and hence to substances like saliva that should not be leaked from the body any more than sexual fluid. It is also the vital essence that creates forms, both on the worldly level, and on the cosmic level of the creative energy that brings about the cosmos from the primordial Void that is *Tao*. It is the essence in the seed that makes things what they are, as much as the essence in the Void that makes the universe what it is. It is also that which permits the wisdom of the sage:

> The vital essence of all things:
> It is this that brings them to life.
> It generates the five grains below
> And becomes the constellated stars above.
> When flowing amid the heavens and the earth
> We call it ghostly and numinous.
> When stored within the chests of human beings,
> We call them sages.[17]

The storage of this essence in our chests, that is to say, in the middle cinnabar field, and not in the lowest cinnnabar field where it is normally concentrated, is necessary for the enlightenment that the sage attains. Increasing it, then, brings health and longevity, decreasing it, illness and death. It is decreased by the involvement of the mind in the world.

Ch'i/qi

Ch'i/qi has wide meanings – anything from the subtle breath of life itself to abdominal wind.[18] Originally, it referred to the steam arising from cooked rice. But its importance lies in the fact that it is the emanation of *Tao* in all aspects of life from the cosmos at large to its expression in the human body itself. It is cause and effect in the changing rhythms of all that exists. Livia Kohn puts this admirably: "It is a continuously changing, forever flowing force, an energy that can appear and disappear, can be strong and weak, can be controlled and overwhelming. *Qi* is what moves on in the changing rhythm of the seasons; *qi* shines in the rays of the sun; *qi* is what constitutes health or sickness; *qi* is how we live, move, eat, sleep."[19] So while it can mean the air that we breath, and the breath itself, it can also be indicative of energy and vitality. Michael Page likens it to a cut diamond that reflects different lights, yet is the same diamond.[20]

The cosmic importance of *ch'i/qi* cannot be overestimated. It is the *One* in the Taoist process of creation, the first subtle entity that emerges from *Tao*. As such it is also *Te*, the expression of *Tao* in the whole cosmos. Divided it is *yin* and *yang*, and therefore informs the rhythms of rise and fall, ascent and descent, advance and retreat and the swing of all things between polarities. It is what makes possible all the changes and transformations in the universe and what, at the same time, interrelates and unites all the changing phenomena. It is also the causative nature of the Five Elements, that which makes Wood the Element of spring, Fire of summer, Metal of autumn, and Water of winter. It is what gives each of the "ten thousand things" its special nature; and the particular nature of it in each individual makes you what you are and I what I am. Ultimately it is the subtle link between all things and *Tao*.

Medics of ancient China were less interested in the organs of the body than in the fluids and energies that pervaded it: healing the *ch'i/qi* energy was the most important facet of restoring health.[21] For health and longevity it is essential, but can only be stirred, nourished and stored when the body is diverted from external emotions and over-involvement with the world. In inner alchemy it will be the crucial link between *ching/jing* and *shen* and is located mainly in the middle cinnabar field between the *ching/jing* in the lowest and *shen* in the uppermost, though T'ang alchemists believed it to be in the lowest field.[22] Breathed into the body it is *yang* and embodies the energies of the sun and fire. Breathed out it is *yin*, and embodies the energies of the moon and water. It circulates in the meridians of the body and is affected by emotions, temperature, rest, exhaustion, so that being over-animated disperses it, and getting tired and exhausted wastes it. Here, it is in its subtle form in the body, but it also condenses into more solid tangible forms such as the vital organs and into even more condensed form as the skeleton, muscles and flesh. In the same way it can be subtle cosmic air or condense to form huge mountains.

While its presence in the body can only be inferred through imbalances, energy loss and gain, and the like, the physical act of breathing, and the necessity of breath for life meant that respiration was the most observable facet of *ch'i/qi* in human existence. It was an observation that prompted breathing techniques as a means of nourishing the *ch'i/qi* in the body. Since health, and life itself, depended on *ch'i/qi*, then it was also thought to be important not to let much of the air out – from any part of the body (hence a need for attention to diet!). Retaining the air that was inhaled and letting as little out as possible became a means to store and nourish *ch'i/qi*, and the Taoist adept was expected to feed on it, and nourish it within the body.

Instead of there being just one breath in the body, there were thought to be many, both subtle and gross, and some pure and some impure. Indeed, from the primordial state of Void came not just one Breath, but nine, which combined to form subtle or gross realms. In the body, different breaths exist, different kinds of *ch'i/qi* with different functions apart from breathing – digestion, circulation of the blood, gland secretion, mind processes, for example.[23] Sexual energy (as opposed to fluids, which are *ching/jing*) is also *ch'i/qi*, for it is the creative energy that produces new life through the emission of sexual fluid. But sexual emissions, too, were seen as a loss of *ch'i/qi* from the body and many Taoists sought to prevent ejaculation of semen or loss of menstrual blood. Inner alchemy aimed to get rid of impure breaths and retain pure ones. It sought to conserve *ch'i/qi*, to nourish it, to circulate it properly, and to refine it. The purpose is no different today in the practice of T'ai Chi Ch'üan/Taijiquan, which aims primarily to direct the flow of energy within the body. Heavenly *ch'i/qi* influences the weather, earthly *ch'i/qi* the lines of energy that pervade the land. Both must be in harmony, for it is imbalance between them that causes disasters. Similarly, every entity has its own special *ch'i/qi*, but that, too, has to be kept in balance with the energies of both Earth and Heaven. How far that balance is inhibited in today's world is put rather well by Mantak Cha and Juan Li:

> Just as the universe is an integrated whole, the body is an integrated whole, with each part connected to and dependent on the other parts. Yet as we become adults leading sedentary lives, we often forget to use all the parts of our bodies. We depend on the head and arms, using the spine, hips and legs only to get us from the car to the elevator to the swivel seat, where we can use the head and arms again. By restricting our movement, we

forget how to move strongly, lithely, and efficiently. When we forget how to live fully in our bodies, we overly restrict the way we move, and eventually we forget who we really are.[24]

Even if viewed at its most superficial level, T'ai Chi Ch'üan/Taijiquan is an excellent way of overcoming the stagnant energies that have built up through habitual lifestyles, exercising every fibre and part of the body in a balanced way.

Shen

Shen is spirit, the soul, the psyche, the spiritual aspect in the self. Cosmically, it is the Void, the undifferentiated *Tao* of primordial Chaos. In the body, *shen* is associated with the heart, the seat of emotions, with the mind, the deepest consciousness, and with the nervous system. However, though connected with the heart, it functions through other organs also. Thus, for example, spirit of ambition is associated with the kidneys, intention with the spleen, the higher spirit with the lungs, and the lower with the liver.[25] As consciousness it is not of the kind that is attracted to the stimuli of the world, though it makes such consciousness possible. Rather, it is consciousness in itself, in natural stillness. The goal of inner alchemy, and of T'ai Chi, is to purify, nourish and transmute *ch'ing/jing* and *ch'i/qi* into *shen*. *Shen* is the part of us that is intimately *Tao* and the means by which we can experience *Tao*. It is the means of return to the primordial state of *Tao* from whence we sprang. Located in the uppermost field of the body, in the head, it is the flower that needs to develop from the roots of *ching/jing* and the stem of *ch'i/qi*.

The Spirit Embryo

At the beginning of his classic *Understanding Reality* the eleventh century Taoist Chang Po-tuan/Zhang Boduan began his teaching with the following words:

> If you do not seek the great way to leave the path of delusion, even if you are intelligent and talented you are not great. A hundred years is like a spark, a lifetime is like a bubble. If you only crave material gain and prominence, without considering the deterioration of your body, I ask you, even if you accumulate a mountain of gold can you buy off impermanence?[26]

As an inner alchemist, the impermanence of the self was an encumbrance that Chang Po-tuan/Zhang Boduan sought to overcome. But it was not the survival of the spiritual self as opposed to the bodily one. As pointed out earlier, there was no separation of spirit and body in Chinese thought. The creation of a *new* and *physically spiritual* body was the ultimate aim of the inner alchemists. Before examining the intricacies of inner alchemy, then, it is important to pause and look at this ultimate goal.

It was as early as Han times that the belief arose in the possibility of developing an immortal foetus, an embryo, within the body. It was thought to be subtle, light, and yet physical. It was given many names – the Golden Embryo, the Holy Embryo, the Immortal Embryo, Golden Elixir, the True Person Cinnabar of the North, the Golden Pill, the Pearl. It is formed after a long period of inward concentration. Chang San-feng/Zhang Sanfeng is reputed to have written: "At this time a point of absolutely positive vitality crystallizes within the centre. It is stored in the time when desires are cleared and emotions are stilled, yet it has appearance and form. When you get to this stage, the breath stays in the 'womb'. Incubation inside and out with unerring timing is called the ten months' work."[27] It is the True Self and is formed when *shen* is purified and unified with *ch'i/qi* and *ching/jing*, the Three being indistinguishable and united. The proper circulation of energies in the body feed and nourish it until, when fully developed, it is able to leave the body like the butterfly that leaves the chrysalis.

The point at which the Spirit Embryo is formed is synonymous with the opening of what is called the *Mysterious Pass* or *Gate*. For this to occur there must be an emptying of the self, in the sense of a cessation of egoistic involvement with the world. Such a state is sometimes also called the *Mysterious Female*, the imagery being of the emptiness of the womb into which the embryo is planted. It is described, too, as the "centre", but not so much as the centre of the body as the central equilibrium of the self, "an undefined opening anywhere in the eternity of time and the infinity of space".[28] As such it is the central "point" of the universe, too, the same axis as the *Tao* that is centripetal to all life. But it is an opening that has to be worked for:

> Nourish yourself thus within,
> Tranquil and still in the void,
> While at source concealing brilliance
> Which illuminates within your whole body.
> Shut and close up the mouth,
> Repressing within the spiritual trunk,

The senses all swallowed up
To gently support that pearl so young.
Observe it there, the unobvious –
So close by and easy to seek.[29]

The whole process of creating and then nourishing the Spirit Embryo through its "conception", its growth, and its birth into the Void is what inner alchemy entails.

Harmony of body and mind

The harmony of the inner body, a calm inner state, a still mind, and freedom from extraneous influences are general characteristics of inner alchemy and T'ai Chi Ch'üan/Taijiquan that are reminiscent of the *Tao Te Ching/Daodejing* and the *Chuang-tzu/Zhuangzi*, especially the former. Liu I-ming/Liu Yiming wrote about cultivating the reality that is within the physical body, the reality that is the nature of *Tao* and primordial:

> The physical human body is like an alchemical workshop, the organs in the body are like vessels. The physical body has a real body hidden in it, the organs have five forces hidden in them. Cultivating reality does not mean cultivating the physical body and its organs; it means cultivating the real body and refining the five forces. It is simply a matter of borrowing this artificial body and its organs to cultivate the forces of the real body.[30]

Chapter 10 of the *Tao Te Ching/Daodejing* talks about making breathing as soft and gentle as an infant's, a purified vision of the inner self, of realizing the feminine through control of the "gates", and of the mysterious white light that penetrates all within. These are concepts highly akin to the practices of inner alchemy. The harmony advocated by texts such as the *Tao Te Ching/Daodejing* is brought about in the body by the union of opposites, creating utter equilibrium. The goal is to preserve, restore and transmute the energies within into their natural state that existed at conception, to their natural primordial state of *Tao* that existed before awareness of the world dissipated them. It is a spiritual refinement that aims to produce from such purified energies, an immortal, spiritual body within the physical outer frame:

Serene, unstirring,
One emerges with true eternity;
Dissolving all obscurities

Spontaneously restores the light.
In stillness the will
Fosters the spiritual being;
In concentration consciousness
Weds unconditioned knowing.
Inwardly stable in the midst of peril, energy grows;
Action coming from calmness, vitality's ebullient.
In the silver river
There's not the slightest shadow;
The gold moon appears alone,
Shining with spiritual light.[31]

These words describe the experience of the end goal (though in slightly Buddhist tones). By a process that wards off conscious knowledge, that is to say knowledge involved with the stimuli of the world, real knowledge accumulates within to a point of utter stillness when the Spirit Embryo is fully formed. Such training of the mind is, generally, a characteristic facet of inner alchemy, and of T'ai Chi Ch'üan/Taijiquan.

Respiration techniques

While there were many proponents of inner alchemy that dissociated themselves from what they regarded as extraneous techniques such as breathing, gymnastics and dietetics, others saw such practices as essential in the process of refining the self and creating an immortal body. Robinet made a neat distinction between the two, however, by pointing out that inner alchemy texts *always* use chemical terminology to depict its processes, while texts on respiration and gymnastics, as in *chi-kung/qigong*, do not.[32] On the other hand, Needham certainly associated gymnastic exercises with inner alchemy,[33] and today's practice of T'ai Chi Ch'üan/Taijiquan, in which respiration is critical to the movements, combines respiration techniques with the inner alchemical tradition. However, breathing exercises are not specifically Taoist, but belong to the wider context of Chinese interest in health and longevity.

The earliest text on breathing meditation is a Chinese Jade Tablet Inscription, which dates back to fourth century BCE, though its date is disputed. It describes circulating the vital breath, swallowing and collecting it, and nurturing it until it descends and stabilizes. What is interesting is that the inscription then states that the firm breath will then "sprout", grow and return.[34] The language is similar to the idea of the beginning and nurturing of the Spirit Embryo. The *Yellow Emperor's*

Classic of Internal Medicine, the *Huang-ti Nei-ching/Huangdi Neijing* (fourth century BCE), also states that through controlling breathing the mind becomes quiet, and the inner body is strengthened against disease. The importance of breath in promoting inner stability is, therefore, a long-established concept in China. Breath breathed into the body gives health, while expelled breath gets rid of what is impure. In the process of inner alchemy, the breath is the means by which the "firing process" is effectuated, with fast *yang* and slow *yin* breathing. Alchemically, breath is capable of unifying the whole body, and building inner harmony. Catherine Despeux writes: "Since breathing is a constant exchange of the inner and the outer, it also plays an important role in setting the inner circulation of *qi* in motion and in eliminating eventual blockages on the way. It also serves to harmonize the movements into a proper rhythm and to maintain a given posture."[35]

The link between breaths in the body and the cosmic primordial breath reinforces the body as the microcosm of the macrocosmic universe. As noted above, in the primordial, chaotic state there was the potential for nine breaths which, when creation occurred, separated. Coarser ones sank to form Earth, and more subtle ones rose to form Heaven. Human beings were thought to contain mainly impure breaths but also the vital breath, the *ch'i/qi*, which combined with the special essence that makes a human being what he or she is. When these come together the individual is animated with life; when they separate, death occurs. To attain immortality, the impure breaths have to be replaced with the pure, cosmic *ch'i/qi*. It is important to retain the pure breath in the lowest cinnabar field where, combined with pure essence, the Spirit Embryo can form.

While there were a variety of techniques, nourishing the *ch'i/qi* within by retention of breath was notable. In such a practice, air was breathed in and retained longer and longer – up to a count of 120. When the breath was retained for the count of a thousand, immortality was achieved. And as the breath was taken in and out, it was so smooth that the hairs of the nostrils remained still, or a goose feather placed under the nose did not move. In T'ang/Tang times and thereafter such practices became more physically internalized. The breath was "guided" internally. Guiding the breath meant moving it at the behest of the adept to whatever part of the body was desired. The whole process was called "womb breathing" or "embryonic breathing", though the term was wide enough to include different practices. It is what is aimed at today in the practice of T'ai Chi. "Womb breathing", from the idea of the foetus "breathing" in the womb, was also thought to be through the umbilical cord, the space between the kidneys or the whole body, and the *Chuang-tzu/Zhuangzi* even mentions through the heels. The breath was also "swallowed" by being held at the back of the throat and gulped into the alimentary canal with saliva, a combination called "jade broth", to nourish the body and aid the change of impure breaths into subtle and pure ones. Thus, the breath was circulating around the body without any apparent external breathing taking place. In womb breathing the breath is particularly guided to the region of the lower abdomen, and there the attention of the mind is also settled, so that mind and breath became one. Other practices included breathing in energies from the Five Elements and appropriating them in their respective organs in the body; breathing in the energies of the sun or moon, or of the constellation of the Big Dipper. All such practices were accompanied by ritual methods conducted at special times.[36] Chang San-feng/Zhang Sanfeng is reputed to have said in his *Commentary on Ancestor Lü's Hundred Character Tablet*:

> It is said that when you breathe out you contact the Root of Heaven and experience a sense of openness, and when you breathe in you contact the Root of Earth and experience a sense of solidity. Breathing out is associated with the fluidity of the dragon, breathing in is associated with the strength of the tiger.
>
> As you go on breathing in this frame of mind, with these associations, alternating between movement and stillness, it is important that the focus of your mind does not shift.
>
> Let the true breath come and go, a subtle continuum on the brink of existence. Tune the breathing until you get breath without breathing; become one with it, and then the spirit can be solidified and the elixir can be made.[37]

Breathing techniques were often independent of the kind of inner alchemy that used the language of the laboratory to depict its praxis. As such, they were part of the regime that promoted physical and mental health. However, inner alchemy had to be dependent on breathing techniques for its practices. Outer alchemy referred to the bellows that fanned the fires of the cauldron, regulating the temperature in line with the seasons and the *yin* and *yang* of the year. In inner alchemy, breath became the bellows, the means by which the Elixir of life could be formulated in the inner cauldron of the body. The "vapour" produced by inner alchemical practice was the Primordial Breath that existed before creation, and its circulation in the body was necessary in the creation, nurture and maturing of the Spirit Embryo.

Gymnastic exercises

Despeux traces the origins of gymnastic exercises to the shamanism of ancient China, particularly in the dances of the shamans.[38] While breathing cannot be separated from inner alchemy, gymnastic exercises for promoting health and longevity are less obviously connected with inner alchemy. However, there is some measure in accepting that Chang San-feng/Zhang Sanfeng saw his "martial" art as an inner process as much as an external one. The association between breathing and gymnastic exercise, *tao-yin/daoyin*, is also a firm one. While, too, there is an absence of alchemical language in the following words of Schipper, they nevertheless provide the same kind of concentration on the inner body that characterizes inner alchemy:

> At every moment, the body changes; it floats through time, and the regulation of our life can never exist without the cyclical time structure. The daily preparatory exercises already constitute an entrance into the cosmic rhythm, a way of participating in the spontaneous evolution of nature. As soon as the practitioner enters into this universal moment, he becomes one with the great mutation of all beings.[39]

Such exercises complemented the circulation of the breath because they unblocked areas that prevented the passage of the breath. Gymnastic exercises were the beginning of all kinds of associative practices for making the body supple, massaging the inner organs, and calming the mind.

Returning to *Tao*

The major philosophy underpinning inner alchemy and T'ai Chi Ch'üan/Taijiquan is the idea of *return* to *Tao* by *reversal* of the process of creation. It is a reversal that starts with the state of the human self as it is, and refines it back to its state in the Void, as *Tao*. The idea is adapted and reversed from the conception, gestation and birth of the child. Before a child is conceived, it is the undifferentiated *Tao* existing only in potential. At conception, it is no longer undifferentiated, but becomes a manifestation of *Tao*, and from that point on the separation of that embryo from *Tao* becomes accentuated. At birth, it faces the world for the first time, and its energies are separated from its mother – it has its own *ch'ing/jing*, *ch'i/qi* and *shen*. As the ability to understand the world grows and the multitude of stimuli affect the mind, the child's emotions develop and, gradually, the energies of the body are weakened and lost. Sexual activity, anger, desire, aversion – all cause the weakening of the internal energies and lead to ill health. Sickness, ageing and, eventually, death are the results of the leakage of energy. The process of return sets out to reverse this.

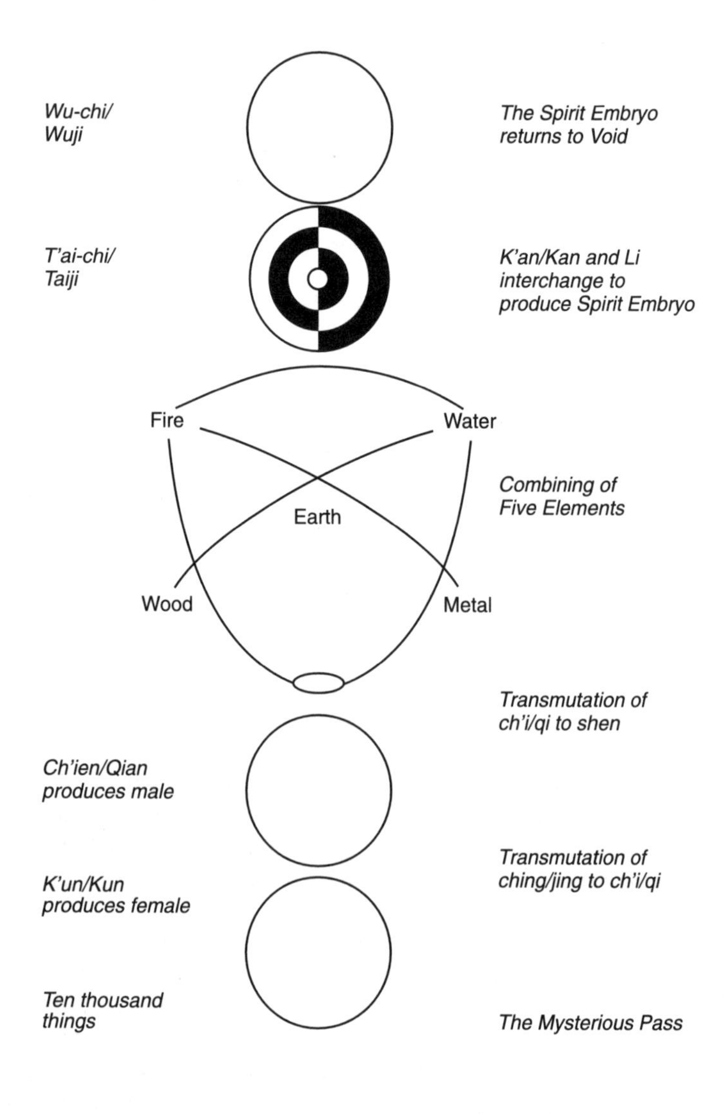

The goal of returning, then, is a return to the Source that one really is. To do this one has to become empty like the depth of a valley, pure *yin*, devoid of ego and differentiation of dualities, still, silent and at the point into which all pours – microcosmically the valley, macrocosmically, *Tao*. It is a return from some point on a circle to the centre of it. As opposed to evolution from the Void to the gross manifestation of the ten thousand things, and the generative cycle of the Five Elements that we examined in chapter 5, *involution* occurs. This is back from the gross, the *yang*, to the subtle *yin* of the Void, and the reverse, destructive order of the Five Elements. So the process of subtle, pure spirit to gross form in the human body has to change from the gross back to pure, subtle spirit, from coarse *ching/jing* to subtle, from whence it is able to transmute into *ch'i/qi*. Coarse *ch'i/qi* is transmuted into its subtle state, and is then transmuted into *shen*. At this point *ching/jing*, *ch'i/qi* and *shen* are undifferentiated. *Shen* is then dissolved into Void. The interaction of the Three Treasures here is pure and wholly subtle. This is the transmutation process of reversal of inner alchemy. So, just as the gestation of *Tao* produces the One, the Two and the Three, and then the ten thousand things, there is a gestation within the self in the sense of a rebirth that reverses the process and returns to *Tao*.

The Void, as we saw in chapter 3, is called *Wu-chi/Wuji*, *wu* indicating the negative "not", and *chi/ji* being the ridgepole at the highest point of a building – the ultimate part that holds it together. Thus, *Wu-chi/Wuji* is the ultimate, non-manifest source of all. Diagrammatically, the processes of evolution and involution are shown on the previous page. Looked at from top to bottom, it represents evolution from Void to outward forms, the ten thousand things. Read from the bottom up, it represents reversal from outward form, back to *Tao*.

Creatively, from *Wu-chi/Wuji* comes *T'ai-chi/Tai-ji*, which represents the movement and rhythm of *yin* and *yang*. From these come the Five Elements. The energy these produce create the *yang* male from the trigram *Ch'ien/Qian* that is Heaven, and the *yin* female from *K'un/Kun* that is Earth. From the union of these two come all phenomena in the universe – the ten thousand things. Interpreting the diagram from the bottom up, we have the reversal of the gross back to *Wu-chi/Wuji*. At the bottom, the place representing the ten thousand things, is also the "Mysterious Gate", the "Mysterious Female", the "Valley Spirit", the place that has to be generated in the self that is the "gate" of return, the first opening. From here, *ching/jing* has to be changed or transmuted into *ch'i/qi*. When *ch'i/qi* becomes sufficiently subtle it is transmuted into *shen*, spirit. Spirit is capable of filling those organs of the body associated with the Five Elements and all other parts of the body. At the next stage, the stage depicted by the *T'ai-chi/Taiji* symbol, Water and Fire interact to produce the Spirit Embryo that is nourished until it is ready to leave the body and merge with *Wu-ch'i/Wuji*.

Meditation

Essentially, T'ai Chi is a meditative practice and is the legacy of a long tradition of meditation that reaches far back into Chinese and Taoist history. The earliest form of meditation goes back to Han times and was called the "ingestion of the five sprouts" and was connected with visualization of the Five Elements within the body.[40] An early, fourth century BCE text *Inward Training*, also points to early mystical practices,[41] particularly circulating the breath as a meditative practice,[42] as well as the circulation of vital energy.[43] A text like *Inward Training* illustrates rather well how the holistic nature of practices of breathing, exercises, diet and meditation inform the journey back to the Source and, at the same time, stresses the stilling of the mind as the crux of all meditation. The *Tao Te Ching/Daodejing* spoke of emptying the mind in the same way. In the much later *Book of Balance and Harmony*, the words of Li Tao-ch'ün/Li Daoqun illustrate, too, how essential control of the mind became:

> Clearing the mind, dissolving preoccupations, purifying thought, forgetting feelings, minimizing self, lessening desire, seeing the basic, embracing the fundamental – this is meditation of the Transformative Way. When the mind is clear and freed of preoccupations, it is possible to fathom the design of reality; when thoughts are ended and feelings forgotten, it is possible to fathom the essence of reality. When selfishness and desire disappear, it is possible to arrive at the Tao; when one is plain and simple, pure and whole, it is possible to know the celestial.[44]

These words certainly reflect the ideas of the ancient Taoist philosophers like Lao-tzu/Laozi, and would only need the addition of alchemical language to link the meditative process with inner alchemy. Chuang-tzu/Zhuangzi, too, spoke of sitting and forgetting, of listening with the breath and not the ears, of abandoning consciousness of the outer world. Essentially, it is the "I" forgetting its "me". It is necessary for inner alchemists to employ meditative techniques in the internal processes of transmutation of the Three Treasures for, ordinarily, the "me" that is enmeshed in the world is too egocentric to bring about the transmutation process. There is a transcendence of ordinary subjective consciousness, a forgetting of who the self is in the world. In the words of the *Huai-nan-tzu/Huainanzi* from the late Warring States and early Han period:

> When the mind does not worry or rejoice,
> This is the perfection of inner power.
> When it is absorbed and does not alter,
> This is the perfection of stillness.
> When lusts and desires do not fill it up,
> This is perfection of emptiness.
> When there is nothing liked or disliked,
> This is the perfection of equanimity.
> When it is not confused by external things,
> This is the perfection of purity.[45]

Since the inner body is seen as mirroring the macrocosm, meditation and visualization of its inward nature are tantamount to understanding of the cosmos itself. Inner stillness, quietude and tranquillity are necessary to nourish inner health, power, unobstructed pure energy and essence that are of the nature of *Tao* and *Te*. The well-being and harmony of the inner self need to be brought in line with the harmony of the universe. Then, all objects cease to be objects that are separate from the self, the interrelation of all is experienced and all is seen as a movement of *Tao* in life and interfused with it as the Source of all. Transcending the senses is the key to such inner harmony. The senses involve the individual in ordinary consciousness that is subject–object, "I–that" orientated. *Real* consciousness is of the reality of *Tao*. Cleary writes: "The Taoist aim is to open consciousness and thereby allow greater access to reality, bypassing mental habit, stabilizing conscious knowing by real knowledge so that it is not subject to distorting influences. This is also expressed in terms of making real knowledge conscious and conscious knowledge real."[46]

In Ishida's study of body and mind in Chinese thought, he states that the mind was seen as fluid, "part of the eternally moving flux of the human physis". It was not a static aspect of the self, but could pervade the whole body, function with it and, therefore, affect any part of it. The normal mind has a tendency to be distracted by things outside the body, and hence to leave it. Thus, the inner self is not cared for.[47] Seduced by worldly concerns, the inner nature is forgotten. The beginnings of inner alchemy, therefore, consist of governing the mind, controlling the desires and emotions that pervade it. The transmutation process can only occur when the mind is still, empty and serene.

The firing process

Inner alchemy uses the language of outer alchemy to express the transmutation of *ching/jing* to *ch'i/qi* and *ch'i/qi* to *shen* in order to produce the Spirit Embryo. Instead of refining metal to produce gold, there is an internal refinement of the artificial self into a real and pure self. Such language, then, is symbolic language, and this factor, together with the secretive nature of the schools, oral tradition, the complex anatomy of the body with its many symbolic names, and the variety of traditions, serves to make the "firing process" a complicated area. The firing process is the term used for the means, the process, of transmutation. The outward nature of the trigrams *Li* as Fire, and *K'an/Kan*, Water, were described in chapter 2 on the *I Ching/Yijing*. But it is not the outward, overall trigram that is important in inner alchemy as much as the *middle line* of the trigrams. In the firing process, then, we have the interchange of the Dragon, which is the middle line of the trigram *Li*, ☲, with the Tiger, the middle line of the trigram *K'an/Kan* ☵. A point worth remembering is that ordinarily, water sinks and fire rises up. However, given the aim of reversal in inner alchemy, fire will need to *descend* and water *rise up*. The four alchemical necessities, then, are the Dragon and Tiger (the ingredients), and the Cauldron and Furnace (the means). Their equivalents are as follows:[48]

Dragon: The trigram *Li* is predominantly *yang*, but the important middle line is *yin* and so the Dragon is female. It is the *yin* essence in *yang*, Water in Fire, the female in the male, the moon in the sun. It is referred to as Green Dragon, Cinnabar, True Mercury, the Golden Raven in the Sun, the Golden Flower, the Jade Maiden, amongst others. It is water that rises, being heated, and is therefore fiery but yielding, rising to Heaven.

Tiger: The trigram *K'an/Kan* is Water and predominantly *yin* and female. But the middle line is *yang* and alchemically is the *yang* in the *yin*, the White Tiger, the Red Raven, or the Jade Rabbit in the moon. It is associated with True Lead and its function is to descend to Earth when fire reacts with it. It is the Fire in Water.

Cauldron: The cauldron or crucible is the mind, the head, and the space between the kidneys. Liu I-ming/Liu Yiming equated the cauldron with Heaven. In this case the trigram *Ch'ien/Qian*, symbolized by the three *yang* lines, suggested firmness, strength and stability or, at a deeper level, "single-minded concentration of will, by which one can bear the Tao".[49] The lowest cinnabar field is a cauldron for *ching/jing*, the middle one for *ch'i/qi* and the uppermost one for *shen*, but the lowest one is the place where the Spirit Embryo is "conceived".

Furnace: The furnace is the stove, the body, the abdomen, and *ch'i/qi*. Liu I-ming/Liu Yiming equated the furnace with Earth and, therefore, with the trigram *K'un/Kun* and its three, broken, *yin* lines, representing the warmth, flexibility, evenness and peace of the "Jade Furnace", which is able to effectuate gradual change.[50]

With language like: "Knock on bamboo to call the tortoise to ingest jade mushroom"; "Strum the lute to call the phoenix to drink from the medicinal spoon"; "the yellow woman"; "the metal man"; "single cavity of the mysterious gate" and so on, it is no wonder that interpretations could be wide.

The *I Ching/Yijing* is of immense importance in the understanding of inner alchemy. As Robinet commented: "Diverted from their divinatory uses, the trigrams are taken as stylized, abstract forms of fundamental truths, as ways of speaking concisely, of bringing together several levels of truth in one single sign."[51] Harmonizing *yin* and *yang* was the key to the formation of the Spirit Embryo. Liu I-ming/Liu Yiming depicted such harmony of the two in the following language of inner alchemy:

> On the peak of Sacred-Flower Mountain, the male tiger roars;
> At the bottom of Sun-Mulberry Ocean, the female dragon howls.
> The matchmaker of the center spontaneously knows how to join them together;
> They become husband and wife, sharing the same core.[52]

In the firing process, the middle *yin* and *yang* lines in the trigrams of *Li* and *K'an/Kan* respectively are interacted with each other to effectuate the restoration of the new, pure *yin* and *yang* trigrams of Heaven and Earth. The process is sometimes referred to as the "immersion of Fire in Water". It is through such interaction that transmutation of the Three Treasures takes place. All the *yin* and *yang* balances in the body must first be harmonized – the back (*yang*) with the front (*yin*); the left (*yang*) with the right (*yin*); the upper (*yang*) with the lower (*yin*). We can see here how meticulous the balance of *yin* and *yang* in the performance of T'ai Chi needs to be in order to accomplish such harmony. When the *yin* and *yang* energies combine in the lowest cinnabar field, they are referred to as the "dragon and tiger swirling in the winding river". When they combine in the middle field "the sun and moon reflecting on each other in the Yellow Palace", and in the uppermost cinnabar field, "the union of husband and wife in the bedchamber".[53] The Spirit Embryo that is produced is sometimes called the "Dragon-Tiger Pill", and the total harmony of *yin* and *yang* the "Valley Spirit". However, since the human being is a blend of Heaven and Earth in makeup, and since he or she leans towards the earthly stimuli rather than the spiritual heavenly ones, there has to be a certain *yangization* of the self in the process of inner alchemy. That is to say, there has to be a focus on the spiritual, heavenly *yang* and the stilling of the earthly desires and passions, the *yin*.

If we cast our minds back to the two *Pa-kua/Bagua* diagrams that were examined in an earlier chapter, the first was an arrangement of trigrams in the original, primal "Yellow River Map" (*ho-t'u/hetu*) of Fu Hsi/Fu Xi. The second was King Wen's arrangement that represented the motion of change throughout the cycle of the year. In inner alchemy, the earlier one is regarded as the state of purity that needs to be brought about by the alchemical process. The later one represents the pattern of life as it is, the process of ageing. Changing from the latter to the former is what the process of reversal is all about.

In the earlier arrangement *Ch'ien/Qian* is at the top of the circle in, to the Chinese, the South, and *K'un'Kun* at the bottom, in the North. *K'an/Kan* is in the West and *Li* in the East,[54] *Li* is the sun and *K'an/Kan* is the moon. The later arrangement has *Li* and *K'an/Kan* on the South–North axis with *K'un/Kun* following *Li* and *Ch'ien/Qian* preceding *K'an/Kan*. The aim of inner alchemy is to transform the later arrangement to the primal. This is done by the extraction of the middle *yin* and *yang* lines of *K'an/Kan* and *Li* respectively and the use of them to recreate pure *Ch'ien/Qian* and *K'un/Kun* but on a reversed North–South axis. The process is, thus, one of separation and restoration. A new, *yang Ch'ien/Qian* has to be generated as the means to allow the immortal to rise to Heaven.[55]

Put in another way, the *yang* in the middle of Water is taken to fill the *yin* in the middle of Fire, so reproducing Heaven. The *yang* in Water is the ultimate vitality within the body; the *yin* in Fire is the energy of mind. In the transmutation process, the *yang* vitality is what is changed into subtle form. Of course, the other trigrams also have to be transformed until the primal arrangement of the *Pa-kua/Bagua* is achieved.[56]

Li and *K'an/Kan* are the products of the union of *Ch'ien/Qian* and *K'un/Kun*. That union causes the middle lines of the trigrams *Li* and *K'an/Kan*. The *yin* in the middle of the trigram *Li* is called "True Lead", and is descending. The *yang* in the middle of *K'an/Kan* is "True Mercury" and is rising. They are dynamic representations of the original, primal *yin* and *yang* in the pure trigrams of Heaven and Earth. Ordinarily, the *yang* has the tendency to rise towards Heaven, or the head in the human body, and the *yin* is striving to descend to pure Earth and to the lowest cinnabar field of the body. Bringing the two together in a central place of the body is the goal. In the alchemical process, the *yang* in the Water is used to settle the *yin* in Fire: the Water rises and the Fire descends, inverting their normal functions. Thus, the solid *yang* line is taken out of the Water to replace the middle *yin* line in Fire, thus producing Heaven. The *yang* being within the *yin* represents the enlightened real consciousness being entrapped in worldly consciousness. Extracting it and replacing the middle *yin* line of *Li* restores the ultimate reality of Heaven.

Ch'ien/Qian and *K'un/Kun* are the cauldron and furnace within. *Li* and *K'an/Kan* are the ingredients that are brought together within them. All the other trigrams and the hexagrams indicate the firing times in the process of transmutation.[57] For example, two upper *yang* lines and a lowest *yin* one indicates two parts *yang* to one part *yin* in terms of the blend of heat and cold.[58] Being a key factor in the firing process, Fire has to be carefully controlled. Whereas in outer alchemy this was done with the bellows, in inner alchemy the breath – its pace and depth – provides the same role. In the language of inner alchemy, Hsü Ts'ung-shih/Xu Congshi describes the process thus:

> Heaven and earth set the stage,
> Whilst Change travels in their midst.
> Heaven and earth take as images Qian and Kun,
> They set the stage for the fitting together of the separate Yin and Yang.
>
> Change is shown through Kan and Li:
> Kan and Li are the two functions of Qian and Kun.
> These two function beyond established lines,
> Altogether streaming through the six empty spaces;
> Coming and going without settling,
> Rising and falling without regularity.[59]

The transmutation process

In the transmutation process of inner alchemy, the Three Treasures of *ching/jing*, *ch'i/qi* and *shen* are transmuted from their coarse states to their refined and subtle states in the furnace of the body and in the cauldrons, the cinnabar fields. Throughout the process, the stilling of the mind is essential. Initially, coarse *ching/jing* is gathered in order to build up energy. The "gate" to the lowest cauldron is opened and, there, the coarse *ching/jing* is then refined or transmuted into a subtle state. Once refined, it is able to pass through the second "gate" into the middle cinnabar field. Here, *ch'i/qi* is nourished and refined in the same way by means of the subtle *ching/jing*. These subtle forms then pass through the third "gate" to the uppermost cinnabar field for the same transmutation process of coarse *shen* – the animating spirit of the mind – to subtle *shen*. Now, all the "gates" are open and subtle *ch'i/qi* is able to move to all three fields uninterrupted. It does this in two orbits or circuits, a microcosmic, lesser one, and a macrocosmic, greater one. These we shall look at below. The Three Treasures are now united in subtle form. They become one, and it is through their union that a Spirit Embryo is able to be born, nourished and eventually liberated. The whole process of refinement or transmutation reverses the evolution of creation, Void > spirit > vitality > essence > form, to one of involution, form > essence > vitality > spirit > Void. According to Chang San-feng/Zhang Sanfeng:

> The absolute is the Way of nonresistance and spontaneity. The two modalities are yin and yang. The absolute is the basic spirit; the two modalities are vitality and energy. The absolute is the matrix of the alchemical elixir; the two modalities are true lead and true mercury. Symbolized by a circle, the absolute is itself infinite. This is also called the Great Transmutation, which is none other than the countenance before birth. "Absolute unity containing true energy" is a reference to the state of the universal inception, prior to the division of the two polar energies."[60]

Energy in T'ai Chi Ch'üan/Taijiquan

The harmonizing of movement, breath and concentration lies at the core of T'ai Chi. For T'ai Chi is a Taoist alchemical exercise for developing and refining the universal energy, *ch'i/qi*, through its moving form of meditation. In fact, it effectuates the transmutation processes outlined above. Sometimes, sitting meditation is used to bring this about. Here, the mind is gradually brought into a state of stillness by concentrating on breathing. Such stillness takes a considerable time to develop but, once achieved, the mind can be used to circulate the energy around the body. Using the mind to direct the *ch'i/qi* through the body increases *chin/jin*, a word meaning "power". The difficulty in moving meditation is that the physical movements that make up the particular style or *form* have to be developed first – not only co-ordination of hands and feet moving at the same time, but also the perfection of balance. Some of the movements in the *form,* for example, ask the individual to balance on one leg, and it takes time to perfect such actions, bearing in mind that the ultimate aim is that movements should flow smoothly one into the other. But Taoists believe that physical movements are a superb tool for bringing the mind under control. Indeed, as the postures become more difficult and take longer to learn, the mind needs to concentrate more. Hence, the mind is trained to become still and focused. Ideally, it helps to combine both sitting and moving meditation as a way of speeding up the connection of mind and body. But, as far as T'ai Chi is concerned, once the level has been reached whereby it is possible to flow smoothly through the *form* without losing concentration, when combined with breathing techniques, *ch'i/qi* is developed, harnessed, refined and circulated.

Alignment

The circulation of energy around the body is affected by postural alignment. Bad posture, misalignment, hinders the circulation and may cause it to stagnate, resulting in many adverse health conditions – joint problems, high blood pressure etc. In the practice of T'ai Chi there are some guidelines that must be adhered to in order to prevent poor posture and encourage energy flow. For example:

- *The head* should have a slight lifted feeling, as if the top of the head were suspended from above.
- *The eyes* lead the mind's "intent" and are the first to move, so they should focus on the arm or leg performing the most important movement at the time.
- *The spine* must be kept upright; there should be no leaning forwards or backwards.

- *The shoulders* sink downwards and should not lift.
- *The chest* should be naturally relaxed and arched in slightly, in order to reduce pressure on the lungs, so allowing deeper respiration. The arching of the chest allows the back to round slightly.
- *The waist* is the central movement for all the body's joints as it connects both the upper and the lower body. It is important to keep the waist flexible and loose.
- *The elbows* must droop downwards towards the ground; this allows the shoulders to relax and stops the elbows from locking and causing joint stiffness.
- *The fingers* are gently extended and *the wrist* settles, helping to stretch the muscles and tendons. But, in relation to energy, the motion of the wrist and fingers helps bring the attention of the mind in leading the *ch'i/qi* to the fingertips. Some of the most beautiful movements in T'ai Chi are gentle, but specific, hand movements.
- As far as *the legs* are concerned, fullness and emptiness are guidelines in the achievement of agility. There should be smoothness in shifting weight from one leg to another, and centredness and balance need to be maintained.

When performing T'ai Chi the body must be kept relaxed, the muscles should not tense up in any way, as this will restrict the flow of energy through the body. Further, there should be no locking or stiffening of the joints of the upper and lower body; like the muscles, the joints also should be kept relaxed, and the arms and legs must have a slight bend so as to allow strong energy circulation to the extremities.

The real reason for proper posture alignment in the practice of T'ai Chi is to allow the *ch'i/qi* to flow internally through the acupuncture meridians and channels that are its natural pathways. It is when these pathways are hindered by misalignment of the body that the *ch'i/qi* stagnates or becomes blocked. An adverse effect on the physical, emotional, and mental aspects of the individual then occurs. So, correct posture in the practice of moving meditation is very important, not just for outward, physical appearance but because of what is happening internally. In Taoist inner alchemy the Golden Elixir is circulated through the three cinnabar fields by way of three energy gates. As noted above, the lowest *tan-t'ien/dantian* is located just below the navel, the middle *tan-t'ien/dantian* in the centre of the chest between the two nipples, and the uppermost *tan-t'ien/dantian* between the eyes – what some people call the "third eye", "sky eye" or "wisdom eye". In the practice of T'ai Chi, since these three energy areas are also used to store and refine the

Golden Elixir, they must be kept in alignment. So through correcting posture and perfecting the movements of the *form* the internal energy pathways are brought into alignment, and the energy gates of the body can open.

Fire and Water energy schools

In the Taoist practice of developing energy there are two main schools of thought. These are known as *K'an/Kan* and *Li*, or the Fire and Water schools, respectively. Something of the characteristics of the schools are suggested by their naming elements, the Fire schools adopting more aggressive methods and the Water schools gentler ones. There are many different Taoist Fire schools, but they are characterized by similar forceful approaches in working towards union with *Tao* – extensive holding of the breath, and suffering physical pain and mental discomfort, for example. The mind is used to push *ch'i/qi* forcefully around the body through the microcosmic and macrocosmic orbits, which we shall examine below. Visualization is adopted as the inner means to accomplish this. It is believed that such methods open the mind and the energy gates of the body very quickly. But it can be a dangerous practice, causing adverse side effects in physical and mental health. A strong flow of energy is directed around the microcosmic and macrocosmic orbits of the body – all powered by visualization in the mind. Lack of concentration or tiredness may cause the energy to stagnate. Physical obstructions like muscle tensions through over-alignment of the body, or mental/emotional obstructions such as fear, anger or grief, may also cause stagnation of energy. With the Fire method, the energy usually forces its way through like a giant fire burning up everything in its path. But severe headaches, hallucinations, palpitations and the like, may result, which is why it is important to find an experienced and talented teacher in the Fire tradition.

The Taoist Water tradition is much gentler and safer since it is cultivated over a long period of time. The process is a natural one, though involving many long hours of repetitive sitting or moving meditation where the intent is on dissolving energy blockages and feeling the energy develop naturally without forcing it through the body. The Water method uses many breathing exercises to harness *ch'i/qi*, and to circulate it around the body – a skill that is built up gradually over a period of time which varies from one individual to another. The *feeling* of energy moving around the microcosmic and macrocosmic orbits is the aim of the practice. Here, energy sensations vary, but the most common is the feeling of warmth or heat building up in the body. Some people actually feel the vital energy moving up the back, *yang*, governor vessel, but this usually takes some time to experience.

The Taoist Water tradition of energy development is said to have originated with Lao tzu/Laozi, the father of Taoism. He describes the softness of water overcoming hardness in the *Tao Te Ching/Daodejing*. The Fire tradition was supposedly developed much later by Neo-Taoists. Both are used in the practice of T'ai Chi. Teachers of the Fire tradition encourage students to practise seated meditation in order to open the microcosmic orbit quickly, before proceeding to the moving meditation. However, many teachers of the Water tradition dispense with seated meditation and start the student immediately with the moving meditation practice of T'ai Chi – a longer route, but a natural one.

The microcosmic orbit or small heavenly circuit[61]

The microcosmic orbit, or small heavenly circuit, refers to the circulation of *ch'i/qi* around the torso or upper body. It passes through two acupuncture meridians, eight major acupuncture points and three main energy gates. The two acupuncture meridians are the back, *yang*, governor vessel and the front, *yin*, conception vessel. These two meridians are also known as *K'an/Kan* and *Li*. The eight acupuncture energy points of the microcosmic orbit consist of the following, which are used both in Taoist meditation and acupuncture theory:

1 *Ch'i-hai/qihai*
2 *Hui-yin*
3 *Ming-men*
4 *Ling-t'ai/lingtai*
5 *Yü-ch'en/yuchen*
6 *Pai-hui/baihui*
7 *Yin-t'ang/yintang*
8 *Shan-chung/shanzhong*

The lowest *tan-t'ien/dantian* point is located two inches below the navel on the conception vessel. In acupuncture the *ch'i-hai/qihai* point corresponds to the same area and is often used as the name for the lowest *tan-t'ien/dantian* itself. But the real *tan-t'ien/dantian* lies deep inside, to the centre of the body. The middle *tan-t'ien/dantian* is located directly in the middle of the chest; some people call this the "Heart Energy Centre", and link it with the *shang-chung/shanzhong* point. The uppermost *tan-t'ien/dantian* is located between the eyes, and is known as the "third eye" or "Heaven's Gate" and corresponds to the *yin-t'ang/yintang* point.

The circulation of energy around the body is effectuated by the power of breathing and visualization. The route starts with a *yang* half-circuit beginning in the abdomen, in the lowest cinnabar field at the base of the spine, at the *ch'i-hai/qihai* point. It runs along the *tu/du yang* meridian. The energy is directed along this meridian downwards towards the *hui-yin* point and the perineum, then up the back to the coccyx, and up the spine to the thorax, passing through the *ming-men* and *yü-ch'en/yuchen* points. Then it is directed to the crown of the head, the occiput, and the *pai-hui/baihui* point, from where it feeds the brain. Its journey then is downwards to a point between the eyebrows, then to the mouth where it is mixed with saliva. At this point, half the circuit is completed and the *tu/du* meridian ends. Then, the *yin* begins its increase by descending, as is its nature, to the throat, down past the heart to the stomach, and to the *shang-chung/shangzhong* point. The journey of the energy runs along the *jen/ren yin* meridian at the front of the body until it joins the *tu/du*. When energy is thus circulated without hindrance through this orbit, it creates what is sometimes called the "waterwheel". Connecting the two meridians enables the water of *K'an/Kan* in the *yin* lowest cinnabar field to meet the fire of *Li* in the *yang* of the head. The fusion of the two produces the original Heaven and Earth trigrams.[62] One complete circuit is said to take three and three-quarter hours, and can be either clockwise or anti-clockwise, with different benefits. The clockwise direction is necessary for the transmutation process above. The anti-clockwise direction nurtures and stimulates *ch'i/qi*, which in turn nurtures and stimulates *ching/jing*. The circuits generate heat. The *tu/du* and *jen/ren* meridians, respectively, control all the *yang* and *yin* channels of the body.

There are two difficult stages that can slow down the progress of opening the microcosmic orbit. The first is when the vital energy travels from the lowest *tan-t'ien/dantian* to the *ming-men* point. The difficulty here lies in being able to pass the vital energy through the tailbone coccyx area. Since this area is composed of small bones the energy may stagnate or slow down. Once the vital energy has passed through the coccyx to the *ming-men* point, the second difficult area is the *yü-ch'en/yuchen* point. This part of the body is known as the occipital bone; Taoists call it the "Jade Pillar". It is a problematic point because it takes a long time for the vital energy to pass through it. It can also be a dangerous point, since the vital energy may stagnate, causing a feeling of pressure around the head.

The microcosmic orbit

The macrocosmic orbit or large heavenly circuit

To circulate the vital energy around the whole body combines the microcosmic orbit of the upper body with the lower body, meaning the legs. This wider circulation is the macrocosmic orbit or large heavenly circuit. The circulation of energy into the legs passes through the *yang* heel vessel, and upward through the *yin* heel vessel. The two vessels form a balanced loop of energy that flows from the head to the feet and then, again, upward. The *yang* heel vessel is closely connected to the *yang* bladder channel, which starts at the inside corner of the eye and flows all the way down to the feet. The *yin* heel vessel is closely connected to the *yin* kidney channel, which flows from the feet up the inside of the legs, and up the front of the body to the head, where it connects to the *yang* heel vessel. The important acupuncture energy points that correspond with the flow of the vital energy through the macrocosmic orbit are the following:

1 Circle Jump Point, *huan-t'iao/huantiao*, gall bladder 30.
2 Command the Middle Point, *wei-chung/weizhong*, urinary bladder 40.
3 K'unlun/Kunlun Mountain Point, *k'unlun/kunlun*, urinary bladder 60.
4 Bubbling Spring Point, *yung-ch'üan/yongquan*, kidney 1.

The macrocosmic orbit

The Belt/Girdle Vessel

Another important aspect for good energy circulation around the body is the opening of the Girdle Vessel. This vessel acts like a belt that circles around the waist. It is an essential channel that aids the quality of vital energy in its flow from the upper to the lower body and back again. The "Girdle" or "Belt" vessel connects to the gall bladder, liver and kidney meridians. The circulation of energy through this belt channel is maintained by allowing the waist, hips and lower back to be flexible, loose and relaxed. The practice of the T'ai Chi *form* facilitates such flexibility through the turning of the upper torso from side to side.

Breathing techniques

In the practice of the T'ai Chi *form*, deep breathing techniques, in co-ordination with the physical movements and concentration, are important keys in learning to harness and circulate the vital energy around the whole body. It is the pre-natal, or "womb-breathing" described earlier that is essential to the deeper practices of T'ai Chi. When we learn to breathe in T'ai Chi for health and meditation purposes then the breathing will be in through the nose and out through the nose. The tongue softly touches the hard palate just behind the top teeth so that the circulation of the vital energy through the microcosmic orbit is strong and smooth. If contact is too stiff and rigid, the vital energy will stagnate in the tongue, and its circulation through the microcosmic orbit will be hindered. The different positions of the tongue correspond to the Five Elements and their associative organs. The Earth Element is related to the spleen; here, the tongue touches behind the bottom teeth on the lower palate. The Metal Element connects to the lungs. The tongue for the lungs is curled as in the Earth Element position, but does not touch the teeth. The Water Element connects to the kidney; here, the placement of the tongue is curled upward and as far back as possible on the upper palate. The Element Wood is associated with the liver; here, the tongue is placed in the centre of the upper palate in a vertical position. The Fire Element is connected to the heart and the placement of the tongue for this is behind the teeth on the upper palate; it is the main tongue position for the practice of the T'ai Chi *form*.

The above tongue placements are used in the practice of the Five Element *ch'i-kung/qigong* exercises in Taoism. Taoists call the position of the tongue the "Magic Bridge". It is a practice used in both seated and moving meditation to enable a strong current of energy to flow through the whole body. Alongside the tongue placement, the inhalation and exhalation of air through the nose should be deep, soft and gentle. If heavy or forced, the lungs will become tense and the vital energy will stagnate in the lungs. Breathing should be long and deep, but in the practice of the T'ai Chi *form* the breathing rhythm varies depending on the nature of the movement. Sometimes it will be a balanced breath and at other times it might be a long inhalation and a short exhalation.

Pre-natal breathing and T'ai Chi

Pre-natal, or womb breathing, sometimes called embryonic breathing or reverse breathing, has been mentioned above in the section on respiratory techniques. After birth we change from this natural way of breathing to an unhealthy, shallow, method of breathing, but the aim of T'ai Chi is to reverse this. Pre-natal breathing is a method of breathing deeply using the capacity of the lungs to draw positive energy inwards and to expel negative energy outwards. The abdomen is drawn inwards on the inhalation, creating a feeling of lifting and drawing energy upward and inward towards the centre of the body, or the lowest *tan-t'ien/dantian.* It is also called reverse breathing because of returning to what was the natural method. Pre-natal energy is the energy that was received from the parents and is said to reside in the kidneys. By learning to breathe deeply the post-natal energy that is drawn in on inhalation sinks down to the navel where it mixes with the pre-natal energy rising up to the navel. After exhalation, the post-natal breath/energy rises up and out of the lungs, while the pre-natal breath/energy sinks back down to the lower abdomen. Such rhythmic breathing creates total harmony between energy and breath in the body. "When energy reaches this point," Chang San-feng/Zhang Sanfeng is reputed to have said, "it is like a flower just budding, like an embryo just conceived."[63]

Post-natal breathing

Post-natal breathing is what most people use as a method of breathing; the breath is usually shallow, not using the full capacity of the lungs. This type of breathing stores and circulates the *ch'i/qi* in the lungs and does not encourage the breath to sink downward. It is only through the practices of *tao-yin/daoyin* or T'ai Chi Ch'üan/Taijiquan that the individual is taught to breath deeply into the lower abdomen.

Energy circulation through the T'ai Chi Ch'üan/Taijiquan *form*

Through the practice of T'ai Chi, circulation of the vital energy around the microcosmic and macrocosmic orbits is achieved by the lowering, raising, stretching, pushing and hand drawing movements of the T'ai Chi *form*. These invigorate the flow of vital energy to all areas of the body. Combined with the stepping movements of the *form* in all directions, and with the co-ordination of mind and breathing, the vital energy flows not just in a vertical circle around the body but in either backward to forward or forward to backward directions. It also circulates around the body in a horizontal and diagonal plane. To exemplify this, let us look at some postures taken from the T'ai Chi *form*, to show how energy moves around the body.

In the opening movement of the *form* the individual stands with feet shoulder-width apart with the knees slightly bent. Both arms are hanging by the sides. The individual stands quietly in this position, regulating his or her breathing, calming the mind in preparation for commencement of the *form*. It is called the empty-stance posture. The opening posture of the T'ai Chi *form* is known as *Awakening the Energy*. The individual slowly breathes in, while gently raising the arms to shoulder height (figure 1). As the individual exhales he or she slowly lowers the arms back down to the starting position, bending from the knees as both arms are lowered (figure 2).

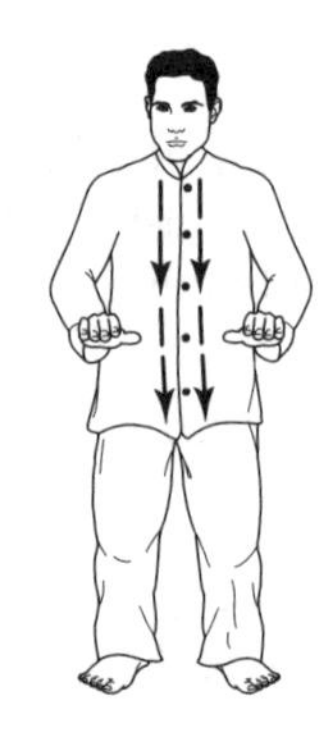

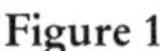

Figure 1 **Figure 2**

In figure 1 the raising of the arms will raise the vital energy from the lowest cinnabar field, or *tan-t'ien/dantian*, up the back, *yang*, governor vessel. In figure 2 the lowering of the arms sinks the *ch'i/qi* down the front, *yin*, conception vessel back to the lowest *tan-t'ien/dantian.* This begins the circulation of the *ch'i/qi* through the microcosmic orbit in a vertical circle around the upper torso, and in a backward to forward direction. It is known as the *Union of K'an/Kan and Li.* A beginner would do this first T'ai Chi posture several times.

Figure 3 **Figure 4**

Once the individual begins to step in any direction, the circulation of *ch'i/qi* is activated through both the microcosmic and macrocosmic orbits. As the individual begins stepping, changing the weight from one leg to another, he or she will generate the circulation of both blood and *ch'i/qi* into the legs in a pumping action. Combine this with the upper arm movements of the *form* and it can be seen how *ch'i/qi* is invigorated throughout the whole body. Once the actions of stepping are incorporated into the postures of the *form*, then the circulation of *ch'i/qi* is integrated to encompass the macrocosmic orbit. The T'ai Chi posture known as *Brush Knee Side Step*, in figures 3 and 4, demonstrates this well.

Apart from backwards and forwards movement, the circulation of *ch'i/qi* within the body also occurs in a sideways direction, either clockwise or anti-clockwise. This is seen in the posture known as *Wave Hands in Clouds* as shown in figures 5 and 6 below:

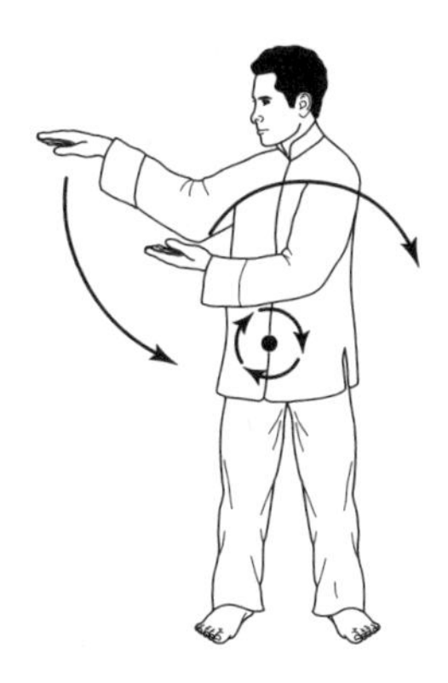

Figure 5

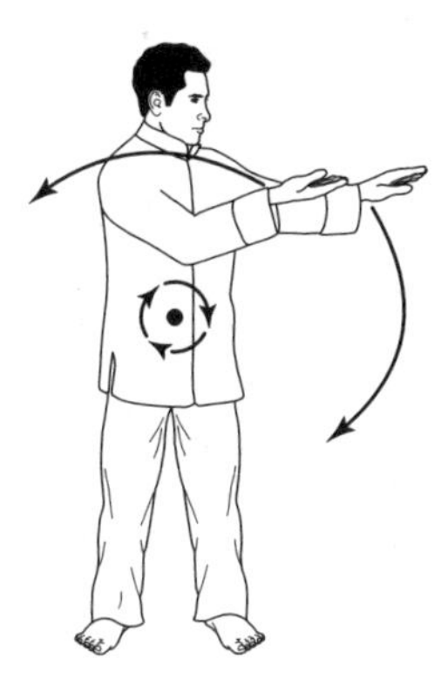

Figure 6

In the *Wave Hands in Clouds* posture, both arms move around in opposite directions to one another in front of the body, and in a sideways circle on a vertical plane. The upper torso sways from side to side as the eyes follow the hand that rises up in front of the face. The legs move in a sideways direction, either to the right or left. This particular posture invigorates the *ch'i/qi* to rotate within the lowest *tan-t'ien/dantian*; Taoists call this *Turning the Wheel of Law from Left to Right*. The practice of *Wave Hands in Clouds* is also beneficial for complaints of the digestive system, because the swaying of the waist, as the upper torso turns from side to side in co-ordination with the hands, stimulates the circulation of blood within the intestines.

Another sphere of *ch'i/qi* circulation within the body during the practice of the T'ai Chi *form* is seen in the posture known as *Fair Lady Weaves Shuttle* illustrated below in figures 7 and 8.

Figure 7

Figure 8

The movement of *Fair Lady Weaves Shuttle* or *Shuttle Back and Forth* turns the body diagonally both to the left and right, and then to the right and left. The succession of pivots and turns that comprise the movements of this posture are used to guide the *ch'i/qi* in a sphere that passes diagonally through the torso. The first part of the posture is a step to the right, pivoting on the left heel to the north-east corner, and taking a small step forward with the right foot. The right hand moves from the belly diagonally up in front of the body to the right upper corner above the head, the right hand pushing directly forward in front of the chest. This movement is then repeated on the other side of the body, this time moving to the north-west corner. The combination of movement guides the *ch'i/qi* upward and diagonally across the front of the body to either the right or left shoulder. Such circulation of *ch'i/qi* during the practice of the T'ai Chi *form* is illustrated in the many different spheres that make up the ancient Chinese astronomical instrument called a "palindrome". Like the many spheres in the instrument, the circulation of *ch'i/qi* during the *form* reaches every single part of the body. Another direction of energy circulation that has not been mentioned is the horizontal sphere. This particular energy circulation forms a spiralling type of energy that rises up from the feet to the hands, moving in either a centrifugal or centripetal direction as shown in figures 9 and 10 opposite.

In turning the body on a horizontal sphere, the leg that carries the weight acts as the axle of a wheel, while the leg that has no weight upon it acts like the wheel. The action brings the circulation of *ch'i/qi* through the "Girdle" or "Belt" vessel that runs around the waist and hips in a circle, and connects the smooth flow of energy from the upper body to the lower body. The horizontal turning of the whole body also develops joint flexibility, especially in the ankle, knee and hip joints of the lower body.

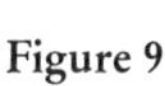

Figure 9

Figure 10

The degree to which the microcosmic and macrocosmic orbits are opened through the practice of T'ai Chi, varies from one individual to another. While progress may be speedier with the Fire tradition, the moving meditation of the Water tradition is the practice that most people will encounter. Here, the microcosmic and macrocosmic orbits open naturally over a long period of time. However, control of *ch'i/qi* by the mind is the aim of both traditions. In the *Thirteen Postures*, therefore, we find the words: "Use the Xin (heart, mind) to transport the Qi, (the mind) must be sunk (steady) and calm, then (the Qi) can condense (deep) into the bones. Circulate the Qi throughout the body, (Qi) must be smooth and fluid, then it can easily follow the mind."[64]

The complexities of the inner alchemy traditions have, thus, fully informed the practice of T'ai Chi Ch'üan/Taijiquan. The ultimate goals of the two are united in the search to gain effective circulation of *ch'i/qi* in the body, along with its refinement to a point of physical spirituality that reverses the individual from one of ten-thousand things to being the primordial unity that is *Tao*.

Becoming the Void

In the quiet room I open the mirror of mind;
In the vacant hall I light the lamp of wisdom.

> Outside is clear and bright,
> Inside is effulgent light.
> A tiny grain appears in the glow,
> The silver moon is clear in the water.
> In the gold crucible, suspended in space,
> A grain of great elixir crystallizes.[65]

Such is the description of the birth of the Spirit Embryo. It is a time of harmony within the self, and with the outer cosmos. The adept "dissolves the imperfect coagulations of the soul, reduces the latter to its *materia*, and crystallizes it anew in a nobler form. But he can accomplish this work only in unison with Nature, by means of a natural vibration of the soul which awakens during the course of the work and links the human and cosmic domains".[66] The "tiny pearl" of the Spirit Embryo is itself the formless and undifferentiated reality that is *Tao*. It is the original energy of pre-creation. Nourished by equanimity, harmony, balance, and stillness of mind it develops. The perception of the self as *Tao* pervades the self and maintains such equilibrium. Once fully developed and able to leave the body, the body remains in the world of the human, but the spirit is liberated to roam in the cosmos, until the body sheds its life. Here, there is what Blofeld called a "relaxation in the totality of being", and "a state of consciousness in which all sense of self and other, of heaven and earth has vanished; there is naught but pure void, a limitless ocean of *ch'i* resembling a panorama of ever-changing cloud-forms".[67]

Experience of *Tao* is experience of the Void, of utter emptiness and yet utter fullness, because *Tao* is the unity of all opposites. There is at once both unconsciousness – of the world as a separate entity from the self – and yet real consciousness of *Tao* as and in all things. It is a return home, a return to the Source, a return to the centre of the circle, the central point between all dualities. The pure energy created in the self returns to the primordial energy of the cosmos.

7 Movement in Stillness

When the Absolute goes into motion, it produces yin and yang.
When motion culminates, it reverts to stillness and in stillness produces yin.
When stillness culminates, it returns to movement.
Movement and stillness in alternation constitute bases for each other.
This is the wonder of Creation, the natural course of the Way.[1]

When you chance upon a lone practitioner or a group of individuals going through their T'ai Chi *form* – smoothly moving forwards, backwards, turning, dropping, gracefully spinning never rushing or pausing, but stringing the movements together like a spider spinning a web – you may suddenly become aware of the stillness in their movement, and the movement in their stillness. The Chinese call the practice of T'ai Chi a moving meditation exercise, where the mind, body and spirit connect and the circulation of *ch'i/qi* flows throughout the entire body. Softness in strength, emptiness in fullness, stillness in movement, non-action in action characterize the highest level of achievement in the practice of T'ai Chi. It takes many years of dedicated practice to develop concentration to a level where consciousness is simplified to the point of unity. The union of non-action and action or *yin* and *yang* constantly alternates irrespective of the many movements performed and whether they are active or non-active postures. Taoists call this level *hsü-ching/ xujing* "emptiness and stillness". According to tradition, in stillness one should be as a mountain, and when in motion one should move like water in a river. So in T'ai Chi, the aim is to become inwardly as still as a mountain while outward movement is continuous without pause or hesitation. Over a period of time, the outer movements will mirror the inner feelings and awareness. Then, the spirit grows, blossoms and becomes tranquil. The ultimate purpose of T'ai Chi, then, is to reach a higher spiritual level that will lead to the realization of *Tao*. Some people choose the route via greater understanding of the martial arts aspect of T'ai Chi, while others just choose the route of T'ai Chi for increased health and self-healing.

Movement in stillness in the martial arts

In the performance of T'ai Chi as a martial art, the level of *hsü-ching/xujing* "emptiness and stillness" is an important level for the individual to attain. If concentration cannot be maintained, then the mind–body connection will be weak, and while in the midst of defence, one is easily defeated. In T'ai Chi as a martial art the mind is considered the general of an army, while the limbs and torso are considered the army. If the general (mind) cannot give the correct commands to his or her army (body), then energy will become wasted and scattered, counter-attacks will be weak, and defence will be easily overcome. The essence of T'ai Chi as a martial art is to strengthen the connections between mind and body in order to direct defence or counter-attacks with greater skill. Operating at an advanced level, it is important to use action as non-action, and softness to overcome hardness. This can only occur when the mind and body connections are strong, and when the mind is calm, still and focused. At the same time, the body is relaxed, alert and aware. In the midst of action the mind is in a state of stillness even though the body is in constant motion. Then, the body flows from defence to counter-attack effectively, in complete co-ordination and balance, and alternating from *yin* to *yang*. What underpins movement at every point is inner stillness. In the same way that *yin* and *yang* alternate so that the one generates the other, so ultimate stillness generates movement and movement generates stillness. The most efficient movement, therefore, comes from stillness, and that high-quality movement in turn maintains stillness. When the body is calm and still the mind is focused and clear, and when the mind is focused *ch'i/qi* will be strong and full. In vigorous movement, the mind becomes excited and loses its concentration, in which case the power being developed within the body will be weak. Using stillness to generate movement makes action strong and powerful.

T'ai Chi develops a high level of manipulative skill and control. These are attained through the many two-person exercises that develop such attributes as co-ordination, balance and sensitivity. However, it is through the practice of the moving meditation exercise of the T'ai Chi *form*, and seated or standing meditation exercises, that an individual can attain greater mind–body connection and reach higher levels of practice. Hence, through T'ai Chi as a martial art, one is even able to reach the highest level of martial art ability, where movements are ultimately natural, skilful and effective. This is the stage of T'ai Chi martial art development known as "fighting with enlightenment". In this stage there is knowledge of the self as well as knowledge of the attackers' responses and actions. *You* are the one who controls the entire situation. Obviously it takes many years of dedicated practice to reach this stage of martial art enlightenment: control of the body, breathing, mind, vital energy and the spirit and the fusing of them into one are essential at this level. Once the stage is reached where the whole spirit is involved in the actions without any effort, then the enlightenment stage or the level of action without action is attained.

Movement in stillness for health

Far more people are drawn towards the practice of T'ai Chi as a way to help maintain and improve their health, vitality and well-being. But some only attain the state of relaxation and of releasing tension and stress from the body. Not many individuals actually learn to discipline the mind and develop a sense of spiritual awareness within themselves and their surroundings. As a health exercise the practice of T'ai Chi helps some to control, or even cure, illnesses such as high blood pressure, poor circulation and arthritis, for example. The beauty of practising T'ai Chi is that it can be performed by anyone of any age, though some people still believe that it is only for the older generation. Perhaps this is because it is more widely practised by older, rather than younger, people. It is an unfortunate misconception, since the earlier training in T'ai Chi begins, the greater the benefit received in good health, vitality and well-being in later years.

It is the concept of stillness generating movement in T'ai Chi training that many people do not understand, as they are taken in only by its beautiful, soft, graceful movements. The stillness aspect of T'ai Chi and the need to regulate the mind are connected to the dark side of *yin* and *yang*; they are the *yin* aspect of T'ai Chi. Through the co-ordinating movements of the T'ai Chi *form* the individual slowly learns to discipline the mind, to concentrate, and to focus for longer periods of time. The health benefits of learning to regulate the mind through T'ai Chi practice are considerable, especially in illnesses like Alzheimer's disease, depression, insomnia, and nervousness, for example. By learning to calm the mind, and by developing stronger connections with the body, a greater effect on the mental functioning of the individual occurs. But T'ai Chi also benefits the emotional aspects of the individual, by helping to balance emotions, by promoting the ability to relax and remain calm for longer periods of time. Here, any blockages of energy that may have built up within the body's emotions are released. As a form of exercise for health maintenance, T'ai Chi is a form of prevention and should be taught and practised from a young age. When this occurs, the immune, circulatory, nervous, respiratory and digestive systems are strengthened; the development of vital energy, *ch'i/qi*, is strong, smooth and balanced. The circulation of the blood is also smooth and flowing.

Movement in stillness for prolonging life

Longevity, and slowing down the ageing process, are aspects of T'ai Chi that not many people achieve or even work towards, since most people practise T'ai Chi either for martial art ability or health maintenance. However, regular disciplined training, on a day-to-day basis, slowly regulates the body, energy, breath, mind and, finally, the spirit. Through the practice of the T'ai Chi *form,* the aim is to prolong life through harmony of stillness and movement or strength and flexibility. Through stillness we gain inner strength and through movement we gain flexibility. As we grow older the importance of maintaining our health also increases. T'ai Chi is the tool to help in prolonging life. To the Taoists of old and to those who call themselves Taoists in our present age, prolonging life was, and still is, very important. In China today, you can see elderly people who are well into their eighties and nineties still practising T'ai Chi. It is said that, through regular practice, individuals are rejuvenated and look and feel younger than they are. To achieve such results, however, one must begin the practice of T'ai Chi at a young age.

As we have seen in earlier chapters, the ultimate aim of Taoists was to achieve immortality. To achieve this they experimented with everything from eating certain mushrooms that they believed to be magical and could only be found on sacred mountains, to creating exercises that would develop the Golden Elixir that would bring them immortality. While immortality may seem a remote goal, the practice of T'ai Chi offers us the ability to maintain youthfulness, vitality and independence in our old age and helps to keep the physical aspects of our body supple

The Yang Style Simplified 24-Step T'ai Chi Ch'üan/Taijiquan Form

Empty Stance:
Wu-chi/Wuji (as 61)

Awakening the Energy

Parting the Horse's Mane

White Crane Spreads its Wings

Brush Knee and Side Step

Play the Lute

Rolling/Reeling Arms

Grasp the Sparrow's Tail (left)

(Ward Off)

(Roll Back)

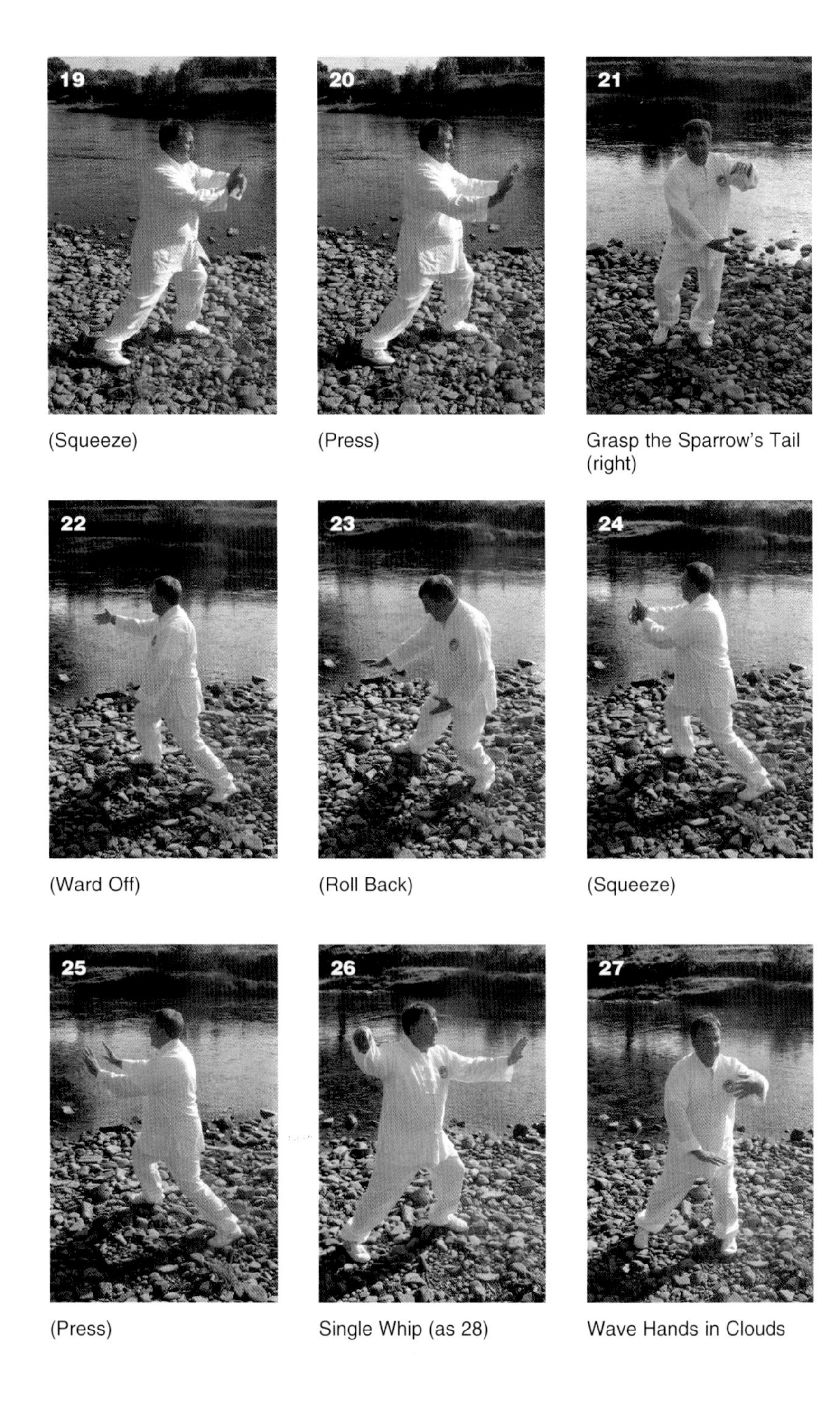

(Squeeze)

(Press)

Grasp the Sparrow's Tail (right)

(Ward Off)

(Roll Back)

(Squeeze)

(Press)

Single Whip (as 28)

Wave Hands in Clouds

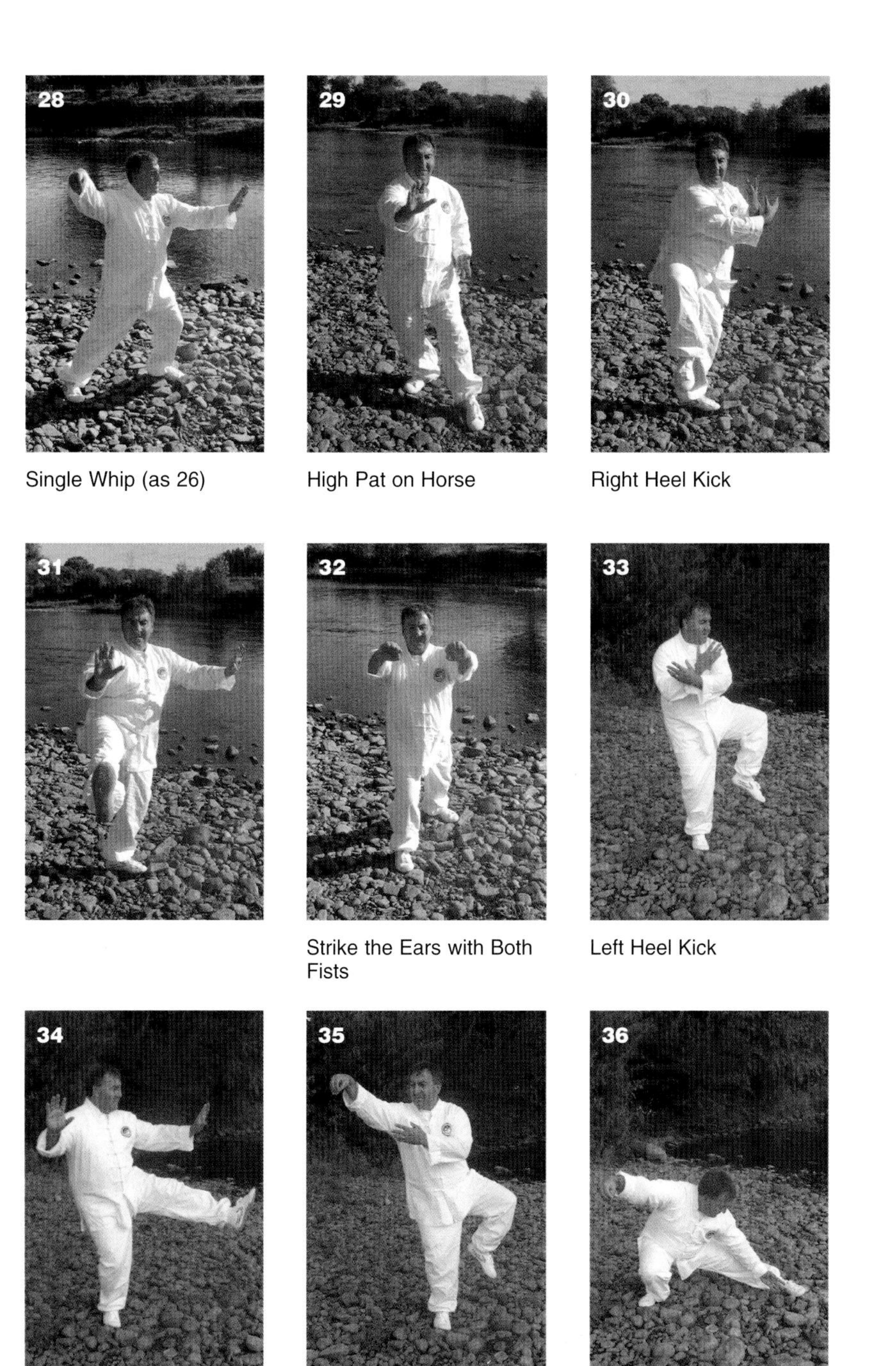

Single Whip (as 26)

High Pat on Horse

Right Heel Kick

Strike the Ears with Both Fists

Left Heel Kick

Snake Creeps Down (left)

Rooster Stand on One Leg

39

Snake Creeps Down (right)

Rooster Stands on One Leg

Shuttle Back and Forth (right)

45

Shuttle Back and Forth (left)

Scoop Needle from Sea Bottom

Fan through the Back

Turn the Body . . .

Deflect . . .

Parry . . .

Punch

Appears Closed

Cross Hands

Sink the Energy Downward

Return to *Wu-chi/Wuji* Empty Stance (as 1)

Standing meditation

Seated meditation

and flexible. It also assists in developing stronger connections of the body and mind as we grow older. Further, the practice of T'ai Chi develops psychic and spiritual awareness in some individuals. T'ai Chi is like a complex symphony of music. At its most advanced stage the body, mind and spirit blend into a unified whole that leads to experience of *Tao*. While the same movements are performed over and over each time, deeper threads are woven into its experience as learning progresses. To summarize, then, spiritual awareness in the practice of T'ai Chi means:

- releasing negative emotional disturbances
- generating positive emotions
- restoring physical, emotional and spiritual balance
- developing psychic potential.

Full spiritual awareness in the practice of T'ai Chi requires learning internal techniques, either solo or with a partner. To Taoists, having true balance and harmony in life means living freely and functioning well from a part within the self that transcends, and is the source of, all *yin* and *yang* relationships. Meditation – either seated (plate 62) or standing (plate 63) – is supportive to serious T'ai Chi practice.

The Yang Style Simplified 24-Step T'ai Chi Ch'üan/Taijiquan *Form*

What follows is a step-by-step guide to the basic postures of the *Yang Style Simplified 24-Step T'ai Chi Form*. While there are many different schools of T'ai Chi, this particular *form* has become very popular. Since it is impossible to include photographs illustrating every aspect of each posture, a video is available that will be useful for the reader to use in conjunction with what follows. For details of how to purchase the video, see p. 271 at the beginning of the *T'ai Chi Further Reading* section. In this book, the 24 postures are illustrated, in colour, in the plate section (after p. 212); the numbers in brackets correspond to the picture numbers. The postures are explained through a set of 63 colour pictures of Shifu Keith Ewers demonstrating each individual movement.

Empty Stance Wu-chi/Wuji

The first posture (1) is called *Empty Stance*. It is an important posture, as it is both the first and the last posture of the T'ai Chi *form*. It is necessary to stand in this posture for a few moments in order to collect oneself both mentally and physically, to relax and centre the mind, and to regulate breathing and gather the vital energy. The individual stands with his or her feet shoulder-width apart. Knees are slightly bent and the body weight is distributed evenly between both legs. Both arms hang from the shoulders alongside the body, but should not be touching. The palms face to the rear with the fingers pointing downward. The torso is relaxed and upright, with the spine straight and the head held up as if suspended from above. The individual then becomes aware of opening certain energy gates within, through which the vital energy is circulated around the entire body. Below is a reminder of a few of the many acupuncture energy points that are used in the practice of T'ai Chi:

- the *pai-hui/baihui* located on the governor meridian which is at the crown of the head.
- the *shan-chung/shanzhong* located in the middle of the chest on the conception meridian.
- the *ch'i-hai/qihai* located just below the navel on the conception meridian.
- the *ming-men/mingmen* located on the spine opposite the navel on the governor meridian.
- the *hui-yin/huiyin* located between the legs on the conception meridian.
- the *lao-kung/laogong* located in the centre of both palms on the pericardium meridian.
- the *yung-ch'üan/yongquan* located on the soles of both feet on the kidney meridian.

Posture one *Awakening the Energy*

From the *Empty Stance* posture the individual begins to lift his or her arms up to shoulder height. The elbows are slightly bent and the wrists gently hang. The palms and fingers are concave (2). He or she then bends from the elbows and gently presses down with both palms towards the waist, the centres of the palms open and the fingers gently extended, at the same time as sinking slowly down from the knees. All the time, while the arms and knees move, the torso remains upright (3).

Posture two *Parting the Horse's Mane*

The left foot is drawn up on the ball of the foot towards the right foot. The body weight should be fully placed onto the right leg. At the same time the waist is slightly turned to the right. The arm and hand positions are as if a ball were being held between both hands. The right palm is above the left palm, with the right elbow pointing downward, the right wrist and fingers are bent as if embracing the ball to the right side. Shoulders should be relaxed and sink downward, but the torso and head are upright (4).

From the position in 4, the left leg is lifted and rotated from the hip as a step is taken towards the left side, lowering onto the heel first, then lowering the ball of the foot, and then the toes, as the body weight begins to transfer from the right leg to the left. The left knee comes over the toes. As weight is beginning to be transferred onto the left leg, the waist is also turned towards the left side, sweeping the left arm round in a circle to finish in front of the left shoulder. The left palm is facing upward and the fingers are pointing in the direction that the body is facing. The right hand will gently press downward to end up alongside the height of the right hip. The palm should face downward and the fingers point out slightly to the side as shown in 5. The *Parting the Horse's Mane* posture is then repeated twice more, switching from right side to left, moving in the same direction (6 and 7). The individual should end up in the same posture as that seen in 4.

Posture three *White Crane Spreads its Wings*

Step up with the right foot and place it behind the heel of the left foot. The toes of the right foot touch the floor first and then the heel is lowered; at the same time the body weight is fully transferred onto it. Step up with the right foot, at the same time embracing the imaginary ball in front of the torso with both hands, the left palm on top of the right, both palms facing each other. The left arm is then lowered, ending up alongside the left hip, palm facing the floor and the fingers pointing forward. At the same time the right arm is raised up the front of the body, with the arm slightly stretched upward, fingers pointing up and the right palm facing in towards the head. Then the left knee is raised and the ball of the left foot is lowered towards the floor. The left heel is kept raised and only the ball of the foot is kept in contact with the ground (8). It is important not to lock the elbow of the raised arm in the *White Crane Spreads its Wings* posture; both arms should be kept concaved with the shoulders having the feeling of sinking downward. The weight is fully on the rear leg; both knees are bent and the hips sit, as if sitting on a high stool. The spinal column is upright, and the eyes look forward.

Posture four *Brush Knee and Side Step*

The right palm is lowered to come directly in front of the face with the palm facing inward towards the body, and continues to be lowered down the centre of the body to the waist. At the same time the left hand begins to circle from the left hip across the chest to end up in front of the right shoulder with the palm facing downward. As the left palm comes alongside the right shoulder the right hand is circled and raised up to shoulder height pointing the fingers and arm towards the rear and diagonally to the right corner. The right palm faces upward, fingers pointing forward to the right corner. The waist turns slightly to the right with the head turning at the same time so that the eyes are looking towards the right rear hand (9). A step forward is taken with the left leg, placing the heel of the left foot onto the ground first then lowering the toes as the body weight transfers from the right leg forward onto the left leg. The left knee is over the toes of the left foot. As the body weight transfers from the rear leg to the front leg, the left arm circles down from the left shoulder across the waist to gently brush the left knee, ending up just outside of the left thigh/hip with the palm facing downward and fingers pointing forward. The right arm also circles forward at the same time as the left arm is moved and as the weight transfers forward, but the right hand circles over the right shoulder, fingers pointing forwards and level with the eyes as it passes over the shoulder. The right arm ends up stretched out in front of the right shoulder, palm facing gently forward, fingers upward, elbow slightly bent (10). The waist turns back to the left as the body moves forward. The eyes follow the movement of the right hand so that the whole body turns in one complete smooth action, finishing with the hips and shoulders square, head facing forward, the right palm stretched forward and the left palm facing downward. Both feet remain in contact with the ground with both knees slightly bent. The *Brush Knee and Side Step* posture is repeated another twice moving in the same direction, switching from right side back to left (11 and 12), ending up in the same posture as seen in 10.

Posture five *Play the Lute*

The right rear leg steps up and is brought into a position just behind the left heel, placing the toes of the right foot down first and then the heel as the weight transfers from the left leg to the right leg. The left hand circles forward, moving upward from the left hip to come in front of the left shoulder. The palm faces inward towards the right with the little finger edge of the hand pointing down and fingers pointing forwards. The elbow is slightly bent and points downward to the ground. At the same time as the left arm is moved forward in a circle, the right arm is circled backwards from the right shoulder to come in front of the navel, with the palm of the right hand facing towards the left side; again the fingers point forward.

Both hands turn, as if rotating a wheel to the right, and both palms gently squeeze inward. As both hands simultaneously move in a circle, the left knee is raised and the left heel slowly lowered onto the ground with the toes pointing upwards, but keeping the body weight fully on the rear leg (13). The torso should be kept upright with the spinal column straight, head held up and the eyes looking forward. The hips sink as if sitting onto a high stool or chair with the weight on the rear leg.

Posture six *Rolling* or *Reeling Arms*

From the last posture, both arms are slowly raised up to shoulder level. Both palms must be facing upward. The head is turned to look at the rear hand. The elbows are slightly bent so that they droop, and the shoulders sink downward. As the arms are raised, the contact area of the left foot is transferred from the heel to the ball of the foot to retain the contact with the ground. The weight remains on the rear right leg and the waist is turned slightly to the right (14). From the position in 14, the right hand is then rolled over the right shoulder, bending from the elbow joint and pointing the fingers directly forward. Then, the right hand is rolled over the left palm, as if gently pushing a ball off the left hand that had been balancing on it.

As the right hand passes over the left hand, the left hand is drawn back alongside the left hip, palm facing upward. The arm should not be touching the body. The action of the hands passing above each other in a gentle pushing and pulling movement is then coordinated with stepping backward with the left leg. Gently making contact with the toes, the body weight is then transferred onto the leg as the left heel is slowly lowered to the ground, so ending in the position shown in 15. The action of raising both arms and rolling them over each other, while continuing to step backward is repeated another three times. This makes a total of four stepping back actions with the legs, ending up with the left leg in front, the left hand stretched out, and the right hand drawn back alongside the right hip. The weight is on the rear right leg.

Posture seven *Grasp the Sparrow's Tail (left)*

From the previous posture, the left leg is drawn back onto the ball of the foot. At the same time the waist is turned slightly to the right side, drawing both arms to the left hip as if holding a ball between both hands. The right hand is above the left with elbows bent. *Grasp the Sparrows Tail* is made up of four movements, which are called *Ward Off*, *Roll Back*, *Squeeze* and *Press*. From the holding the ball position (16), a step is taken diagonally to the left front corner with the left leg. This stepping is done with a heel-to-toe action as the left foot is lowered onto the ground. Rocking the weight from the rear leg to the front, simultaneously, the left arm is moved in a sweeping movement from the right hip. It finishes in front of the chest, as if embracing a ball, with the arm bent at the elbow and the palm facing inward towards the chest. This action is known as *Ward Off* (*p'eng/ peng*). While the left arm is swept across the body, the right hand begins to press downwards alongside the right hip, with the centre of the palm facing the ground (17).

The second movement of *Grasp the Sparrow's Tail* is known as *Roll Back* (*lu*). The left palm is pointed downward towards the right palm, which is then turned to face upward toward the left palm. The weight is then rocked onto the rear leg as the left hand is pulled towards the right hip, as if pulling someone off balance (18).

The third movement of *Grasp the Sparrow's Tail* is termed *Squeeze* (*chi/ji*). The left arm again performs the *Ward Off* movement by sweeping from the left hip across the front of the body at chest height. But the right hand rises up to shoulder height and gently follows the movement of the left arm in a pushing action, where it then makes contact with the wrist of the left arm. Simultaneously, the weight is rocked forward onto the front leg, ending with the right palm squeezing gently against the left wrist. Both elbows are rounded with the tips pointing downward, and the shoulders have a feeling of sinking (19).

The fourth movement of *Grasp the Sparrow's Tail* is called *Press* (*an*). The weight is rocked backward onto the rear right leg and allows the toes of the left foot to point upward, so that the heel is the only part of the foot in contact with the ground. Both hands are separated and begin to press downward towards the waist with the palms facing down. Then, the weight is transferred forward again onto the front left leg. When rocking forward, both arms begin to circle forward in an arc from waist height, finishing in front of the chest with both palms facing forward (20).

Posture eight *Grasp the Sparrow's Tail (right)*

The weight is transferred onto the rear right leg, as the right hand is swept out to the right. The eyes should be following the back of the hand. As the outstretched right hand sweeps out, the waist is allowed to turn fully around to the right. The weight is transferred from the left leg to the right leg and the body turns from the waist, while pivoting on the heel of the left foot. This helps the whole body to turn further around in a 180-degree circle. The weight is then transferred back to the left leg as the right foot is drawn up onto its ball (21). The right hand continues its sweeping circular action, in coordination with the turn of the whole body to end up underneath the left hand, as if holding a ball alongside the left hip. The four movements that were explained in *Grasp the Sparrow's Tail* to the **left** are then repeated on the **right** side of the body, moving in the opposite direction (*Ward Off*, *Roll Back*, *Squeeze*, *Press*, 22, 23, 24 and 25).

Posture nine *Single Whip*

At the end of *Grasping the Sparrow's Tail* the body is in the *Press* position (25) with the right leg forward and the weight on it. The weight is then transferred onto the rear left leg, pivoting on the heel of the right foot, which allows the whole body to turn again in a 180-degree circle to the left. As the body is turned, the left hand sweeps across the chest in an anti-clockwise direction with the palm facing forward and the little finger edge upward. At the same time, the right hand also circles across the body at waist height, in a clockwise direction, with the palm facing inward towards the body. Both hands arrive at the same time alongside the right shoulder, with the right hand stretched out at shoulder height, and the four fingers and thumb touching together in a claw position. The left palm is in front of the right shoulder with the palm facing inward. While both hands circle in their opposite circles, both arriving in front of the right shoulder, the body's weight is simultaneously transferred back onto the right leg, with the left leg drawn up and on the ball of the foot. The eyes are looking at the open left hand.

The left leg then steps with a heel–toe action of the left foot. Transferring the body's weight onto it as the toes are lowered onto the ground, at the same time, the left hand is swept round in a horizontal circle to the left as the body turns around. The left hand is kept at eye level, with the palm facing inward towards the body, and the eyes fixed on the palm. The left hand arrives in front of the face to the left side, with the whole body turning and moving in the same direction. The right hand is still outstretched at shoulder height to the right side, still in its claw position. Then, the left hand is slowly turned around, as if to gently push something away, allowing that left hand to draw a small circle moving from the wrist and finishing with the palm in an upright position facing away from the body (26).

Posture ten *Wave Hands in Clouds*

In this posture, the body begins to move in a sideways direction shifting the weight from one leg to another in a swaying action from side to side, while both hands draw circles in opposite directions to each other. Proceeding from the *Single Whip* posture, both hands are lowered down towards the hips as the body weight is transferred from the left leg to the right leg. The toes of the left foot point inward so that the position is side-on, making contact with the toes first, then the ball of foot and then the heel onto the ground. The body weight begins to be transferred onto the left leg, bending slightly from the knee, which gives the feeling of sinking and connecting with the ground. The left hand circles across the body from the right side, moving in front of the chest with the palm facing inward. It then completes an anti-clockwise circle by lowering down to the left hip, where its palm then faces towards the ground at waist height. The right hand also circles round in front of the body moving in a clockwise direction; again the palm of the right hand faces inward at chest height, but faces the ground as it circles round at waist height. Transferring weight from one leg to another should be timed just as either the left or right hand circles in front of the chest. For example, the weight transfers onto the left leg as the left hand rises in front of the chest and *vice versa* This is shown in 27, where the direction of the *Waving Hands in Clouds* movement is towards the left. The complete *Waving Hands in Clouds* posture is made up of three stepping actions of the left and right feet moving in a sideways direction to the left. In coordination with the movements of the hands circling in opposite directions and the turning of the waist, the head moves from side to side. The eyes follow the hand that is in front of the chest.

Posture eleven *Single Whip*

Proceeding from the *Waving Hands in Clouds* posture, as the body weight transfers onto the right leg and the right hand circles across the chest, the right hand forms a claw position with the four fingers and thumb touching. The arm is stretched out to the right side above shoulder height, while the left-hand circles up in front of the right shoulder, facing inward towards the body. Eyes are directed at the palm. The weight is then drawn up onto the ball of the left foot. Then, the left leg is raised and a step taken to the left side in a heel–toe action, transferring the body weight onto it. The left hand sweeps outward in front of the left shoulder. The hand is turned round in a circle so that the palm of the hand faces forward. The waist turns to the left as the left hand is swept out, at the same time as pivoting on the back heel to help square up the hips and shoulders so that the whole body is moving in the same direction (28).

Posture twelve *High Pat on Horse*

Moving on from the *Single Whip* posture in 28, both arms stay out at shoulder height, with the left hand ahead of the right. The back right leg steps up behind the heel of the front left foot in a toe–heel action, transferring the body weight from the front left leg to the back right leg. As the body weight rocks onto the back leg both palms are pointed upward towards the sky. Both elbows are slightly bent, with the tips of the elbows pointing downward and with the shoulders having a relaxed, sinking feeling. The eyes are looking straight ahead at the left hand. The rear right arm rolls over the right shoulder towards the left hand, where it passes over the top of it, as if gently pushing a ball off the left hand. As the right hand passes over the top of the left hand, the left hand draws back alongside the left hip with the palm facing upward, but the arm should not be touching the body. The left leg then raises up from the knee and lowers down again onto the ball of the foot so that all of the body weight is on the back leg (29).

Posture thirteen *Right Heel Kick*

A small step is taken to the left side with the left foot and the body weight is immediately transferred onto it. As the step is taken to the left side, the left wrist crosses over the back of the right wrist and both hands expand outward and downward in a circle moving from the shoulders. They should end up crossed in front of the chest with the right arm on the outside of the left, but with both palms facing inward towards the body. The right leg is then raised up so that the knee is level with the hip in coordination with the crossing of the arms (figure 30). Then, the right leg is slowly kicked out, extending the leg as if kicking out with the heel so that the toes point upward. Simultaneously, both arms are extended outward, sweeping out with the little finger edge of both hands. The left arm extends outward at shoulder height towards the left, and the right arm extends outward in front of the right shoulder above the extended right leg. Both palms face outward, with the hands upright and fingers pointing upward. The elbow tips point downward and the shoulders also sink downward as well. The standing leg is slightly bent at the knee, allowing the body weight to sink downward, lowering the centre of gravity (31).

Posture fourteen *Strike the Ears with Both Fists*

Proceeding from the *Right Heel Kick* the right leg is bent as both palms are turned upward, brought together in front of the chest, and then drawn backwards towards the hips. At the same time the right leg is lowered down onto the ground making contact with the heel; toes are raised off the floor. Both hands coil round underneath the armpits and form two hollow fists, where they then circle round from the hips to come level with the head. Both palms of the fists face forward. As the fists circle forward the body weight is transferred forward onto the front right leg at the same time. The eyes are looking straight ahead and the body is kept upright and should not lean forward. Both elbows are bent and the shoulders sink downward (32).

Posture fifteen *Turn the Body and Left Heel Kick*

From the previous posture of *Strike the Ears with Both Fists* (32), the eyes are focused on the left hand as both palms are opened. The body begins to turn to the left, by transferring weight from the right leg to the left, and pivoting on the right heel in an anti-clockwise direction. At the same time a circle is drawn with both arms, lowering the arms down towards both hips and quickly transferring the body weight back onto the right leg. Both arms are then crossed in front of the chest, with the left arm on the outside of the right arm. Both hands face inward towards the body, wrists gently touching. As both arms are raised and crossed, the left knee is also raised to about the height of the left hip (33). Then, the left leg is slowly extended out, as if kicking with the bottom of the heel. The toes should point upward and the knee is slightly bent. At the same time as extending the left leg, both arms also sweep out. The right arm sweeps out to the right side at shoulder height, while the left arm sweeps out in front of the left shoulder. The elbows of both arms point downward, towards the ground. Both palms face outward. The sweeping of the arms and the extending of the leg should be co-ordinated together (34).

Posture sixteen *Snake Creeps Down to the left and Rooster Stands on One Leg*

The left knee is bent and at the same time the left arm is brought in a downward arc to finish in front of the right shoulder with the palm facing inward. The right hand bends at the wrist with the four fingers and thumb coming together in a claw position as in the *Single Whip* posture (35). The left leg is lowered down onto the ground keeping the body weight on the right leg. As it is lowered, the left arm is swept along the inside of the left leg (figure 36). The body weight is transferred forward onto the left leg, scooping the left arm up in front of the shoulder with the palm facing forward. As the body weight moves forward, the back right leg slides up slightly. In order to help maintain balance the right hand is lowered alongside the right hip, still in a claw position (37).

From the *Snake Creeps Down* posture as shown in 37, we move on to *Rooster Stands on One Leg*. Again, the weight is transferred onto the right leg. The left hip is opened by pivoting on the left heel, pointing the toes outward. Then, weight is transferred back onto the left leg, lowering the left hand to the left hip, with the palm facing downward towards the ground. Immediately, the weight moves forward onto the left leg. The right knee is slowly raised to hip height, at the same time raising the right arm. The right hand finishes in front of the right shoulder, fingers pointing upward and the palm facing sideways towards the left. The eyes look straight ahead, with the body in an upright position (38).

Posture seventeen *Snake Creeps Down to the right and Rooster Stands on One Leg*

From *Rooster Stands on One Leg* we now move to the right. The right leg is slowly lowered onto the ball of the foot but still keeping the body weight on the left leg. The following movement involves pivoting on the balls of both feet towards the left so that the body is turned side on (39). Another step forward is taken with the right leg, but the body is lowered towards the ground, as in posture 16. But this time it's the right hand that sweeps along the inside of the right leg (40). The body's weight is transferred forward onto the right leg, scooping the right arm upward in front of the right shoulder with the palm facing forward, and sliding up on the left leg slightly in order to help maintain balance (41). The left arm then lowers down towards the left hip, still maintaining the claw position. Again this is a repeat of posture sixteen, but with the left arm and knee raised (42).

Posture eighteen *Shuttle Back and Forth* or *Fair Lady Weaves Shuttle*

A small step is taken to the left side with the left leg in a heel–toe action, transferring the body weight onto the left leg. Drawing up onto the ball of the right foot, the body is turned slightly towards the left side. The arm position is as if a ball were held between both hands, with the left hand on top of the right hand (43). Then, a diagonal step towards the right front corner is taken, with the right leg moving in a heel–toe action, again transferring the body weight forward onto it. The right arm moves in an upward arc above the head, with the palm facing forward. At the same time as the right arm sweeps above the head, the left hand pushes forward in front of the chest, again with the palm facing forward (44). The body's weight is then rocked backwards onto the left leg, and the right hip is opened by pivoting on the right heel, turning the toes outward.

Then, immediately, the body weight is again transferred onto the right leg and the left leg is drawn up towards the right leg, moving onto the ball of the foot. At the same time, the body is turned to the right side. The arms appear as if holding a ball between both hands. The right hand should be above the left (45). Then, with the left leg, a diagonal step is taken towards the left front corner in a heel–toe action, transferring the body weight forward onto the left leg. The left arm sweeps upward in an arc above the head with its palm facing forward. Immediately, the body pushes forward with the right hand directly in front of the chest with the palm facing forward (46).

Posture nineteen *Scoop* or *Pick up Needle from Sea Bottom*

From the previous posture of *Shuttle Back and Forth* (46), step up with the right foot behind the heel of the left foot in a toe–heel action, transferring the body weight backward onto the right leg. Then, both arms are lowered to the waist, with the left palm facing the ground alongside the left hip. The right arm sweeps downward towards the waist and then arcs upward to the right shoulder. The left knee is raised to hip height. The right hand then extends forward towards the ground, with the fingers pointing downward and the palm facing sideways. As the right hand is extended towards the ground the left leg is lowered onto the ball of the foot at the same time, making sure to co-ordinate the movement of the right hand and left leg together (47).

Posture twenty *Fan through the Back*

Moving on from the previous posture, both hands are raised in front of the chest with the right hand above the left, but with the fingers of the left hand pointing upward towards the right wrist palm of the left hand, which is facing forward. Both arms are bent. At the same time as both arms are raised, the left leg is also raised. A step forward is then taken with the left leg, in a heel–toe action, transferring the weight forward at the same time. The right hand is pulled back over the head, with the palm facing outward. The left palm is extended forward in a gentle pushing action in front of the left shoulder (48).

Posture twenty-one *Turn the Body, Deflect, Parry and Punch*

The body is turned in a 180-degree turn to the right, shifting the body weight onto the right leg, and pivoting on the heel of the left foot so that the body is side on. The right hand circles in a clockwise direction from above the head to finish up in front of the left shoulder in a fist, with the palm facing downward. As the right hand arrives in front of the left shoulder, the body weight is rocked onto the left leg (49). This completes the *Turn the Body* part of the posture.

The left hand circles upward above the head with the palm facing upward. At this moment, the left knee is bent and carries the weight of the whole body. The turning of the body must be in co-ordination with the arrival of the left hand above the head and the right fist ending up in front of the left shoulder as the body weight rocks from right to left leg. The left palm continues to lower until it arrives level with the abdomen. The right fist continues its sweeping, arcing movement down the front of the body in a downward fist action, where it finishes at the right hip. As this is all happening the right knee is raised, with the toes of the right pointing outward towards the right side (50). This is the *Deflect* part of the posture.

For the *Parry* part of the posture the right foot is placed onto the ground in front of the body and the body weight transfers onto it. This is deflective movement. The left hand then does a circular movement of the arm and hand across the chest, as if to brush something aside. The left palm is side on, with the fingers pointing upward (51).

For the *Punch* part of the posture, a step forward is taken with the left leg, placing the left foot in a heel–toe action onto the ground; the body weight is immediately transferred forward onto it. The left hand is still in the *Parry* position in the centre of the chest. Then, slowly, the right fist is extended forward in a punching action in front of the chest (52).

Posture twenty-two *Appears Closed*

The left hand is rotated to the outside of the right arm's forearm. The left hand is slid down the length of the right arm from elbow to wrist until it faces up as shown in 53. The weight is shifted onto the right leg while the toes of the left foot point upward. Both palms are pulled back towards the body in a circular action, as if following the lines of a large ball, in a horizontal circle. Then, both palms are lowered downward towards the waist, alongside the abdomen (54). Both palms then push forward, while shifting the weight forward to the left leg. Both hands push forward from the abdomen to shoulder height in an arcing movement. Both elbows are bent with the hands upright (55).

Posture twenty-three *Cross Hands*

The weight is shifted to the right leg, lifting the ball of the left foot and beginning a turn of the body 180-degrees to the right. The left foot is turned until it points forward, and then the right foot is turned out. While the body rotates, the right hand is extended to the right, and the left hand is pulled slightly to the left (56). The weight is shifted back to the left leg and both arms begin to lower. The right foot is brought closer to the left until both feet are about shoulder-width apart, while both hands scoop down and upward, crossing both wrists in front of the face with the right hand on the outside of the left. Keeping both knees bent, the body then comes to a slightly standing position (57 and 58).

Posture twenty-four *Sink the Energy Downward*

Both hands are rotated until they are facing downward. Then, the hands are separated until they are shoulder-width apart, with the elbows bent and the palms facing downward (59). The hands are lowered downward to the hips. As the arms lower down towards the hips the body also gently sinks downward from the knees, which should give the feeling of sinking or lowering the energy downward towards the abdomen. Both palms gently press downward as the arms lower (60). An upright position is then taken and the arms are allowed to hang down with the finger tips pointing downward, but the arms should not be touching the body. This position is held for a while, so allowing the energy to circulate and balance itself within the whole body (61). The closing position is, thus, the *Empty Stance* position that preceded the *form*.

This nearly completes the explanation of the *Yang Style Simplified 24-Step T'ai Chi Form.* Two remaining points need to be mentioned. The first is a question of direction. The *form* outlined above has been described moving in one direction as a whole. After completing it, the twenty-four postures are then done in the opposite direction. This will mean altering the movements so that the effect is a mirror image of the first set. The second aspect is breathing. Breathing should be soft, silent, deep and smooth: it should not be loud, forced or held. Breathing is inhaled and exhaled through the nose, and the tongue should gently touch the hard palate just behind the top teeth, but the tongue should not touch the teeth. Breathing mainly works on a balanced *yin/yang* method where the inward breath is as long as the outward breath. But there are some movements where the inward breath is slightly longer than the outward breath. In the practice of the Tai Chi *form*, when movements bring the arms closer towards the body, inhalation takes place. When arms or legs are extended further away from the body then exhalation occurs. Such a rhythm allows breathing to be co-ordinated with the opening and closing actions of the body's joints. It will bring about the feeling of shrinking and expanding of internal energy from the centre of the body, so allowing the energy points within the whole body to fully open and close. When this happens, the negative and positive energies of Heaven and Earth within are better exchanged and balanced. In chapter 15 of the *Yang Family Forty Chapters* are the following words:

> The human ability to interpret energy relies on the senses to respond to changing conditions and naturally produces marvelous results. Our body achieves perfect clarity without effort, and our movement becomes supremely sensitive. When your skill reaches this level, whatever you do will come easily and you can move without thinking.[2]

Yang Jwing Ming points out that, while T'ai Chi is a meditative practice it promotes peacefulness, calm, clarity of mind and a greater ability to see into the depth of things: the "spiritual side of things starts to open up", he says. So, in his view, the inner spiritual abilities acquired in martial arts have their wider effects in attitudes and wisdom in life itself.[3] Thus, the beginning of the pathway to wisdom comes through a practice such as T'ai Chi Ch'üan/Taijiquan.

8 Unity

Taoism has accumulated a store of mythologies that are not only unique to its own development, but which also have to be seen against the wider setting of Chinese tradition and culture. Traditions about ancestors, deities, immortals and sages have been handed down for generations not only by Taoists themselves but by Confucians, Buddhists and ordinary folk, and with considerable overlap of these religious cultures. Thus, the myths and legends of ancient historical and legendary personages of human or divine form have been embellished down the centuries with contributions from wider Chinese contexts than Taoism itself. Many practice T'ai Chi Ch'üan/Taijiquan without the need to explore such a background. For others, however, T'ai Chi Ch'üan/Taijiquan is one expression of religious practice and cannot be separated from its religious roots. We need, then, to glimpse something of the religious backdrop from which Taoism sprang. While it is not within the remit of this book to deal with the major religious sects of Taoism, a glance at the ultimate fate of the adherents of such sects in a life beyond Earth will provide some insight into the religious beliefs of Taoists. Ancestors reflect the very roots of Taoism in ancient Chinese customs, well before its advent as a religion. Deities reflect the origins and growth of religious Taoism, and the establishment of ritual patterns. Immortals reflect the search for ultimate goals in a non-reincarnating life beyond Earth, and the search for inner means to immortality. And sages reflect the internalization of the means to a full life beyond death. It is with the sage that T'ai Chi Ch'üan/Taijiquan in its present forms shows the greatest affinity. While T'ai Chi may set aside religious Taoism its concepts remain close to the tenets of philosophical Taoism, and to the sage as the outcome of its practice. Let us now look at each of these in turn.

Ancestors

The veneration of ancestors was essential to Chinese culture. It provided the link between the living and the dead that made sense of life, and it accentuated the role of the family unit by encouraging respect of the younger for the elder and for the deceased, entrenched by customary rites. With justification, considering its influence, Thompson describes the presence of the veneration of ancestors in China as "the very warp of a high culture throughout millennia of time".[1] I have used the term "veneration" to avoid the pitfalls that the more frequently used expression "worshipped" suggests. For in fact, while ancestors of the great emperors frequently found themselves deified and ritually approached as such, in the wider context of family life, ancestors were respected and venerated, but hardly worshipped, though reciprocal aid might be expected between the living and the dead. Such a concept was the foundation of much Chinese belief and practice from ancient times, and remained so throughout its long history. Ancestor veneration provided a continuum and unity between life and death on the one hand, and permitted the dead a continued role in the context of life in the world on the other. Stephen Teiser puts the position succinctly:

> If the system works well, then the younger generations support the senior ones, and the ancestors bestow fortune, longevity, and the birth of sons upon the living. As each son fulfills his duty, he progresses up the family scale, eventually assuming his status as revered ancestor. The attitude toward the dead (or rather the significant and, it is hoped, benevolent dead – one's ancestors) is simply a continuation of one's attitude towards one's parents while they were living. In all cases, the theory goes, one treats them with respect and veneration by fulfilling their personal wishes and acting according to the dictates of ritual tradition.[2]

This succinct statement of the nature of the case shows very clearly that worship is not an appropriate term for the relationship between the living and their ancestors.

Deities

It is religious Taoism that has built up and collected a numerous variety of deities of all kinds, deities that have been gleaned from traditions, local stories of heroes, of magical places, and ancient legends. The whole gamut of nature, officialdom, history, legend, fact, shamanism and fame, has contributed to an enormous pantheon of gods and spirits. Some are celestial, some stellar. Some are connected to mountains, streams and the like, some are historical people who have become immortal. Some incarnate on Earth, some are human, and others are not. Even Taoist Masters have been deified. Providing the credibility of the deity is maintained by a belief in its power, then that deity is recognized through ritual practice. Conversely, where such power appears to have waned, the deity becomes obsolete.

There is a certain pragmatism attached to the polytheistic worship of deities that has characterized Chinese religion in general from its ancient past. Early belief in the deities and spirits associated with natural forces, along with localized gods of the earth, locality, city, district and home, indicate well how much deities were associated with the ongoing lives of the people. Given the emphasis on the family and importance of territorial safety, each area had its own traditions about gods so that consistency in legends is impossible to find. Yet, at a deeper level, it has to be said that however much pragmatism informs the worship of many deities, philosophically they are all united by *Tao*, emanate from *Tao*, and are infused by *Tao*: the kaleidoscope of myriad divinities must, ultimately, be united as one. However, in some ways philosophical and mystical Taoism was an intrusion into a world of polytheistic animism, which has never really left the ordinary folk. Palmer and Zhao Xiaomin aptly state: "In a world where every year has its own deity, each day is watched over by good and bad spirits and when every hour has its good luck or bad luck influence, the physical world is wrapped and encapsulated in the spiritual world. What remains consistent is that the old shamanistic understanding that the spirit world is more powerful, even more real than this physical one, remains. Life has to be undertaken by negotiating your way through with the aid of the gods."[3] These words illustrate well the pragmatism of belief in a plurality of deities rather than more philosophical contemplation of a mystical unity that underpins them. As the same authors go on to say: "Believing in the Taoist deities is a little like playing the lottery. You just never know when you might be blessed!"[4]

While Taoism has a vast array of deities they are not essential to the designation of a person as a Taoist. Blofeld commented: "The fact is that deities entered the body of Taoism more or less accidentally and may be regarded or disregarded at will."[5] While the first part of this statement is debatable given the deep shamanistic influence on Taoist thought and its natural interdependence of human and supernatural, the second part is certainly valid. Indeed, those attracted to Taoism in the West, for example Masters or practitioners of T'ai Chi Ch'üan/Taijiquan, and those inspired by philosophical Taoism, have little knowledge or awareness of the deities that proliferate religious Taoism past and present. But the statement still stands that deities can be accepted or disregarded entirely. Given theories like the transforming changes of the *I Ching/Yijing*, the theories of *yin* and *yang* and the Five Elements, there was no need for a creator deity, and the world could operate in unending change quite by itself. Where they were important, however, was in the revelations they were believed to give humankind. This was especially so with the sacred texts of the different schools of religious Taoism, each being associated with a particular divine patron. At the popular level, nevertheless, ordinary Taoists would propitiate a number of deities – earth, local, district or city, for example – and would pay their respects to different deities on special days throughout the year.

Immortals

In its long history, Taoism courted a number of theories about immortality and the means to procure it. The *Tao Te Ching/Daodejing* does not seem to contain immortality as a major theme of its text. The *Chuang-tzu/Zhuangzi*, too, regards death as a balance of life, part of the natural rhythm and order of things, and an unavoidable end to life that only the enlightened sage can take in his stride. But the text also refers to *shen-jen/shenren*, "divine men". Alchemical Taoism, as we saw in chapter 6, had an altogether different view. Longevity was the aim of the alchemists and, by extension, eternal life in immortality, accomplished through return to *Tao* by the means of a Spirit Embryo that would mature within. Then, too, the ordinary mortal, the ordinary Taoist, would not contemplate everlasting life. Rather, he or she would hope for a good and blessed present one. To these ideas must be added the concept of life as very anthropomorphic immortals, in tune with *Tao* but able to live a colourful life on Earth or in the heavens. Of these, eight are especially famous (see pp. 235–7).

Origins and early nature

The idea of immortality in China is an ancient one, with legends of those who have transcended death to live in heavenly realms, or of those who live in lonely parts of mountains and forests. Some were believed to have had apparent rather than real deaths. Such concepts were widespread in

Chinese thought in the third century BCE. But, according to Robinet, the belief in physical immortality is witnessed on Shang bronze inscriptions dated to as early as the eighth century BCE, and talk of the isles where plants for immortality grew was present in court circles in the fourth century BCE.[6] In time, the status of immortals rose to exceed that of the earth gods. It came to be believed that, through excessively good merit, some mortals could by-pass the hells after death, and take their place in the ranks of heavenly beings, from where they would be able to rise in status, eventually becoming full immortals.

The Chinese character for immortal is *hsien/xian*, which is usually translated as "immortal", even as "genie". It can also mean "perfected" or "transcendent". It refers to a person who has lived such a holy and spiritual life that he or she has transcended normal patterns of existence and has taken on the nature of a saint. The Chinese character *hsien/xian* is itself composed of two characters, one for "human being" and the other for "mountain". Put together, the image is of a mortal being who dwells in the mountains, or of one who transcends. Thus, as Schipper points out: 'Phonologically, the word *hsien/xian* derives from the root meaning "to change, evolve, go up," or even "to dance." This recalls the themes of transformation, of ascension to heaven, and of dance which, in the ritual, allows one to take possession of a sacred space.'[7] Schipper's words here are reminiscent of the shamanic dances and flights of the shaman to the realms of the spirits and gods. But one characteristic seems to pervade the concept of an immortal, and that is the easy-going, free and spontaneous nature of those who realize such a level of spirituality. A variant form of the character for *hsien/xian* in the *Book of Songs* means "to dance with flying sleeves", a superb picture of the free immortal. Kohn notes that, according to the commentary on the *Book of Songs*, the combination of the human being and the mountain in the Chinese character can mean "to reach old age and not to die". Thus, Kohn comments: "The obvious basic implication of the term *xian* is therefore twofold. It connotes, first, the idea of a take-off, a separation from normal life, be it in an ecstatic dance or by going into the mountains; and, second, the notion of longevity and the complete avoidance of death."[8]

In particularly graphic words, Robinet described the immortals thus:

> Immortals prefer to live in hiding, far from the world, withdrawn into the mountains and often living in caves. . . . They are masters of the rain and the wind, like the wu sorcerers, and . . . they can pass through fire without burning and through water without getting wet. These are the signs that

> they know how to control Yin and Yang (water and rain, fire and wind). They move up and down with the clouds, as they please. They have wings, on which feathers grow, and they ride either cranes or fish (air-yang and water-yin). They know the future. They are masters of time and space. They can, at will, reduce the world to the size of a gourd, or turn a gourd into a world as vast as the universe. They are evanescent, disappearing and appearing in the wink of an eye.[9]

These are words that portray many of the characteristics of the early shamans, and immortals combine the skills of the latter in healing and magical practices. They are usually portrayed as being eternally youthful, with soft skin, shining eyes, square pupils, elongated head, long ears, a luminous body, and movement as swift, nimble and fleet as a deer. Their figures cast no shadow, though they can exist disguised as ordinary mortals. They seem to be astride the human and divine realms and able to function in either. But at a deeper level they are at one with the universe, with *Tao*. The shamans, especially, were known to be able to travel out of ordinary existence into the divine world. Immortals do the same; indeed, Kohn sees this feature as the significant connection between shamans and immortals.[10] The "free and easy wandering" of the *Chuang-tzu/Zhuangzi* – the ability to traverse the earth and the heavens – is characteristic of immortals. And they have a freedom of movement and a joyous naturalness that are often exhibited in dance.

Much literature supported the belief in immortals. The *Shen-hsien chuan/Shenxian zhuan* "Biographies of Spirit Immortals" was one important post-Han text written by Ko Hung/Ge Hong in the fourth century.[11] The literature concerned with immortals gives not only an account of their lives but, also, some description of the method by which immortality was achieved in each case. These methods, as Schipper notes, are not uniform: "There are as many ways to become immortal as there are Immortals, and there is nothing systematic about it."[12] Some of the literature connected with immortals clearly points to the legendary nature of many of them. On the other hand, some were historical figures. Some of the latter obviously died naturally, but are believed to have had their physical being and spirit reunited after death.

Sipping dew and riding on clouds

Not all immortals are portrayed as secretive, mystical beings. They might ride the winds and sip dew, but many are depicted as colourful characters. It is especially in the popular mind that these more accessible immortals are held dear. These are the immortals that engage in earthly events, appearing to uphold justice and defend the weak. It is these who are artistically portrayed in art and iconography, and who take on profoundly anthropomorphic personalities. They sip dew, which might also, on occasions, be wine, or be seen playing the lute. They are merry people, at ease with each other and with themselves, existing in perfect contentment. Unlike deities and ancestors, they are not confined to particular locations like temples, for their "free and easy wandering" is a major facet of their nature. Blofeld noted that immortals are often likened to floating clouds that *are* without making any effort to *be*: "The filmy lightness of an idling summer cloud is suggestive of the sensation of weightlessness that characterises immortals, a sensation born of absolute freedom from care and anxiety."[13] Immortals thus epitomized the ultimate goal for mortals – in whatever way that goal was visualized. Physical contentment in a physical body could be the end product of one's spiritual efforts, as much as life in the abodes of the immortals, or passage into the ultimate non-being of *Tao*: it was simply a matter of degree. But the path was not an easy one, and this point is reflected in the portrayal of some immortals as old men, representing the years of arduous pursuit of the spiritual goal.

The Eight Immortals (*Pa-hsien/Baxian*)

Of all the immortals, eight are particularly special. They are found in a prominent position in most Taoist temples, where they have the special function of warding off evil. They are to be seen in the home, at celebrations like weddings and anniversaries, or represented in dance at the beginning of theatrical performances. They are depicted on paintings, vases, plates, teapots, and can be found in shops and garden centres in the West. Such is their importance that they are not just a Taoist phenomenon, but are popular in the wider context of Chinese religious life as a whole. Since these Eight Immortals defend the weak and uphold justice they illustrate that the life-condition of the truly good person can be turned from one of poverty to riches or from oppression to joy. In short, they provide hope, and the Immortals are always ready to intervene in the human situation to turn hope into reality. Given the hardship of the peasants and lowest strata of Chinese society, the tales of the Eight Immortals were welcomed as illustrations of how persecutors could themselves be punished and how the rich could be brought low. The tales of the Immortals are ones in which happiness follows sadness for those who are virtuous.

The Eight Immortals are examples of those who have reached the ultimate goal but who have remained in the world, or returned to it, to help others. They participate in the lives of ordinary folk, disguising themselves to perpetrate justice. They are funny, happy, free and very different individuals, who were often drunk! Their purpose in the many tales and anecdotes about them is manifold. Apart from championing justice, for example, sometimes an explanation for a geographical feature like the grottoes of Ching Ling/Jingling is explained by a story about them – in this case their digging and burrowing through the mountain in search of a precious pearl.[14] But they are champions of Taoism, helping people to understand the functioning of *Tao* in the world. Then, too, the characters in the stories reflect the daily life of ordinary people – the oil seller, woodcutter, beggar, local commissioner, for example. Of the Eight, however, some have always been more popular than others: Lü Tung-pin/Lü Dongbin, Li T'ieh-kuai/Li Tieguai and Chang Kuo-lao/Zhang Guolao, the first three, are far more important than the rest.

Some of the Eight only occur in the context of the others in their group, but the important ones are portrayed in tales individually. Their characters span social boundaries of rich and poor, official and peasant, male and female, old and young, the healthy and the sick. The origins of the tales of the Eight Immortals date back to T'ang/Tang times, though the tales about them were developed more significantly in Sung/Song times. But it was not until Ming times that the official legends about the Immortals were finalized.

While the Taoist adept is able to leave his or her body for flights to Heaven, to the stars, or to ride on the winds, ultimately there is a final transcendence of all worldly life and the passage into full immortality. Those who remain in contact with the earthly sphere are a constant reminder of the spontaneity and naturalness of the liberated person, and of the necessity for turning away from worldly conventions to lose the self in nature, and the spirit in *Tao*. The message of the immortals is put remarkably well by Schipper, who writes:

> Every human being, whether big or small, humble or great, young woman or old man, musician, herbalist, clown, or scholar, may – on the sole condition of finding his or her own mountain – quit the treadmill of progress towards death and discover the return towards life. It is not even necessary to act intentionally: luck and a certain predisposition may sometimes be the only needed conditions, but nothing is guaranteed. It is necessary, however, to at all times be open and prepared to recognize, at a given moment of one's life, the mountain or the initiating Immortal,

which some day is to be found on everyone's life path. It is in this readiness and openness that we find all possible latitude for individual free will and faith.[15]

Sages

Much has been written about the sage in previous chapters, and it is my purpose here simply to draw together the various strands. Indeed, the Taoist sage is the culmination of years of effort by the adept, and is the true conclusion of life on Earth that culminates in immortal life beyond it. There are many terms used for the sage – *sheng-jen/shengren*, "sage" or "saint", the term used in the *Tao Te Ching/Daodejing*; *chen-jen/zhenren*, "true", "real" or "perfect being"; *shen-jen/shenren*, "spirit being"; *chih-jen/zhiren*, "perfect being",[16] the terms found in the *Chuang-tzu/Zhuangzi*. While inhabiting Earth, the sage has the means to traverse beyond it in the same way as immortals. He is at one with *Tao*, but his involvement in human affairs can range from the rulership of the sage-king of early texts like the *Tao Te Ching/Daodejing* to instruction of disciples on lonely mountainsides. This two-fold nature of the sage epitomizes the distinction between those involved in life, and those who withdrew from it to solitude. The term "sage" is, therefore, an all-embracing one, though it encompasses for all sages the status of imminent immortality, and the ability to be both this-worldly and other-worldly, the perfect pivot between Heaven and Earth.

It is the ability to be astride this and the other world beyond ordinary life that links sages with the shamans of the ancient past. With the sage we find none of the ecstatic and wilder activities of the shaman, but the thread of continuity between the two is not that difficult to see. Indeed, when they become immortals they will have all the skills of shamans, many of which they acquire in pre-immortal state. They acquire power over nature and time, and act in unconventional ways. So, in a way, we have come full circle from the shamans of ancient times to the sage as the ultimate goal of the Taoist adept: both sages and immortals display so many of the characteristics of the old shamanic practices.[17] In particular, it is the flights of the sage beyond his mortal body to the corners of the universe, flying on clouds and dragons, which are so reminiscent of the shamans.

It is with the sage that we find much in affinity with the ultimate goal of T'ai Chi Ch'üan/Taijiquan. The sage has transcended the dualities of life that bind the human mind to the world. Easiness of mind, naturalness of life and spontaneity of action are the outcome of a life rooted in *Tao*, and of a human who has transcended the limitations of ordinary existence and is cosmic in nature. The nature of the sage in the *Tao Te Ching/Daodejing* and in the *Chuang-tzu/Zhuangzi* was discussed in chapter 3, but the *Huai-nan-tzu/Huainanzi* sums up well the early view of the sage, as well as pointing forward to the later concept:

> Therefore, those who penetrate the Way return to purity and quiescence.
> Those who look deeply into things end in doing nothing.
> If you nourish your innate nature through calmness
> And stabilize your numen through stillness,
> You will enter the Gateway of Heaven. . . .
> Therefore the sage does not allow the human to becloud the Heavenly,
> And does not allow desires to disrupt his true responses (qing).
> Without planning he hits the mark;
> Without speaking he is trusted.
> Without deliberating he attains,
> Without acting he succeeds,
> His vital essence is absorbed into the spiritual storehouse,
> And he is a companion of the Creative Force (the Way).[18]

Inner stillness

The sage is the culmination of earthly life and the medium for transcendence to the heavenly one. He is at the same time in the world and beyond it at the pinnacle of reality, *Tao* itself, and he has the freedom to wander at will from one to the other. His egoistic self has vanished, and he is ageless like the sun and moon. Like the shamans of old, the Taoist sages left the confines of the world for the splendours of the heavens. Mount K'un-lun/Kunlun was the *axis mundi* of the world, the point at which travel between Heaven and Earth was possible. Thus, it was the place where the Taoist sage could best transcend the world and fly to the heavenly realms:

> My body not submerged,
> My bones not heavy,
> I spur a blue simurgh,[19]
> And harness a white phoenix.
> Pennants and parasols whirling upward, I enter the cool void.
> A celestial wind sighs and soughs; the Starry River moves.
> Turquoise watchtowers jagged and serrated: Amah's household.
> Playful and relaxed beside storied buildings and platforms:
> Congealed red lacquer clouds.

Five sets of three little transcendents ride dragon chariots.
Before her audience hall, they grind flowers of the coiling peach tree into mush.
Turning my head, I look back once more to the summit of P'eng-lai
A single dot of thick mountain mist within a deep well.[20]

Here, the adept ascends to the palace of The Queen Mother of the West (Amah) where he is given the elixir of immortality made from ground peaches. Thence, he ascends so high that the mountain he left is like a dot at the bottom of a well. Such wandering in the universe "leads out of the entanglements of given laws into a freedom in which the rules of tradition no longer prevail".[21] Symbolic flights through the heavens were a particular feature of Shang-ch'ing/Shangqing Taoism. Here, they were facilitated by the vividness of the scriptures and the meditational visualizations deep within the self. Robinet wrote of sages:

They know the exact location and structure of the spirit routes. The scriptures revealed by the gods inform them of the roads of the divinities, the ways of the Yin and Yang, the passes and the gates of the various heavens, the landmarks of the earth. They become familiar with the paths and the directions leading from the earth to the heavens, they learn to navigate along the stations of the sun and the moon, they know the exact ways by which the sun brings light to the earth and by which the stars and the moon draw shining patterns and constellations on the nocturnal sky.[22]

It is a journey to the furthest reaches of the universe, a journey beyond the ordinary self, or even the transcendent self. It is a journey that ultimately loses the self in utter tranquillity and serenity, stillness and emptiness. Such is the ultimate aim of T'ai Chi Ch'üan/Taijiquan.

The sage is a truly "perfected" being, perfectly poised in all situations, and in harmony with himself within and with the world without. Experiencing all things as *Tao*, and immersed in a reality that is both within the world and transcends it, his nature has become cosmic like *Tao* itself. He acts spontaneously, not having to think or plan responses to situations. The *Huai-nan-tzu/Huainanzi* says of the sage:

In his life proceeds with Heaven,
In his death transforms with other things.
In stillness he closes up with the Yin,
In motion he opens up with the Yang.
His Numinous Essence is placidly . . . limitless
It is not dispersed amidst phenomena
And the entire world naturally submits. . . .

> He knows without studying.
> He sees without looking.
> He completes without acting.
> He regulates without disputing.
> When stirred he responds
> When pressed he moves. . . . [23]

Because the sage has become empty of individual personality and self-hood, he is like a pure tube through which the light of *Tao* pours into his being. The rhythm of the universe floods through him, linking him to the ten thousand things with which he is in total harmony and unity. Perfect simplicity and innocence to all things pervades the mind and being of the sage. Thus, he conforms to the transformations of *Tao* as they occur in the universe, knowing that they will take their own courses in an orderly rhythm: he is totally harmonized with such rhythm. All conventional knowledge is dispelled for a state of ignorance that, paradoxically, opens the mind to the entire universe. It is a process of "forgetting the forgetting", that is to say forgetting all conventional knowledge even to the extent that you have forgotten that you have forgotten it. Thus, the mind becomes truly empty and freed from its own volition. It is in this state of no-self, of utter emptiness and void, that *Tao* is found.

The essence of the sage is pure *Tao*, and, as such, the self is desireless. The senses perceive in every way, but there is no reaction from the self in terms of desire or aversion. Loss of the self-assertive ego is the hall-mark of the enlightened being. While pleasure or anger may occasionally be expressed by the sage, as Fung Yu-lan commented: "But since his mind has an impersonal, objective, and impartial attitude, when these feelings come, they are simply objective phenomena in the universe, and are not especially connected with his self. When he is pleased or angry, it is simply the external things, deserving of either pleasure or anger, that produce corresponding feelings in his mind."[24] As Fung Yu-lan goes on to say, when the object initiating the emotion is removed, the emotion itself is also removed, just as the reflection in a mirror vanishes when we move our position. Thus: "In a bright mirror, a beautiful object produces a beautiful reflection, while an ugly object produces an ugly one. But the mirror itself has no likes or dislikes."[25] Just so, the self and the mind do not hang on to images once they are removed. What the ordinary mortal does, of course, is to hang on to the impression, the emotion and the reactions to them. The sage is spontaneous in the moment, but does not hold on to the moment once it has gone. The mind is cosmic, not individual. Livia Kohn writes: "The resulting personality is entirely unbound by physical limitations, by emotional values, and arguments of reason. Any conscious ego-identity that was there before is lost. The Tao takes over the identity that once was the individual's alone."[26] Gazing out into the vastness of the universe with its myriad stars and galaxies, the sage is an atom of that whole being, flowing with it, unified with it, feeling its cosmic energy within. It is a return to one's cosmic beginnings and tuning of the self to the ongoing pulses of creation.

The goal of unity in T'ai Chi Ch'üan/Taijiquan

The ultimate goal of the serious practitioner of T'ai Chi is the realization of the same kind of enlightened balance and harmony of the sage. The goal is the fusion of *yin* and *yang* to a point of perfect balance, perfect equilibrium, where the *is-ness* and *such-ness* of each moment, each life phase is experienced. Here, like the related practices of *ch'i-kung/qigong* and *pa-kua/bagua*, T'ai Chi is a pathway to losing the ego, the "I" that drives each moment, and that causes reactions to events around us. It has been pointed out many times in the previous pages that T'ai Chi is a meditation practice. As such, it teaches the unity of body and mind. So often, we are outside our minds, projecting our thoughts to outside concerns. What T'ai Chi does is to encourage the mind to be contained in the body, with awareness of concentrated thought within, not beyond, the self. So instead of the mind being wrinkled with things to do, with activities that are ahead, with pleasant or unpleasant emotions, it is smoothed out, calmed and contained. This is what meditation is all about. But more than that, when the mind is controlled in this way, it lets go of its reactions to stimuli. If we were to sit still for a few minutes, and attempted to stop the mind from thinking, we would find it well nigh impossible. But when focusing the whole mind on the postures of the *form*, it becomes easier to hold single-pointed concentration, and free the mind from its normal reactions to stimuli. And when the mind is free from reactions, the whole self is free. T'ai Chi, then, is the art of moving meditation that moves us towards inner self-cultivation. In itself it is a unity that develops unity between self and cosmos. In Sophia Delza's words:

> T'ai-chi ch'üan is a complete entity, composed to answer the needs to which it is directed. Total in concept, it is a synthesis of form and func-

tion. With the elements of structure and movement so consummately composed, it is an art in the deepest sense of the word. Aesthetically, it can be compared to a composition by Bach or a Shakespearean sonnet. However, t'ai-chi ch'üan is not art directed out to an audience. It is an art-in-action for the doer; the observer, moved by its beauty, can only surmise its content. The experience of the form in process of change makes it an art for the self.[27]

These words illustrate so well that T'ai Chi is a symphony of levels that are themselves unified into total balance and harmony. And once mastered, the balance and harmony of the meditative movement are integrated into the depths of the self.

If we had to single out one of the most important concepts underpinning T'ai Chi, it must surely be that of energy, *ch'i/qi*. When our minds are occupied with external things, our energies are constantly being depleted. We recover in sleep, rest and relaxation – the *yin* aspects that balance the *yang* energetic times of our lives. But how many of us can claim we have peace, serenity and contentment in our life, indeed, at the very core of our being? Harnessing the natural vital energy within, instead of dissipating it in a variety of ways, increases the ability to understand our own being, and to work with it harmoniously and naturally. Vincent Chu points out just how valuable T'ai Chi is for promoting harmonious living through control of vital energy:

Through the practice of Taiji quan, we can learn how to move this qi, how to control this qi, how to emit this qi into our environment. We can create harmony from within ourselves and project this harmony into our surroundings, feeling healthier and more whole within and living in better alignment with the world and the people around us.[28]

Texts attributed to Chang San-feng/Zhang Sanfeng also centre on the control of *ch'i/qi* in the body. In "Taiji Alchemy Secrets" the author points out that: "When myriad thoughts disappear and the soul alone is present, this is called right mindfulness."[29] The same text points out that when the spirit becomes quiet within, *ch'i/qi* abounds, while at the same time, the accumulation of *ch'i/qi* strengthens the spirit.[30] But the key to building that essential energy within, and to circulating it through the body, lies in the mind. In another text (allegedly, though doubtfully) written by Chang San-feng/Zhang Sanfeng, the author says:

All toilsome, rambling, and random thoughts are to be dismissed as soon as you become aware of them. If you hear slander or praise, or anything good or bad, brush it all off right away; don't take it into your mind. If

> you take it in, your mind will be full, and there will be no room for the Tao. Whatever you see and hear, see and hear it as if you did not see or hear. Then right and wrong, good and bad will not enter your mind. When the mind does not take in externals, this is called emptying the mind. When the mind does not pursue externals, this is called pacifying the mind. When the mind is peaceful and empty, the Tao comes of itself to dwell therein.[31]

Since T'ai Chi is a moving *meditation* it serves to encourage the mind to focus within, emptying itself of outside stimuli. At the same time, breathing becomes "a subtle continuum on the brink of existence".[32] Mind, movement and breathing become unified so that thoughts do not arise within the mind to be extended outward into the world, and no intrusion of stimuli enters the mind from without. Since T'ai Chi is essentially concerned with self-cultivation, it promotes cultivation of an inner self that is natural, free from egoistic involvement in the world, fulfilled, and enlightened. It has the same goals as the Taoist sage. The closing words of the last chapter of the *Yang Family Forty Chapters* on T'ai Chi put this superbly. "Wisdom and knowledge, sagehood and immortality, these are what we mean by fulfilling our intrinsic nature and establishing life. Herein lies the perfection of spirit and divine transformation. The way of heaven and the way of humanity is simply sincerity."[33]

Basing his words on an old song about T'ai Chi Ch'üan/Taijiquan, Yang Jwing Ming says that at the higher levels of meditative T'ai Chi, the physical body seems not to exist. Instead, there is a sensation of being a ball of energy, and of being an inseparable part of the whole natural world, into which all actions blend spontaneously. The mind is free of desires, intentions, and the influence of the surroundings: it is clear and under control.[34] He writes:

> When practicing *Taijiquan* you must let go of everything. Your mind must be clear and centered. No concepts (preconceptions) should cloud your vision, no thoughts should hinder your action. The body must be relaxed and stable so that you can be light and agile. Forget your surroundings and just do what needs to be done . . . your mind must be clear, your head held as if suspended from above, and your body as stable and rooted as a great mountain.[35]

The aim is unity of the energy within with the energy of the universe. Yang Jwing Ming puts the ultimate goal superbly when he writes:

> The final goal of spiritual cultivation in Taijiquan practice is reaching spir-

> itual enlightenment. Through practicing Taijiquan, you understand the meaning of life until you reach the stage of clarity about your life and the natural universe. When you have reached this stage, your actual practice will no longer be important, since its essence will be infused into your very being.[36]

Whether we would want to describe the ultimate goal as a spiritual rebirth from a Spirit Embryo, immortality, enlightenment or sagehood, the means to all these ends are the same – the loss of the egoistic self through the stilling of the mind. And with that loss and that stillness comes the discovery of the unity of the self with the whole universe. It is the sage that embodies the perfection of this goal for both Taoism and T'ai Chi.

The sage has the perfect balance between *yang* outer activity and *yin* inner passivity. The English poet Wordsworth captured this when he wrote: "With an eye made quiet by the power of harmony and the deep power of joy, we see into the heart of things". And with inner serenity, the sage is able to act in the world without ever losing the calm serenity and stillness within. For the sage is at the centre of the circle, he is at that point where dualities cease to exist. He is the equipoise, the balance between the this and that of all opposites and all things, and between *yin* and *yang*. The sage has not *found Tao* for he had never really lost it. He simply experiences it as himself and all things. It is in the living, breathing and eating of the day, in the clouds, the moon, the winds, the morning mists, the song of the bird. *Living* is *Tao* but to experience that, one has to transcend the countless egoistic thoughts that pervade the mind, one has to experience the interconnectedness and unity of all. "The ultimate oneness of existence is perceived as being at work within and through oneself. By becoming fully one with all, the individual dissolves completely in the process of existence. Oneness with the Tao is attained; a complete alignment is reached with the principle of the universal life working through human and all life."[37]

The sage offers the example that stillness and quietude, serenity, calmness and harmony are the qualities that we should develop in the self. To nourish the inner being, to enable it to grow, to reach its full spiritual potential, we have to nurture these qualities. We suffer only when we move away from harmony; we suffer only when we strengthen our likes and dislikes, when we forget that we are parts of the wholeness of the universe. Taoism is a process of the evolution of the individual's consciousness, a refining of consciousness throughout life so that the real self, the self devoid of ego and desire, is free. T'ai

Chi is one pathway to such an end. In the rather poignant words of John Blofeld:

> A mind fed on words such as heaven, earth, dew, essence, cinnabar, moonlight, stillness, jade, pearl, cedar, and winter-plum is likely to have a serenity not to be found in minds ringing with the vocabulary of the present age – computer, tractor, jumbo jet, speedball, pop, dollar, liquidation, napalm, overkill! . . . And how full of wisdom is a philosophy that draws man away from the rat race, from the tooth-and-claw struggle for status, wealth, power or fame, to live frugally and contentedly in harmony with nature, reaching effortlessly for the tranquillity that flowers in a heart nurtured in stillness![38]

This is, indeed, a hectic post-modern world, but to survive in it one does not have to retreat to the mountains in meditative solitude. Shifu Keith Ewers thinks of himself as a Taoist. His teacher was a Taoist who opened Keith's eyes to ways in which he could express his Taoist beliefs while living in a fast-paced world. He taught him two guiding rules:

- Think well, and do well, every minute of every day, and learn to help others as much as possible without thought of thanks or possible reward.
- Never hinder, never harass, never harm, and never hurt anyone by thought or deed.

By following these two rules, and practising T'ai Chi, Keith was assured by his teacher that *Tao* would become known to him. Spiritual growth only comes from physical and mental discipline and maintained health. In time, there are some practitioners of T'ai Chi who will come to understand its connection with Taoist principles and see the benefit of their practice in dietary habits, in improved interaction in the workplace, in better social engagement and in balanced emotional and psychological expression. Greater conscious awareness of the beauty of nature usually ensues, along with greater awareness of one's special place in the whole interconnected universe.

Living in harmony with all things, being able to operate in the world from a calm stillness within is the goal. And yes, the dream seems impossible, but as the *Tao Te Ching/Daodejing* says, the tree as large as a person's embrace starts only from a small shoot, and a nine-storied terrace begins with a small pile of earth. The journey of a thousand miles starts under one's feet: the first footstep can always be taken. The path to harmony is the path to peace, the path to experience of *Tao* on Earth.

Notes

Introduction

1 Paul Crompton, *Tai Chi: An introductory guide to the Chinese art of movement* (Shaftesbury, Dorset and Boston, Massachusetts: Element, 2000, first published in different format in 1990), p. 119.

1 What is Taoism?

1 Julia Ching, *Chinese Religions* (Basingstoke and London: The Macmillan Press, 1993), p. 85.
2 Timothy H. Barrett, *Taoism under the T'ang: Religion and empire during the Golden Age of Chinese history* (London: Wellsweep, 1996), p. 17.
3 Buddhism, having been introduced from India, was a very different phenomenon.
4 Isabelle Robinet, *Taoism: Growth of a religion* translated from French by Phyllis Brooks (Stanford, California: Stanford University Press, 1997, first published as *Histoire du Taoïsme des origines au XIVe siècle*, Paris: Cerf), p. 1.
5 Derk Bodde, *Essays on Chinese Civilization*, edited and introduced by Charles Le Blanc and Dorothy Borei (Princeton, New Jersey and Guilford, Surrey: Princeton University Press, 1981), p. 133.
6 Marcel Granet, *The Religion of the Chinese People* translated and edited by Maurice Freedman (Oxford: Basil Blackwell, 1975), p. 46.
7 Martin Palmer, *The Elements of Taoism* (Shaftesbury, Dorset and Rockport, Massachusetts: Element, 1991), pp. 17–18.
8 Donald Bishop, "Introduction" in Donald H. Bishop (ed.), *Chinese Thought: An introduction* (Delhi: Motilal Banarsidass, 2001, first published 1985), p. 174.
9 Bodde, "Dominant Ideas in the Formation of Chinese Culture" in Bodde, *Essays on Chinese Civilization*, p. 133.

10 See Conrad Schirokauer, *A Brief History of Chinese Civilization* (San Diego, New York, Chicago, Austin, Washington, D.C., London, Sydney, Tokyo, Toronto: Harcourt Brace, 1991), p. 5.
11 John Blofeld, *Taoism: The quest for immortality* (London, Boston, Sydney, Wellington: Unwin, 1989, first published 1979), p. 19.
12 Sarah Allan, *The Shape of the Turtle: Myth, art and cosmos in early China* (Albany, New York: State University of New York Press, 1991), p. 1.
13 Bishop, "Chinese Thought before Confucius" in Bishop (ed.), *Chinese Thought*, p. 7.
14 Henri Maspero, *Taoism and Chinese Religion*, translated by Frank A. Kierman, Jr. (Amherst: University of Massachusetts Press, 1981, first published as *Le Taoïsme et les religions chinoises* in 1971), p. 12.
15 *Ibid.*, p. 4.
16 The year was based on the cycles of the moon, with the addition of an extra lunar period from time to time in order to harmonize with the solar year.
17 Kenneth J. DeWoskin, *Doctors, Diviners, and Magicians of Ancient China: Biographies of Fang-shih* (New York: Columbia University Press, 1983), p. 2.
18 Joseph Needham, *Science and Civilisation in China, Vol. 2: History of scientific thought* (Cambridge: Cambridge University Press, 1956), p. 437.
19 See, for example, Julian F. Pas in cooperation with Man Kam Leung, *Historical Dictionary of Taoism* (Lanham, Middlesex and London: The Scarecrow Press, 1998), p. 187.
20 Talismans, or *fu*, apart from being sacred and magical texts, diagrams and documents that had command over certain spirits, were also registers of the particular powers of Taoist Masters, who could use them to ward off evil. Many texts that were talismans were handed down in the later Taoist canon, the *Tao-tsang/Daozang*. Scriptures were often regarded as having talismanic spiritual powers because they were thought to be drawn from original talismanic symbols given to Earth from Heaven. It was the Celestial Masters School and Chang Tao-ling/Zhang Daoling, especially, that created written talismans as guarantees of divine protection. These were then handed down and copied by disciples, later to be reproduced by block printing and, today, by modern printing. The power invested in a talisman can only be as effective as the energy of the person who creates it.
21 Livia Kohn, *Early Chinese Mysticism: Philosophy and soteriology in the Taoist tradition* (Princeton, New Jersey: Princeton University Press, 1992), pp. 112–13.
22 Robinet, *Taoism*, p. 134.
23 Patricia Buckley Ebrey, translator, from *Chinese Civilization and Society: A Sourcebook* (Columbia University Press, 1986, cited in Deborah Sommer (ed.) *Chinese Religion: An anthology of sources* (New York and Oxford: Oxford University Press, 1995), p. 200.
24 Michael Saso, *Blue Dragon White Tiger: Taoist rites of passage* (Washington, D.C.: The Taoist Center, 1990), p. 16.

25 Douglas Wile, *Lost T'ai-chi Classics from the Late Ch'ing Dynasty* (Albany, New York: State University of New York Press, 1996), p. xv.
26 Paul Crompton, *Tai Chi: An introductory guide to the Chinese art of movement* (Shaftesbury, Dorset, Boston, Massachusetts and Melbourne, Victoria: Element, 2000, first published in different format in 1990 as *The Elements of Tai Chi* also by Element), p. 7.
27 Sophia Delza, *T'ai Chi Ch'üan Body and Mind in Harmony: The integration of meaning and method* (Albany, New York: State University of New York Press, revised edn 1985, first published 1965), p. 14.
28 Stuart Alve Olson, *T'ai Chi According to the I Ching: Embodying the principles of the Book of Changes* (Rochester, Vermont: Inner Traditions, 2001), p. 38
29 Yang Jwing Ming, *Advanced Yang Style Tai Chi Chuan, Vol. 2: Martial application* (Jamaica Plain, Massachusetts: Yang's Martial Arts Association, 1986), p. 3.
30 Catherine Despeux, "Gymnastics: The Ancient Tradition" in Livia Kohn (ed.) in cooperation with Yoshinobu Sakade, *Taoist Meditation and Longevity Techniques* Michigan Monographs in Chinese Studies, vol. 61 (Michigan: Center for Chinese Studies, The University of Michigan 1989), p. 241.
31 *Ibid.*, p. 239.
32 See Kunio Miura, "The Revival of *Qi*: Qigong in Contemporary China", in Kohn (ed.), *Taoist Meditation and Longevity Techniques*, pp. 353–4.
33 Despeux, "Gymnastics", p. 249.
34 *Ibid.*, p. 255.
35 For a full account of the literature, as well as the earliest sources, see Despeux *ibid.*, pp. 226–30.
36 Benjamin Pang Jeng Lo, Martin Inn, Robert Amacker, Susan Foe, translators and editors, *The Essence of T'ai Chi Ch'uan: The literary tradition* (Berkeley, California: North Atlantic Books, 1979), pp. 9–10.
37 Pas, *Historical Dictionary of Taoism*, p. 218.
38 Olson, *T'ai Chi According to the I Ching*, p. 39.
39 Yang Jwing Ming in his preface to the first edn of *Tai Chi Theory & Martial Power: Advanced Yang Style Tai Chi Chuan* (Jamaica Plain, Massachusetts: Yang's Martial Arts Association, 1996 second revised edn), p. xi.
40 Yang Jwing Ming, *Advanced Yang Style Tai Chi Chuan, Vol.* 2, p. 9.
41 *Ibid.*, p. 10.
42 Dan Docherty, *Complete Tai Chi Chuan* (Ramsbury, Wiltshire: The Crowood Press, 2001 impression of 1997 edn), p. 49.
43 Anna Seidel, "A Taoist Immortal of the Ming Dynasty: Chang San-feng" in William Theodore de Bary and the Conference on Ming Thought, *Self and Society in Ming Thought*. Studies in Oriental Culture no. 4 (New York and London: Columbia University Press, 1970), p. 483.

44 See Seidel, *ibid.*, p. 499.
45 See Wile, *Lost T'ai-chi Classics from the Late Ch'ing Dynasty*, pp. 108–11 for a full discussion of this connection.
46 Seidel, "A Taoist Immortal of the Ming Dynasty", p. 485.
47 *Ibid.*, p. 501. For a balanced and full account of his life see Seidel *ibid., passim.*
48 See Douglas Wile, *Art of the Bedchamber: The Chinese sexual yoga Classics including women's solo meditation texts* (Albany, New York: State University of New York Press, 1992), pp. 146–7.
49 See Thomas Cleary, *The Taoist Classics: The collected translations of Thomas Cleary, Vol. 3* (Boston, Massachusetts: Shambhala, 2003, first published 1988), pp. 185–6.
50 Translator Olson, *T'ai Chi According to the I Ching*, p. 37.
51 *Ibid.*, p. 46.
52 Wile, *Art of the Bedchamber*, p. 171.
53 Translator Wile, *ibid.*, p. 188.
54 See Wile, *ibid.*, pp. 178–87.
55 Seidel, "A Taoist Immortal of the Ming Dynasty", p. 507.
56 Olson, *T'ai Chi According to the I Ching*, p. 39.
57 Seidel, "A Taoist Immortal of the Ming Dynasty", pp. 504–5.
58 *Ibid.*
59 *Ibid.*, p. 508.
60 See Olson, *Lost T'ai-chi Classics from the Late Ch'ing Dynasty*, pp. 101, 108–9 and 109–10.
61 *Ibid.*, p. 116.
62 See Seidel, "A Taoist Immortal of the Ming Dynasty", pp. 504–6 for a full account. Dan Docherty also deals at length with the intricacies of the history of T'ai Chi in *Complete Tai Chi Chuan*, pp. 29– 60.
63 Docherty, *Complete Tai Chi Chuan*, p. 32.
64 Wile, *Lost T'ai-chi Classics from the Late Ch'ing Dynasty*, p. 111.
65 *Ibid.*, p. 9, see also pp. 5–8.
66 *Ibid.*, p. xv.
67 Kristofer Schipper, *The Taoist Body*, translated by Karen C. Duval (Berkeley, Los Angeles, London: University of California Press, 1993, first published in 1982 as *Le corps taoïste*), p. 138.
68 Yang Cheng-fu, *Yang's Ten Important Points*, translated by Lo, Inn, Ammacker and Foe, *The Essence of T'ai Chi Ch'uan*, p. 89.
69 Wile, *Lost T'ai-chi Classics from the Late Ch'ing Dynasty*, pp. xvi–xvii.
70 Docherty, *Complete Tai Chi Chuan*, p. 31.
71 See Wile, *Lost T'ai-chi Classics from the Late Ch'ing Dynasty*, p. 21.
72 *Ibid.*, p. 24.
73 *Ibid.*, p. 23.
74 *Ibid.*, p. 24

75 *Ibid.*, p. 25.
76 *Ibid.*, p. 27.
77 Yang Jwing Ming, *Advanced Yang Style Tai Chi Chuan, Vol. 2*, pp. 3–4.
78 Wile, *Lost T'ai-chi Classics from the Late Ch'ing Dynasty*, p. 38.
79 Translator Wile, *ibid.*, p. 45. See also the longer *Song of the Thirteen Postures* pp. 51–2.
80 *Ibid.*, p. 50.
81 "An Explanation of the Essence and Application of T'ai-chi" from the *Yang Family Forty Chapters* translator Wile, *ibid.*, p. 70.
82 See the photographs in Lawrence Galante, *Tai Chi: The Supreme Ultimate*, edited by Betsy Selman (York Beach, Maine: Samuel Weiser, Inc., 1981), pp. 90–193.
83 *Ibid.*, p. 23.
84 Crompton, *Tai Chi*, p. 18.
85 The *form* usually refers to the whole series of movements, though in some schools the plural, *forms*, is used to depict the whole series. See for example Delza's use of the term in *T'ai-chi Ch'üan*, *passim*, and Yang Jwing Ming, *Advanced Yang Style Tai Chi Chuan, Vol. 2*, p. 9.
86 Delza, *ibid.*, p. 21.
87 *Ibid.*, p. 22.
88 Docherty, *Complete Tai Chi Chuan*, p. 51.
89 Galante, *Tai Chi*, p. 13.
90 "The Five Mental Keys to Diligent Study", translated by Yang Jwing Ming, *Tai Chi Theory and Martial Power*, p. 232.
91 *Ibid.*, pp. 19–20.
92 Olson, *T'ai Chi According to the I Ching*, pp. 11–12.

2 Harmony

1 Laurence G. Thompson, *Chinese Religion: An Introduction* (Belmont, California: Wadsworth Publishing Company, 1989 reprint of 1979 edn), p. 3.
2 Sarah Allan, *The Shape of the Turtle: Myth, art, and cosmos in early China* (Albany, New York: State University of New York Press, 1991), p. 17.
3 *Ibid.*, p. 73.
4 *Ibid.*, p. 176.
5 Henri Maspero, *China in Antiquity*, translated by Frank A. Kierman Jr. (London: Dawson, 1978, originally published as *La Chine Antique*, Paris 1927, revised edn 1965), pp. 165–6.
6 See Julian F. Pas in cooperation with Man Kam Leung, *Historical Dictionary of Taoism* (Lanham, Middlesex and London: The Scarecrow Press, 1998), pp. 371–2.
7 A. C. Graham, *Yin-Yang and the Nature of Correlative Thinking*. Occasional Paper and Monograph Series no. 6 (Singapore: The Institute of East Asian Philosophies, 1989 reprint of 1986 edn), p. 73.

8 See Fung Yu-lan, *A History of Chinese Philosophy, Vol. 1: The period of the philosophers (from the beginnings to circa 100 B.C.)*, translated by Derk Bodde (Princeton, New Jersey: Princeton University Press, 1983 reprint of second English edn 1952), p. 163.
9 See Graham, *Yin-Yang and the Nature of Correlative Thinking*, pp. 12–13.
10 See Fung Yu-lan, *A History of Chinese Philosophy, Vol. 2: The period of classical learning (from the second century B.C. to the twentieth century A.D.)*, translated by Derk Bodde (Princeton, New Jersey: Princeton University Press, 1983 reprint, first published in English in 1953. First published in Chinese in 1934), p. 9.
11 Translator Fung Yu-lan, *A History of Chinese Philosophy, Vol. 1*, p. 160.
12 Jean Cooper, *Taoism: The Way of the mystic* (Wellingborough, Northamptonshire: Crucible, 1990 revised edn, first published 1972), p. 40.
13 From Liu I-ming, *Eight Elements of the Spiritual House*, translator Thomas Cleary, *The Taoist I Ching* (Boston, Massachusetts and London: Shambhala, 1986), p. 20.
14 From Huang Yuan-ch'i, *Annals of the Hall of Blissful Development*, translator Cleary, *ibid.*, pp. 15–16.
15 From Liu I-ming, *Eight Elements of the Spiritual House*, translator Cleary, *ibid.*, p. 20.
16 *Tao Te Ching/Daodejing* 2.
17 Fritjof Capra, *The Tao of Physics: An exploration of the parallels bewteen modern physics and eastern mysticism* (London: Flamingo, 1990 impression of 1983 edn, first published 1975), p. 157.
18 *Tao Te Ching/Daodejing* 36.
19 Jean Cooper, *Yin and Yang: The Taoist harmony of opposites* (Wellingborough, Northamptonshire: The Aquarian Press, 1981), p. 17.
20 *Tao Te Ching/Daodejing* 22.
21 Derk Bodde, *Essays on Chinese Civilization*, edited and translated by Charles Le Blanc and Dorothy Borei (Princeton, New Jersey: Princeton University Press, 1981), p. 239.
22 Examples here are "albino members of a species; beings that are part-animal, part-human; women who die before marriage and turn into ghosts receiving no care; people who die in unusual ways like suicide or on battlefields far from home; and people whose bodies fail to decompose or emit strange signs after death". See Stephen Teiser, "Introduction" in Donald S. Lopez, Jr., *Religions of China in Practice.* Princeton Readings in Religion (Princeton, New Jersey: Princeton University Press, 1996), p. 35.
23 Cooper, *Taoism*, p. 37.
24 Isabelle Robinet, *Taoism: Growth of a religion*, translated from French by Phyllis Brooks (Stanford, California: Stanford University Press, 1997, first published in Paris, 1992 as *Histoire du Taoïsme des origine au XIVe siècle*), p. 7.

25 *Ibid.*, pp. 7–8.
26 Cheng Xinnong (ed.), *Chinese Acupuncture and Moxibustion* (Beijing: Foreign Languages Press, 1999 revised edn, first published 1987), p. 14.
27 From the *Yellow Emperor's Classic of Medicine*, translated by Mark Coyle, "The Interaction of Yin and Yang", in Patricia Buckley Ebrey (ed.), *Chinese Civilization and Society: A sourcebook* (New York: The Free Press and London: Collier Macmillan, 1981), p. 37.
28 Wu Ju-ch'ing/Wu Ruqing, *Treatise on T'ai-chi Ch'üan*, translated by Douglas Wile, *Lost T'ai-chi Classics from the Late Ch'ing Dynasty* (Albany, New York: State University of New York Press, 1996), p. 47.
29 Chang San-feng, "T'ai Chi Ch'uan Ching" in Benjamin Lo, Martin Inn, Robert Amacker and Susan Foe, *The Essence of T'ai Chi Ch'uan: The literary tradition* (Berkeley, California: North Atlantic Books, 1979), p. 21.
30 *Ibid.*, p. 22.
31 *Tao Te Ching/Daodejing* 41.
32 See Graham, *Yin-Yang and the Nature of Correlative Thinking*, p. 15.
33 Robinet, *Taoism*, p. 14.
34 *Ibid.*, p. 9.

3 The Way

1 Joseph Needham, *Science and Civilisation in China, Vol. 2: History of Scientific Thought* (Cambridge: Cambridge University Press, 1956), p. 35.
2 For a full account of traditions about the life of Lao-tzu/Laozi, see Jeaneane Fowler, *Pathways to Immortality: An introduction to the philosophy and religion of Taoism* (Brighton, Sussex and Portland, Oregon: Sussex Academic Press, 2005), chapter 4.
3 Jacob Needleman "Introduction" in *Lao Tsu Tao Te Ching* translated by Gia-fu Feng and Jane English (New York: Vintage Books, 1989, first published 1972), p. v.
4 Chad Hansen, *A Daoist Theory of Chinese Thought: A philosophical interpretation* (Oxford: Oxford University Press, 1992), p. 201.
5 Richard Wilhelm, translator and commentator, *Lao Tzu Tao Te Ching: The book of meaning and life*, translated into English by H. G. Ostwald (London, New York, Ontario, Toronto, Auckland: Penguin, Arkana, 1990 reprint of 1985 edn), p. 98.
6 For a full account of the traditions concerning Chuang-tzu/Zhuangzi, see Fowler, *Pathways to Immortality*, chapter 4.
7 Martin Palmer, translator, with Elizabeth Breuilly, Chang Wai Ming and Jay Ramsay, *The Book of Chuang Tzu* (London, Ontario, Victoria, Auckland: Penguin, Arkana, 1996), pp. xix–xx.
8 *Ibid.*, p. xiii.
9 *Ibid.*, p. xv.
10 Henri Maspero, *China in Antiquity*, translated by Frank A. Kierman Jr. (Folkestone, Kent: Dawson and Massachusetts: University of

Massachusetts, 1978. Originally published in French as *La Chine Antique*, vol. 4 of *Histoire du Monde* by E. De Boccard (ed.), Paris 1927 and revised in 1965 as part of the *Annales du Musée Guiment Biblioteque d'Etudes*), p. 306.

11 *Tao Te Ching/Daodejing* 25.

12 Alan Watts, *Tao: The watercourse Way* (London, New York, Victoria, Ontario, Auckland: Penguin, 1975), p. 39. Watts likened the movement to going (*yang*) and pausing (*yin*).

13 R. H. Mathews, *Mathews' Chinese–English Dictionary* (Cambridge, Massachusetts: Harvard University Press, revised American edn 2000, first published 1931), p. 884.

14 *Ibid.*, p. 882.

15 Jonathan Star, translator and commentator, *Lao Tzu Tao Te Ching: The definitive edition* (New York: Jeremy P. Tarcher, 2001), p. 272.

16 *Tao Te Ching/Daodejing* 1.

17 The word *tao/dao* occurs three times in the first line, and in the second case is normally translated as "told", "spoken of", "expressed".

18 Fung Yu-lan, *A Short History of Chinese Philosophy* edited by Derk Bodde (New York: The Free Press and London: Collier Macmillan, 1966, first published 1948), p. 95.

19 *Tao Te Ching/Daodejing* 34.

20 *Chuang-tzu/Zhuangzi*, chapter 2, translator Angus Graham, *Chuang-Tzu: The Inner Chapters* (London, Boston, Sydney, New Zealand: Unwin Paperbacks, 1989, first published 1981).

21 Chang San-feng/Zhang Sanfeng, "Discourses on the Teachings of Wang Che: Attaining the Tao", translator Thomas Cleary, *The Taoist Classics: The collected translations of Thomas Cleary, Vol. 3* (Boston, Massachusetts: Shambhala, 2003, first published 1988), p. 199.

22 Julian F. Pas in cooperation with Man Kam Leung, *Historical Dictionary of Taoism* (Lanham, Middlesex and London: The Scarecrow Press, Inc., 1998), p. 309.

23 *Tao Te Ching/Daodejing* 42.

24 *Chuang-tzu/Zhuangzi*, chapter 12, translator James Legge, *The Texts of Taoism, Vols 1 & 2* (Scotland: Tynron Press, 1989, [1891], p. 315.

25 Graham, *Chuang-Tzu*, p. 18.

26 See Pas, *Historical Dictionary of Taoism*, p. 78.

27 The first movement of the *form*.

28 Yang Jwing Ming, *Tai Chi Theory & Martial Power: Advanced Yang Style Tai Chi Chuan* (Jamaica Plain, Massachusetts: Yang's Martial Arts Association Publication Center, 1996), p. 215.

29 Translator Yang Jwing Ming, *Tai Chi Secrets of the Wu & Li Styles* (Jamaica Plain, Massachusetts: Yang's Martial Arts Association Publication Center, 2001), p. 25.

30 See Livia Kohn, *Early Chinese Mysticism: Philosophy and soteriology in the Taoist tradition* (Princeton, New Jersey: Princeton University Press, 1992), p. 47, and Terry F. Kleeman "Daoism and the Quest for Order", in Norman J. Girardot, James Miller and Liu Xiaogan (eds), *Daoism and Ecology: Ways within a cosmic landscape* (Cambridge, Massachusetts: Harvard University Press, 2001), p. 62.
31 John Blofeld, *Taoism: The quest for immortality* (London, Boston, Sydney, Wellington: Mandala, 1989, first published 1979), p. 1.
32 Chang San-feng/Zhang Sanfeng, "Summary of the Golden Elixir" translator Douglas Wile, *Art of the Bedchamber: The Chinese Yoga Classics including women's solo meditation texts* (Albany, New York: State University of New York Press, 1992), p. 169.
33 Graham, *Chuang-Tzu*, p. 21.
34 *Tao Te Ching/Daodejing* 32.
35 *Chuang-tzu/Zhuangzi*, chapter 20, translator Fung Yu-lan, *A Short History of Chinese Philosophy*, pp. 114–15.
36 *Tao Te Ching/Daodejing* 45.
37 Chang San-feng/Zhang Sanfeng, "Summary of the Golden Elixir" translator Douglas Wile, *Art of the Bedchamber*, p. 170.
38 Chang San-feng/Zhang Sanfeng, "Discourses on the Teachings of Wang Che: Being Unaffected", translated by Cleary, *The Taoist Classics, Vol. 3*, p. 195.
39 Livia Kohn, *Early Chinese Mysticism*, p. 56.
40 *Chuang-tzu/Zhuangzi*, chapter 13:1, translator Thomas Merton, *The Way of Chuang Tzu* (New York: New Directions, 1965), p. 80.
41 Yang Jwing Ming, *Tai Chi Theory and Martial Power*, p. 211.
42 Chang San-feng/Zhang Sanfeng, "Discourses on the Teachings of Wang Che: Genuine Observation", translator Cleary, *The Taoist Classics, Vol. 3*, p. 196.
43 Blofeld, *Taoism*, p. 15.
44 Star, *Lau Tzu Tao Te Ching*, p. 260.
45 Arthur Waley, *The Way and Its Power: The Tao Te Ching and its place in Chinese thought* (London, Sydney and Wellington: Unwin Paperbacks, 1987 reissue of 1977 edn, first published 1934), pp. 31–2.
46 Needleman, "Introduction" in Gia-fu Feng and English, *Lao Tsu Tao Te Ching*, p. x.
47 Wilhelm, *Lao Tzu Tao Te Ching*, p. 84.
48 Needleman, "Introduction" in Gia-fu Feng and English, *Lao Tsu Tao Te Ching*, p. xi.
49 *Tao Te Ching/Daodejing* 11.
50 Roger T. Ames, "The Local and the Focal in Realizing a Daoist World" in Girardot, Miller and Liu Xiaogan (eds), *Daoism and Ecology*, p. 278.
51 *Tao Te Ching/Daodejing* 22.

52 *Ibid.*, 36.

53 *Lieh-tzu/Liezi* chapter 1, translator Angus C. Graham, *The Book of Lieh-tzu: A classic of Tao* (New York: Columbia University Press, 1990 reprint of 1960 edn), p. 23.

54 *Ibid.*, p. 25.

55 *Ibid.*, p. 26.

56 *Chuang-tzu/Zhuangzi*, chapter 6, translator Graham, *Chuang-Tzu*, p. 86.

57 *Tao Te Ching/Daodejing* 21.

58 *Ibid.*, 53.

59 Mathews, *Mathews' Chinese–English Dictionary*, p. 1048.

60 Paul Carus, translator, *The Teachings of Lao-tzu: The Tao Te Ching* (London, Sydney, Auckland, Johannesburg: Rider, 1999 revised edn, first published 1913), p. 22.

61 *Tao Te Ching/Daodejing* 48.

62 Liu Xiaogan, "Non-Action and the Environment Today" in Girardot, Miller and Xiaogan, *Daoism and Ecology*, p. 334.

63 As a modern example of the unnatural path, consider the following: "One of the main reasons for the continued rain forest conflagration in Indonesia is 'industrialized burning' set by plantation owners and subcontractors, which has devoured at least two million hectares of the world's second-largest region of rain forest. For every hectare of burned land, one hundred hectares is engulfed in smoke stretching from Thailand to the Philippines to New Guinea and the northern coast of Australia. Smoke has affected people's health right across the region. An estimated forty thousand Indonesians have suffered respiratory problems, and up to one million have suffered eye irritations. Smoke has been blamed for ship and air crashes that killed about three hundred people." Liu Xiaogan, *ibid.*, p. 318.

64 Chang San-feng/Zhang Sanfeng, "Discourses on the Teachings of Wang Che: Emptying the Mind", translator Cleary, *The Taoist Classics, Vol. 3*, p. 194.

65 Benjamin Hoff, *The Tao of Pooh & The Te of Piglet* (London: Methuen, 1995 reprint of 1982 edn), p. 96.

66 *Tao Te Ching/Daodejing* 67.

67 *Ibid.*, 63.

68 Merton, *The Way of Chuang Tzu*, p. 142

69 *Lieh-tzu/Liezi* chapter 1, translator Graham, *The Book of Lieh-tzu*, pp. 29–30.

70 Hoff, *The Tao of Pooh & The Te of Piglet*, p. 76.

71 *Tao Te Ching/Daodejing* 78.

72 *Ibid.*, 8.

73 *Ibid.*, 29.

74 Graham, *Chuang-Tzu*, p. 8.

75 *Chuang-tzu/Zhuangzi*, chapter 2, translator Graham, *ibid.*, p. 59.

76 *Lieh-tzu/Liezi* chapter 4, translator Graham, *The Book of Lieh-tzu*, p. 90.
77 *Tao Te Ching/Daodejing* 28.
78 Although anachronistically, see Pas, *Historical Dictionary of Taoism*, p. 237.
79 Needham, *Science and Civilisation in China, Vol. 2*, p. 38.
80 Graham, *Chuang-Tzu*, p. 7.
81 *Ibid.*, p. 6.
82 *Chuang-tzu/Zhuangzi*, chapter 19:12, translator Merton, *The Way of Chuang Tzu*, pp. 112–13.
83 Chang San-feng/Zhang Sanfeng, "Discourses on the Teachings of Wang Che: Attaining the Tao", translator Cleary, *The Taoist Classics, Vol. 3*, p. 200.
84 Sophia Delza, *T'ai-Chi Ch'üan: Body and mind in harmony, the integration of meaning and method* (Albany, New York: State University of New York Press, 1985 revised edn, first published 1961), p. 18.
85 Paul Wildish, *Principles of Taoism* (London: Thorsons, 2000), pp. 22–3.

4 Change

1 Richard Wilhelm, translator, *I Ching or Book of Changes*, translated into English by Cary F. Baynes (London: Penguin, Arkana, 1989 third edn, first published 1950).
2 *Ibid.*, p. xlvii.
3 John Blofeld, translator, *I Ching: The Book of Change* (London, Sydney, Wellington: Unwin Paperbacks), translator's *Foreword*, p. 7.
4 See Wilhelm, *I Ching or Book of Changes*, p. 4.
5 Deborah Sommer (ed.), *Chinese Religion: An anthology of sources* (New York and Oxford: Oxford University Press, 1995), p. 4.
6 Fritjof Capra, *The Tao of Physics: An exploration of the parallels between modern physics and eastern mysticism* (1990 reprint of 1983 edn, first published 1975), p. 121.
7 Fung Yu-lan, *A History of Chinese Philosophy, Vol. 1: The period of the philosophers (from the beginnings to circa 100 B.C.)*, translated by Derk Bodde (Princeton, New Jersey: Princeton University Press), p. 390.
8 Carl Jung, from the *Foreword*, Wilhelm, *I Ching or Book of Changes*, p. xxxix.
9 Jou, Tsung Hwa, *The Tao of I Ching: Way to divination* (Scottsdale, AZ: Tai Chi Foundation, 2000 reprint of 1983 edn), p. 8.
10 *Ta-chuan/Dazhuan* 8:1, trans. Wilhelm, *I Ching or Book of Changes*, p. 304.
11 See Kidder Smith, Jr., Peter K. Bol, Joseph A. Adler, and Don J. Wyatt, *Sung Dynasty Uses of the I Ching* (Princeton, New Jersey: Princeton University Press, 1990), p. 10.
12 See Edward L. Shaughnessy, "I ching" in Michael Loewe (ed.), *Early Chinese Texts: A bibliographical guide* (Berkeley, California: The Society for the Study of Early China, and The Institute of East Asian Studies, University of California, 1993), p. 218.

13 See Richard Rutt, *The Book of Changes (Zhouyi): A Bronze Age document translated with introduction and notes*. Durham East Asia Series no. 1 (London: RoutledgeCurzon, 2002 reprint of 1996 edn), *passim*.
14 *Shuo-kua/Shuogua* 1:1, translator Wilhelm, *I Ching or Book of Changes*, p. 262.
15 Scholars are considerably divided concerning the contribution of Wen and Tan/Dan. Some claim that King Wen devised the hexagrams, others that they existed prior to the Chou/Zhou dynasty. But the particular contributions of Wen and Tan/Dan are blurred. The position taken here is the traditional one.
16 Wilhelm, *I Ching or Book of Changes*, p. liii.
17 Thomas Cleary, translator, in Cheng Yi, *The Tao of Organization: The I Ching for group dynamics* (Boston, Massachusetts and London: Shambhala, 1995 reprint of 1988 edn), p. 217.
18 Blofeld, *I Ching*, pp. 31–2.
19 Thomas Cleary, translator, *The Taoist I Ching* (Boston and London: Shambhala, 1986), p. 7.
20 Hellmut Wilhelm, *Change: Eight lectures on the I Ching*, translated from German by Cary F. Baynes (London: Routledge & Kegan Paul, 1975 reprint of 1961 edn, first German edn 1944), p. 38.
21 A particularly good analysis of the concept of change in the "Great Treatise" appended to the *I Ching/Yijing* can be found in an article by Gerald Swanson, "The Concept of Change in the *Great Treatise*", in Henry Rosemont, Jr. (ed.), *Explorations in Early Chinese Cosmology*, Journal of the American Academy of Religion Studies, vol. 50 no. 2 (Chicago, California: Scholars Press), pp. 67–93.
22 Hellmut Wilhelm, *Heaven, Earth and Man in the Book of Change* (Seattle: University of Washington Press, 1977), p. 100.
23 For an altogether different origin of the word as "lizard", and the association of the lizard's mobility and changeability with transformation and change, as well as wider meanings of *I/Yi* in antiquity, see Hellmut Wilhelm, *Change*, p. 14.
24 Hellmut Wilhelm, *Change*, p. 23.
25 See Wilhelm, *I Ching or Book of Changes*, p. lvi.
26 *Ibid.*, p. 283.
27 *Ibid.*, p. lv.
28 See Hellmut Wilhelm, *Change*, p. 33.
29 See Joseph Needham, *Science and Civilization in China, Vol. 2: History of scientific thought* (Cambridge: Cambridge University Press, 1956), p. 313, and Lama Anagarika Govinda, *The Inner Structure of the I Ching: The Book of Transformations* (Tokyo and New York: Weatherhill and Wheelwright Press, 1981), pp. 46–7.
30 *Shuo-kua/Shuogua* 2:11.
31 *Shuo-kua/Shuogua* 2:3, translator Wilhelm, *I Ching or Book of Changes*, p. 265. See also verses 4 and 6, and Wilhelm's comments on these verses.

32 Translator Cleary, *The Taoist I Ching*, p. 11.
33 Cleary, *ibid.*
34 See Rutt, *The Book of Changes (Zhouyi)*, pp. 97–8.
35 See Shaughnessy, "I ching", p. 217.
36 Xinzhong Yao and Helene McMurtrie, "History and Wisdom of The Book of Changes: New Scholarship and Richard Rutt's Translation", *Journal of Contemporary Religion* 14 (1999), p. 137.
37 Blofeld, *I Ching*, p. 68.
38 Within a hexagram there are also "ruling" lines. The "governing" ruler is the one that sets the whole tone of the hexagram. It is usually in the fifth place, but not always. There is also a "constituting" ruler to add meaning to the hexagram. Sometimes, both governing and constituting ruling lines are in the same place – a most auspicious and favourable occurrence. It is particularly when either ruling line is a moving one that their importance is considerable.
39 Raymond Van Over (ed.), *I Ching*. Based on the translation by James Legge. New York, Scarborough Ontario and London: Mentor, 1971), p. 127.
40 Blofeld, *I Ching*, p. 24.
41 Liu I-ming/Liu Yiming, *The Book of Balance and Harmony*, translator Cleary, *The Taoist I Ching*, p. 17.
42 Joseph Needham, *Science and Civilization in China, Vol. 2*, p. 337.
43 *Ibid.*, p. 336.
44 For a full analysis of the influence of the *I Ching/Yijing* on T'ai Chi see Stuart Alve Olson, *T'ai Chi according to the I Ching: Embodying the principles of the Book of Changes* (Rochester, Vermont: Inner Traditions, 2001), *passim.*
45 Translator Olson, *ibid.*, p. 37.
46 Van Over, *I Ching*, p. 14.
47 Hellmut Wilhelm, *Change*, p. 9.

5 Phases

1 Isabelle Robinet, *Taoism: Growth of a religion*, translated from French by Phillis Brooks (Stanford, California: Stanford University Press, 1997, first published in Paris, 1992 as *Histoire du Taoïsme des origine au XIVe siècle*), p. 11.
2 See R. H. Mathews, *Mathew's Chinese–English Dictionary* (Cambridge, Massachusetts: Harvard University Press, Revised American Version 2000, first published 1931), pp. 409–10.
3 See A. C. Graham, *Yin-Yang and the Nature of Correlative Thinking*. Occasional Paper and Monograph Series no. 6 (Singapore: The Institute of East Asian Philosophies, 1989 reprint of 1986 edn), p. 47.
4 *Ibid.*, p. 74.
5 *Ibid.*, pp. 84–5.
6 *Hung Fan*, translator Fung Yu-lan, *A History of Chinese Philosophy, Vol. 1: The period of the philosophers (from the beginnings to circa 100 B.C.)*, trans-

lated by Derk Bodde (Princeton, New Jersey, Princeton University Press, 1983 reprint of second English edn 1952), p. 163.

7 See Vitaly A. Rubin, "Ancient Chinese Cosmology and *Fa-chia* Theory" in Henry Rosemont, Jr. (ed.), *Explorations in Early Chinese Cosmology.* Journal of the American Academy of Religion Studies vol. 50, no. 2 (Chicago, California: Scholars Press, 1984), p. 96.

8 *Ibid.*, p. 98.

9 Graham, *Yin-Yang and the Nature of Correlative Thinking*, p. 52.

10 *Kuan-tzu* 39, translator Fung Yu-lan, *A History of Chinese Philosophy, Vol. 1*, p. 167.

11 Robinet, *Taoism*, p. 11.

12 Sarah Allan, *The Shape of the Turtle: Myth, art and cosmos in early China* (Albany, New York: State University of New York Press, 1991), p. 102.

13 *Ibid.*, p. 101.

14 Derk Bodde, *Essays on Chinese Civilization*, edited and translated by Charles Le Blanc and Dorothy Borei (Princeton, New Jersey: Princeton University Press, 1981), p. 135.

15 In some texts, the organs are assigned differently – Wood spleen; Fire lungs; Earth heart; Metal liver; Water kidneys. See, for example the order in the list given by Conrad Schirokauer, *A Brief History of Chinese Civilization* (San Diego, New York, Chicago, Austin, Washington, D.C., London, Sydney, Tokyo, Toronto: Harcourt Brace Gap College, Publishers, 1991), p. 74. The order in the chart in the present book is to be found in the *Huang-ti Nei-ching/Huangdi Neijing*, the prestigious medical *Yellow Emperor's Classic of Internal Medicine*, and is that accepted in modern Chinese medical practice.

16 From the *Huang-ti Nei-ching/ Huangdi Neijing*, translator Graham, *Ying-Yang and the Nature of Correlative Thinking*, p. 61.

17 *Ibid.*, p. 62.

18 *Ibid.*

19 *Ibid.*, p. 63.

20 Cheng Xinnong (ed.), *Chinese Acupuncture and Moxibustion* (Beijing: Foreign Languages Press, 1999 revised edn, first published 1987), p. 20.

21 *Ibid.*, p. 24.

22 Schirokauer, *A Brief History of Chinese Civilization*, p. 73.

23 The *Wen Tzu* 139, translator Thomas Cleary, *The Taoist Classics: The collected translations of Thomas Cleary, Vol. 1* (Boston, Massachusetts: Shambhala, 1999 reprint of 1990 edn), p. 261.

24 Chang San-feng, *T'ai Chi Ch'üan Ching/Taijiquan Jing*, translators and eds Benjamin Pang Jeng Lo, Martin Inn, Robert Amacker, and Susan Foe, *The Essence of T'ai Chi Ch'uan: The Literary Tradition* (Berkeley, California: North Atlantic Books, 1979), p. 27.

25 Translator Douglas Wile, *Lost T'ai-chi Classics from the Late Ch'ing Dynasty* (Albany, New York: State University of New York Press, 1996), p. 44.

6 Energy

1 Kristofer Schipper, *The Taoist Body*, translated by Karen C. Duval (Berkeley, Los Angeles, London: University of California Press, 1993. First published as *Le corps taoïste*, Paris 1982), p. 175.
2 Both words *wai* and *nei* are used very differently depending on the contexts in which they are found; see Isabelle Robinet, "Original Contributions of *Neidan* to Taoism and Chinese Thought" in Livia Kohn (ed.) in cooperation with Yoshinobu Sakade, *Taoist Meditation and Longevity Techniques*. Michigan Monographs in Chinese Studies, vol. 61 (Ann Arbour: Centre for Chinese Studies, The University of Michigan, 1989), p. 297 n. 1.
3 Daniel Overmyer, "Chinese Religion: An Overview" in Mircea Eliade (ed.), *The Encyclopedia of Religion* (hereafter *ER*, New York: Macmillan Publishing Company and London: Collier Macmillan Publishers, 1987), Vol. 3 p. 264.
4 Joseph Needham, *Science in Traditional China* (Cambridge, Massachusetts: Harvard University Press, and Hong Kong: The Chinese University Press, 1982 reprint of 1981 edn), p. 14.
5 Nathan Sivin, "Chinese Alchemy and the Manipulation of Time" in Nathan Sivin (ed.), *Science and Technology in East Asia* (New York: Science History Publications, 1977), p. 110.
6 Robinet, "Original Contributions of *Neidan* to Taoism and Chinese Thought", pp. 300–1.
7 See Julian F. Pas in cooperation with Man Kam Leung, *Historical Dictionary of Taoism* (Lanham, Middlesex and London: The Scarecrow Press, 1998), p. 244.
8 Douglas Wile, *Art of the Bedchamber: The Chinese Yoga Classics including women's solo meditation texts* (Albany, New York: State University of New York Press, 1992), p. 10.
9 Sivin, "Chinese Alchemy and the Manipulation of Time", p. 121.
10 Liu I-ming /Liu Yiming commentary on Chang Po-tuan/Zhang Boduan, *Understanding Reality* 1:3, translated by Thomas Cleary, *The Taoist Classics: The collected translations of Thomas Cleary, Vol. 2* (Boston, Massachusetts: Shambhala, 2003, first published 1986), p. 38.
11 Isabelle Robinet, *Taoism: Growth of a Religion*, translated by Phyllis Brooks (Stanford, California: Stanford University Press, 1997, first published in Paris as *Histoire du Taoïsme des origines au XIVe siècle* in 1992), pp. 108–9.
12 A term that is synonymous with Buddhist *nirvana*.
13 For a good summary of the most important points of the anatomy of the body, see Wile, *Art of the Bedchamber*, pp. 36–9.
14 Robinet, *Taoism*, p. 17.
15 Cited in Deborah Sommer (ed.), *Chinese Religion: An anthology of sources* (New York, Oxford: Oxford University Press, 1995), p. 147.
16 See Pas, *Historical Dictionary of Taoism*, p. 80.
17 From *Inward Training* 1, translator Harold D. Roth, *Original Tao: Inward*

training and the foundations of Taoist mysticism (New York and Chichester, West Sussex: Columbia University Press, 1999), p. 46.

18 For its chemical and medical meanings see Nathan Sivin, *Chinese Alchemy: Preliminary Studies* (Cambridge, Massachusetts: Harvard University Press, 1968), p. xviii.

19 Livia Kohn (ed.), *The Taoist Experience: An anthology* (Albany, New York: State University of New York Press, 1993), p. 133.

20 Michael Page, *The Power of Ch'i: An introduction to Chinese mysticism and philosophy* (Wellingborough, Northamptonshire: The Aquarian Press, 1988), p. 11.

21 Hidemi Ishida, "Body and Mind: The Chinese Perspective" in Kohn (ed.), *Taoist Meditation and Longevity Techniques*, p. 45.

22 Livia Kohn, *Taoist Mystical Philosophy: The Scripture of Western Ascension* (Albany, New York: State University of New York Press, 1991), p. 94.

23 For a more extensive account of subtle and coarse *ch'i/qi* in the body, see Page, *The Power of Ch'i*, pp. 14–17.

24 Mantak Chia and Juan Li, *The Inner Structure of Tai Chi: Tai Chi Chi Kung* (USA: Mantak and Maneewan Chia, 1996), p. 1.

25 Wile, *Art of the Bedchamber*, p. 40.

26 Chang Po-tuan/Zhang Boduan, *Understanding Reality* 1:1, translator Cleary, *The Taoist Classics, Vol. 2*, p. 35.

27 Chang San-feng/Zhang Sanfeng, *Zhang Sanfeng's Taiji Alchemy Secrets: The Alchemical Process*, translator Thomas Cleary, *Taoist Meditation: Methods for cultivating a healthy mind and body* (Boston, Massachusetts: Shambhala, 2000), p. 120.

28 Robinet, "Original Contributions of *Neidan* to Taoism and Chinese Thought", p. 322.

29 Wei Po-yang/Wei Boyang, *Ts'an T'ung Ch'i/Cantongqi*, translator Richard Bertschinger, *The Secret of Everlasting Life: The first translation of the ancient Chinese text on immortality* (London: Vega, 2002, first published 1994), p. 104.

30 Liu I-ming/Liu Yiming, *Awakening to the Tao*, translator Thomas Cleary (Boston, Massachusetts and Shaftesbury: Shambhala, 1988), pp. 74–5.

31 From *The Book of Balance and Harmony*, translator Thomas Cleary (London, Sydney, Auckland, Johannesburg: Rider, 1989), pp. 136–7.

32 Robinet, "Original Contributions of *Neidan* to Taoism and Chinese Thought", p. 301.

33 Joseph Needham, *Science and Civilisation in China, Vol. 5, Chemistry and Chemical Technology: Spagyrical Discovery and Invention: Physiological Alchemy* (Cambridge: Cambridge University Press, 1983), pp. 155–81.

34 For full details of the inscription see Roth, *Original Tao*, pp. 161–4.

35 Catherine Despeux, "Gymnastics: The Ancient Tradition" in Kohn, *Taoist Meditation and Longevity Techniques*, p. 257.

36 For an extensive analysis of breathing techniques, see Henri Maspero, *Taoism and Chinese Religion*, translated by Frank A. Kierman, Jr. (Amherst: The University of Massachusetts Press, 1981. First published as *Le Taoïsme et les religions chinoises*, 1971), pp. 459–517.
37 Translator Thomas Cleary, *The Taoist Classics: The collected translations of Thomas Cleary, Vol. 3* (Boston, Massachusetts: Shambhala, 2003, first published 1988), p. 188.
38 Despeux, "Gymnastics: The ancient tradition", pp. 237–40.
39 Schipper, *The Taoist Body*, p. 138.
40 Kohn (ed.), *The Taoist Experience*, p. 193.
41 Roth, *Original Tao*, p. 2.
42 *Ibid.*, pp. 110–11.
43 *Ibid.*, pp. 120–2.
44 From *The Book of Balance and Harmony*, trans. Thomas Cleary, pp. 15–16.
45 From the *Huai-nan-tzu/Huainanzi*, translator Harold D. Roth, "The Inner Cultivation Tradition of early Daoism" in Donald S. Lopez, *Religions of China in Practice* (Princeton, New Jersey: Princeton University Press, 1996), p. 138.
46 Cleary, *The Taoist Classics, Vol. 2*, p. 14.
47 Ishida, "Body and Mind", pp. 71–2.
48 Equivalent terms are widely (and wildly) at variance. I have, therefore, only given those that appear to be consistently held.
49 Liu I-ming/Liu Yiming's commentary on Chang Po-tuan/Zhang Boduan's *The Inner Teachings of Taoism*, translator Thomas Cleary, *The Inner Teachings of Taoism* (Boston, Massachusetts and London: Shambhala, 1986), p. 83.
50 *Ibid.*
51 Robinet, *Taoism*, p. 232.
52 Chang Po-tuan/Zhang Boduan, *Awakening to Perfection*, 20, translator Kohn, *The Taoist Experience*, p. 319.
53 Eva Wong, *The Shambhala Guide to Taoism: A complete introduction to the history, philosophy, and practice of an ancient Chinese spiritual tradition* (Boston, Massachusetts and London: Shambhala, 1997), pp. 175–6.
54 Bearing in mind that the Chinese are facing in the opposite direction with the South (western North, behind them).
55 For a detailed description of such processes, see Needham, *Science and Civilisation in China, Vol. 5, Part 5*, pp. 52–67.
56 For a very concise and clear description of these changes see Eva Wong, translator, *Cultivating Stillness: A Taoist manual for transforming body and mind* (Boston, Massachusetts and London: Shambhala, 1992), pp. 133–4.
57 For the numerology associated with the *Pa-kua/Bagua* see Cleary, *The Book of Balance and Harmony*, pp. 26–8, and for a clear chart of these Wong, *ibid.*, p. 135, with explanations on pp. 132–3.

58 See Eva Wong, *Harmonizing Yin and Yang: The Dragon-Tiger Classic* (Boston, Massachusetts and London: Shambhala, 1997), pp. 20–9 for further discussion on this point in connection with the *Dragon-Tiger Classic.*
59 Hsü Ts'ung-shih/Xu Congshi, from *The Secret of Everlasting Life*, translator Bertschinger, *The Secret of Everlasting Life*, p. 166.
60 Translator Thomas Cleary, *Practical Taoism* (Boston, Massachusetts and London: Shambhala, 1996), p. 26.
61 Texts are remarkably contradictory on this area, and even the same author will give different accounts in different books. We can only give some general indications as to the approximate meanings of terms, which are likely to have varied meaning in different schools of thought.
62 Wong, translator, *Cultivating Stillness*, p. xxiii.
63 From *Zhang Sanfeng's Taiji Alchemy Secrets*, translator Cleary in *Taoist Meditation*, p. 118.
64 Translator Yang Jwing-Ming, *Tai Chi Secrets of the Wu and Li Styles* (Boston, Massachusetts: Yang's Martial Arts Association, 1986), p. 1.
65 From *The Book of Balance and Harmony*, translator Cleary, p. 144.
66 Titus Burckhardt, *Alchemy* (Shaftesbury, Dorset: Element Books, 1987 impression of 1986 edn, first published 1960), p. 123.
67 Blofeld, *Taoism*, p. 153.

7 Movement in Stillness

1 From "The Way of Eternal Life through Perception of Vital Spirit", translator Thomas Cleary, *Practical Taoism* (Boston, Massachusetts and London: Shambhala, 1996), p. 26.
2 From "An Explanation of Interpreting Energy in T'ai-chi", *Yang Family Forty Chapters*, translator Douglas Wile, *Lost T'ai-chi Classics from the Late Ch'ing Dynasty* (Albany, New York: State University of New York Press, 1996), p. 71.
3 Yang Jwing Ming, *Tai Chi Theory & Martial Power: Advanced Yang Style Tai Chi Chuan* (Jamaica Plain, Massachusetts: Yang's Martial Arts Association, 1986), p. 25.

8 Unity

1 Laurence G. Thompson, *Chinese Religion: An introduction* (Belmont, California: Wadsworth Publishing Company, 1989 fourth edn, first published 1979), p. 36.
2 Stephen F. Teiser, "Introduction" in Donald S. Lopez, Jr. (ed.), *Religions of China in Practice* (Princeton, New Jersey: Princeton University Press, 1996), pp. 26–7.
3 Martin Palmer and Zhao Xiaomin, *Essential Chinese Mythology: Stories that change the world* (London: Thorsons, 1997), p. 30.
4 *Ibid.*

5 John Blofeld, *Taoism: The quest for immortality* (London, Boston, Sydney, Wellington: Mandala, 1989 reissue of 1979 edn), p. 90.
6 Isabelle Robinet, *Taoism: Growth of a religion* translated by Phyllis Brooks (Stanford, California: Stanford University Press, 1997, first published in French as *Histoire du Taoïsme des origines au XIVe siècle* in 1992), pp. 37–8.
7 Kristofer Schipper, *The Taoist Body* translated by Karen C. Duval (Berkeley, Los Angeles, London: University of California Press, 1993, first published in 1982 as *Le corps taoïste*), p. 164.
8 Livia Kohn, *Early Chinese Mysticism: Philosophy and soteriology in the Taoist tradition* (Princeton, New Jersey: Princeton University Press, 1992), p. 84.
9 Robinet, *Taoism*, p. 49.
10 Kohn, *Early Chinese Mysticism*, p. 91.
11 The text was later lost, and reconstructed in the sixth century. For other literature concerning immortals, including extracts from texts, see Livia Kohn (ed.), *The Taoist Experience: An anthology* (Albany, New York: State University of New York Press, 1993), pp. 325–32 and 335.
12 Schipper, *The Taoist Body*, p. 164.
13 Blofeld, *Taoism*, p. 60.
14 For the full tale, see Kwok Man Ho and Joanne O'Brien, translators and eds, *The Eight Immortals of Taoism: Legends and fables of popular Taoism* (London, Sydney, Auckland, Johannesburg: Rider, 1990), pp. 61–3.
15 Schipper, *The Taoist Body*, pp. 164–5.
16 Strictly speaking the word "being" should be translated as "man". I have avoided genderized language where possible, but it needs to be remembered that the sage was almost invariably male.
17 See Kohn, *The Taoist Experience*, pp. 280–1.
18 *Huainanzi* 1 cited in William de Bary and Irene Bloom, *Sources of Chinese Tradition: Vol 1, From earliest times to 1600* (New York: Columbia University Press, 1999 revised edn, first published 1960), pp. 270–1.
19 A great bird.
20 From the *Ch'üan T'ang shih* 217, cited in Suzanne E. Cahill, *Transcendence and Divine Passion: The Queen Mother of the West in Medieval China* (Stanford, California: Stanford University Press, 1993), p. 205.
21 Hellmut Wilhelm, *Heaven, Earth, and Man in the Book of Changes: Seven Eranos Lectures* (Seattle and London: University of Washington Press, 1977), p. 179.
22 Isabelle Robinet, "Visualization and Ecstatic Flight in Shangqing Taoism" in Livia Kohn (ed.) in cooperation with Yoshinobu Sakade, *Taoist Meditation and Longevity Techniques*. Michigan Monographs in Chinese Studies, vol. 61 (Michigan: Centre for Chinese Studies, The University of Michigan, 1989), p. 163.
23 *Huai-nan-tzu* 7/4b2–5 and 7/5a12–b2 translated by Harold Roth in "Who

Compiled the *Chuang Tzu*" in Henry Rosemont Jr. (ed.), *Chinese Texts and Philosophical Contexts: Essays dedicated to Angus C. Graham* (La Salle, Illinois: Open Court, 1991), pp. 106–7.

24 Fung Yu-lan, *A Short History of Chinese Philosophy* edited by Derk Bodde (New York: The Free Press and London: Collier Macmillan Publishers, 1996, first published 1948), p. 288.

25 *Ibid.*

26 Livia Kohn, *Taoist Mystical Philosophy: The Scripture of Western Ascension* (Albany, New York: State University of New York Press, 1991), p. 142.

27 Sophia Delza, *T'ai-Chi Ch'üan, Body and Mind in Harmony: The integration of meaning and method* (Albany, New York: State University of New York Press, revised edn 1985, first published 1961), p. 2.

28 Vincent Chu in "A Roundtable Discussion with Liu Ming, René Navarro, Linda Varone, Vincent Chu, Daniel Seitz, and Weidong Lu", compiled by Livia Kohn, "Change Starts Small: Daoist Practice and the Ecology of Individual Lives" in Norman J. Girardot, James Miller, and Liu Xiaogan, *Daoism and Ecology: Ways within a cosmic landsacpe* (Cambridge, Massachusetts: Harvard University Press for the Center for the Study of World Religions, Harvard Divinity School, 2001), p. 386.

29 "Zhang Sanfeng's Taiji Alchemy Secrets: The alchemical process", translator Thomas Cleary, *Taoist Meditation: Methods for cultivating a healthy mind and body* (Boston and London: Shambhala, 2000), p. 118.

30 *Ibid.*, p. 119.

31 Chang San-feng/Zhang Sanfeng, "Discourses on the Teachings of Wang Che: On sitting", translator Thomas Cleary, *The Taoist Classics: The collected translations of Thomas Cleary*, vol. 3 (Boston: Shambhala, 2003), p. 194.

32 Chang San-feng/Zhang Sanfeng, "Commentary on Ancestor Lü's Hundred-Character Tablet", translator Cleary, *ibid.*, p. 188.

33 From the *Yang Family Forty Chapters, 40*, translator Douglas Wile, *Lost T'ai-chi Classics from the Late Ch'ing Dynasty* (Albany, New York: State University of New York Press, 1996), p. 89.

34 Yang Jwing Ming, *Tai Chi Theory & Martial Power: Advanced Yang Style Tai Chi Chuan* (Jamaica Plain, Massachusetts: Yang's Martial Arts Association Publication Centre, second, revised edn 1996), p. 25.

35 *Ibid.*, p. 234.

36 Yang Jwing-Ming, *Taijiquan, Classical Yang Style: The complete form and Qigong* (Boston, Massachusetts: Yang's Martial Arts Publication Center, 1999), p. 106.

37 Kohn, *Taoist Mystical Philosophy*, p. 148.

38 Blofeld, *Taoism*, p. 40.

Glossary

Chang San-feng/Zhang Sanfeng	the traditional founder of T'ai Chi Ch'üan/Taijiquan.
chi/ji	"ultimate", "utmost point", "ridge-pole".
ch'i/qi	energies within and surrounding all things; vitality.
ch'i-kung/qigong	energy circulation through bodily movement.
chin/jin	power.
ching/jing	essence; the liquid element of the body, including saliva, sweat, semen and gastric juices.
Chou I/Zhouyi	*The Changes of the Chou/Zhou*, the early name for the *I Ching/Yijing*.
ch'üan	"boxing", "fist".
Chuang-tzu/Zhuangzi	an early sage, traditional author of the *Chuang-tzu/Zhuangzi.*
Chuang-tzu/Zhuangzi	a Taoist classic said to have been written by Chuang-tzu/Zhuangzi.
chün-tzu/junzi	Confucian term for a superior person, a gentleman.
fang-shih/fangshi	an early diverse group of people who practised divination, magic, medicine, and the like, and who promoted ideas of immortality.
Five Elements/Agents	the basic forces of existence and of patterns of change, rhythms and cycles; they are Wood, Fire, Earth, Metal and Water.

Fu Hsi/Fu Xi	mythical Emperor, the founder of hunting and animal husbandry and reputed to have discovered the eight trigrams.
hexagram	six *yin* and/or *yang* lines, one on top of the other.
ho-t'u/hetu	"Yellow River Map", the primal arrangement of the eight trigrams, traditionally discovered by Fu Hsi/Fu Xi.
hsien/xian	"immortal, perfected being".
Huang-ti/Huangdi	the Yellow Emperor.
Huang-ti Nei-ching/Huangdi Neijing	the *Yellow Emperor's Classic of Internal Medicine.*
i/yi	"intention".
I Ching/Yijing	*Book of Changes*, the ancient Chinese *Classic* concerning change and transformation in the universe.
Ko Hung/Ge Hong	fourth century CE naturalist and alchemist, author of the *Pao-p'u-tzu/Baopuzi.*
kuei/gui	physical forms or ghosts after death.
Lao-tzu/Laozi	early sage, traditionally the founder of Taoism and author of the *Tao Te Ching/Daodejing.*
Lieh-tzu/Liezi	early Taoist sage, traditional author of the text that bears his name.
Ling-pao/Lingbao Taoism	influential school of Taoism in the Six Dynasties period.
macrocosmic orbit	specific circulation of energy around the whole body including a microcosmic orbit around the upper body.
microcosmic orbit	specific circulation of energy around two meridians in the upper torso of the body.
nei-tan/neidan	inner or internal alchemy, the alchemy of the body.
Pa-hsien/Baxian	the Eight Immortals of Taoism.
Pa-kua/Bagua	the basic eight trigrams of the *I Ching/Yijing* arranged in a circular system.
pa-kua-chang/bagua zhang	soft-style martial art based on the eight trigrams.
Pao-p'u-tzu/Baopuzi	literally, "the Master that embraces simplicity", the literary name of the fourth century CE naturalist and

	alchemist Ko Hung/Ge Hong, and the name of a text he wrote.
pa-shou/bashou	eight palm positions used in the T'ai Chi *form*.
p'o/po	the physical *yin* spirits that survive after death and return to the earth.
Shang-ch'ing/Shangqing Taoism	influential school of Taoism in the Six Dynasties period.
Shaolin martial arts	probably the oldest tradition of martial arts in China, dating back to the sixth century CE.
shen	spirit; the spiritual essence of the body.
shen spirits	*yang* spirits that rise from the body at death and that are capable of rebirth.
Shih-i/Shiyi	the *Ten Wings*, the *Appendices* to the *I Ching/Yijing*.
Ta-chuan/Dazhuan	*The Great Treatise*, one of the *Ten Wings* of the *I Ching/Yijing*.
t'ai/tai	"high", "great", "supreme", "remote".
T'ai-chi/Taiji	"Supreme Ultimate".
Ta-mo/Damo	Chinese name of an Indian monk called Bodhidharma, who introduced Shaolin martial arts to China.
tan-t'ien/dantian	a term in inner alchemy for three "cauldrons", three important areas of the body – upper, middle and lower – which are important in the circulation and transmutation of energy in internal alchemy.
Tao	the non-manifest and manifest essence of the universe.
Tao-chia/Daojia	philosophical and mystical Taoism.
Tao-chiao/Daojiao	religious Taoism.
Tao Te Ching/Daodejing	text of eighty-one short chapters attributed to Lao-tzu/Laozi.
Tao-tsang/Daozang	the Taoist canon.
tao-yin/daoyin	gymnastic exercises.
Te/De	the spontaneous, natural and rhythmic expression of *Tao* in the universe.
Thirteen Postures	The postures fundamental to martial art praxis, contained in the *Treatise on T'ai Chi Ch'üan/Taijiquan*.
Three Treasures	*ching/jing* essence, *ch'i/qi* energy, vitality, and *shen* spirit.
transmutation	the alchemical process of the refinement

of *ching/jing*, *ch'i/qi* and *shen* in inner alchemy to produce the immortal Spirit Embryo.

trigram — three *yin* and/or *yang* lines placed one on top of the other.

Tsou Yen/Zou Yan — founder of the combined school of *Yin–Yang* and the Five Elements.

tzu-jan/ziran — naturalness; spontaneity.

wai-tan/waidan — outer or external alchemy, the alchemy of the laboratory.

Wu-chi/Wuji — the undifferentiated Void; absolute nothingness that exists before creation.

wu-hsing/wuxing — the Five Agents, Elements or Phases.

wu-wei — non-action.

yin and *yang* — the two complementary forces in all existence.

Further Reading

Taoism

A comprehensive introduction to Taoism can be found in Jeaneane Fowler's *Pathways to Immortality: An introduction to the philosophy and religion of Taoism* (Brighton, Sussex and Portland, Oregon: Sussex Academic Press, 2005). Contents cover ancient China; the *I Ching/Yijing*; *yin* and *yang*; the historical background to the development of Taoism including the presence of Taoism in the world today; alchemy; philosophical Taoism, with an analysis of key concepts such as *Tao*, *Te*, *wu-wei*, naturalness and spontaneity as presented in the *Tao Te Ching/Daodejing*, the *Chuang-tzu/Zhuangzi* and the *Lieh-tzu/Liezi.* The book also deals with the religious aspect of Taoism with its many deities, its festivals, and its ceremonial rituals.

Taoist texts have been recently gathered together in four volumes, *The Taoist Classics: The collected translations of Thomas Cleary* (Boston: Shambhala, 2003). Volume 1 contains the *Tao Te Ching/Daodejing* and the *Chuang-tzu/Zhuangzi* and volume 4 the *I Ching/Yijing*. There is a range of texts on alchemy to be found in the other volumes. Since translations of Chinese texts vary considerably, the serious student is advised to consult a variety of translations for comparison. This is easily done with short texts like the *Tao Te Ching/Daodejing*. As to the *Chuang-tzu/Zhuangzi*, Angus Graham's *Chuang-Tzu: The Inner Chapters* (London, Boston, Sydney, New Zealand: Unwin Paperbacks, 1989), is excellent, as is Graham's *The Book of Lieh-tzu: A classic of Tao* (New York: Columbia University Press, 1990, first published 1960). Another excellent translation of the *Chuang-tzu/Zhuangzi* is *The Book of Chuang Tzu* by Martin Palmer with Elizabeth Breuilly (London, New York, Victoria, Ontario, Auckland: Penguin, Arkana, 1996). A charming translation by Thomas Merton, *The Way of Chuang Tzu* (New York: New Directions, 1969) is a good introduction to Chuang-tzu/Zhuangzi's thought. For an anthology of Taoist texts *The Taoist Experience: An anthology*, edited by Livia Kohn (Albany, New York: State University of New York Press, 1003), is an outstanding work.

An academic historical survey of Taoism that also encompasses its mystical ritualistic and alchemical dimensions, is to be found in Isabelle Robinet's standard work, *Taoism: Growth of a Religion* (translated by Phyllis Brooks, Stanford, California: Stanford University Press, 1997, first published in French in 1992). Kristofer Schipper's *The Taoist Body* (translated by Karen C. Duval, Berkeley, Los Angeles, London: University of California Press, 1993, first published in French in 1982) is an excellent standard work on Taoism. Recently published and dispelling many of the traditional myths of Taoism is Russell Kirkland's *Taoism: The enduring tradition* (New York and London: Routledge, 2004).

T'ai Chi Ch'üan/Taijiquan

A video by Shifu Keith Ewers demonstrating the *Yang Style Simplified 24-Step T'ai Chi Ch'üan/Taijiquan Form* is available from Bubblingspring Foundation, 3 Kennelwood, Lower Common, Gilwern, Abergavenny, Monmouthshire NP7 OBD and can be used in conjunction with the description of the *form* in chapter 7.

The works of the eminent practitioner and Master, Yang Jwing-Ming, are particularly recommended, and are published by the Yang's Martial Arts Association (Jamaica Plain, Massachusetts). Among these, we might mention *Taijiquan, Classical Yang Style: The complete form and qigong* (1999); *Tai Chi Secrets of the Wu and Li Styles* (2001); *Advanced Yang Style Tai Chi Chuan* (2 vols, 1986); *The Essence of Tai Chi Chi Kung: Health and martial arts* (1990); *Tai Chi Theory & Martial Power: Advanced Yang Style Tai Chi Chuan* (1996). Dan Docherty's *Complete Tai Chi Chuan* (Malborough, Wiltshire: The Crowood Press, 2001, first published 1997), is a thoroughly researched text, with an excellent account of the intricacies of the lineages of the various schools.

Sophia Delza outlines the Wu Style of T'ai Chi in her *T'ai-Chi Ch'üan, Body and Mind in Harmony: The integration of meaning and method* (Albany, New York: State University of New York Press, 1985 revised edn, first published 1985). What is particularly excellent about this source is the philosophical background and comment that Delza supplies in the text. She writes sensitively and very clearly, yet with depth and inspiration. Lawrence Galante's *Tai Chi: The Supreme Ultimate* (York Beach, Maine: Samuel Weiser, 1981), demonstrates very well how the postures of T'ai Chi are embedded in martial art praxis. The photographic support in this text is particularly good. Stuart Alve Olson deals with T'ai Chi in the context of the *I Ching/Yijing* in *T'ai Chi according to the I Ching: Embodying the principles of the Book of Changes* (Rochester, Vermont: Inner Traditions, 2001). Da Liu's *T'ai Chi Ch'uan and I Ching: A choreography of mind and body* (1981 second edn, first published 1972), as its title suggests, also relates T'ai Chi to the *I Ching/Yijing*. The meditative aspects of T'ai Chi are also dealt with by Da Liu in *T'ai Chi Ch'uan and Meditation* (1990, first published in 1986, both books London, New York, Victoria, Ontario, Auckland: Arkana).

A detailed and academic study of the textual traditions underpinning T'ai Chi Ch'üan/Taijiquan can be found in Douglas Wile, *Lost T'ai-chi Classics from the Late Ch'ing Dynasty* (Albany, New York: State University of New York Press, 1996). For more poetic translations without commentary, see Benjamin Pang Jeng Lo, Martin Inn, Robert Amacker and Susan Foe (translators and eds), *The Essence of T'ai Chi Ch'uan: The literary tradition* (Berkeley, California: North Atlantic Books, 1979).

Index